MISSION TRENDS NO. 1

Mission Trends No. 1

Crucial Issues in Mission Today

Edited by
Gerald H. Anderson
and
Thomas F. Stransky, C.S.P.

PAULIST PRESS
New York / Paramus / Toronto
and
WM. B. EERDMANS PUBLISHING CO.
Grand Rapids

Library of Congress
Catalog Card Number: 74-81222

ISBN: 0-8028-1483-2

Published by
Paulist Press
Editorial Office: 1865 Broadway, N.Y., N.Y. 10023
Business Office: 400 Sette Drive, Paramus, N.J. 07652
and
Wm. B. Eerdmans Publishing Co.
255 Jefferson, S.E., Grand Rapids, Mich. 49502

Printed and bound in the
United States of America   *Reprinted, October 1978*

About the Editors

Pennsylvania-born Gerald H. Anderson was a Methodist missionary in the Philippines on the faculty of Union Theological Seminary, Manila, from 1960-70, and president of Scarritt College, Nashville, from 1970-73. He is currently Senior Research Associate in the Southeast Asia Program at Cornell University. A former Fulbright scholar, he studied at the universities of Marburg, Geneva and Edinburgh, and has his Ph.D. from Boston University. Dr. Anderson is president of the American Society of Missiology and serves on the executive committee of the International Association for Mission Studies and the editorial board of *Missiology: An International Review.* He is widely known as an editor and author of such books as *The Theology of the Christian Mission, Christ and Crisis in Southeast Asia, Studies in Philippine Church History, Concise Dictionary of the Christian World Mission* (co-editor), and *Asian Voices in Christian Theology.*

Thomas F. Stransky is the president of the Paulist Fathers, the first missionary society of priests founded in the United States. He did his postgraduate work in Catholic and Protestant mission studies at the Catholic University in Washington, D.C., the University of Münster, and the Gregorianum in Rome. From 1960-70 he was a staff member of the Vatican Secretariat for Promoting Christian Unity. He has visited and lectured extensively in Asia, Africa and Europe. Author of articles on ecumenical and mission subjects for many journals, Fr. Stransky is on the advisory board of the IDOC study series on "The Future of the Missionary Enterprise," and on the editorial board of *Missiology.* He is a consultant to the Vatican Christian Unity Secretariat, and to the Commission on World Mission and Evangelism of the World Council of Churches. He is also a member of the United States Catholic Mission Council.

Contents

Foreword

It has been rightly observed that the "missionary enterprise has undergone more radical change in the last fifteen years than in the previous century." The reasons for this are complex and the results are still ambiguous. Some judge the new situation as a setback for the Christian mission; others—including ourselves—see in it a sign of ferment and vitality in thought, motivation and practice, an opportunity to free Christian communities to find and experience new life in faithful mission. To paraphrase a colleague: "Faithfulness in mission is not the same as doing it as we have always done it."

The crucial issues are fundamental: the meaning of mission today, the message and goals of mission, the missionary vocation, the relation of socio-economic development to discipling, the significance of Church growth *and* decline, the place of humanization and liberation in mission, and the shifting relationships and responsibilities between the so-called older and younger churches—to name a few.

We have brought together recent articles that may help to clarify these issues and suggest "mission trends." The twenty-five contributors represent diverse viewpoints and Church traditions—ranging from the President of Tanzania, to a former Japanese missionary in Thailand, to a Uruguayan Methodist on the staff of the World Council of Churches in Geneva, to an Orthodox theologian in New York and a seminary dean in Pasadena, California.

Not all crucial issues are dealt with, nor is there unanimity. Contrasting views are juxtaposed to provide a sense of the diversity and richness of the Christian experience and reflection, in world perspective. From nearly all of the essays, however, it appears that the major issue for Christians today is not "What is the Church?" but "What is the Church to *do*?" As Dr. W.A.

1

Visser't Hooft observes in his *Memoirs*, there is "a certain shifting of emphases and a reassignment of priorities in order that institutional Christianity may turn outward from institutional preoccupation and spend itself lavishly in the service of all men." This shift does not mean a radical discontinuity with the past, yet it opens the way for new initiatives and a more comprehensive approach toward the world—assessing critically our presuppositions about the way God works through and beyond the Church in the messianic mission of the Son.

In planning this series and in preparing this first volume, we have had the benefit of a wide circle of consultants from six continents. Final responsibility for selection, however, is ours alone. We are particularly indebted to the editors and publishers of the magazines and journals who have graciously permitted us to reprint material which first appeared in their pages. Grateful acknowledgment is also made to the *New Theology* series (Macmillan), edited by Martin E. Marty and Dean G. Peerman, which inspired us to undertake a similar series, but with the focus on Christian mission. Reactions to this initial effort will be welcomed, as we prepare *Mission Trends No. 2*, dealing with "Evangelism in the Modern World."

Gerald H. Anderson

Thomas F. Stransky, C.S.P.

I: Rethinking "Mission"

What Is "Mission" Today? Two Views

Arthur F. Glasser
and Tracey K. Jones, Jr.

One of the most difficult problems today for Protestants as well as Catholics is that of defining what is meant by the Christian "mission," reaching agreement on the aims of mission and what constitutes "missionary activity." The difficulty is demonstrated in these statements by two widely respected and representative missionary statesmen. Arthur F. Glasser served in China and then was an executive of the Overseas Missionary Fellowship (formerly the China Inland Mission) before becoming the dean of the School of World Mission at Fuller Theological Seminary in Pasadena, California. While acknowledging that discipleship includes "solidarity with those who suffer from injustice," Dr. Glasser stresses that the "acid test" of "all activities that claim to represent obedience in mission" is: "Do they or do they not produce disciples of Jesus Christ?" Tracey K. Jones, Jr. served as a missionary in China and in Singapore before becoming an executive of the United Methodist Board of Global Ministries. Dr. Jones, who is also chairman of the World Council of Churches' Commission on World Mission and Evangelism, speaks of mission today in terms of witnessing to the "power" that God has released in Jesus Christ as a source of hope for deliverance from the demonic forces that affect human life. He believes that Christians, both as individuals and as churches, have an authentic missionary responsibility "to use their social, economic and political strength for the sake of disadvantaged people." He also sees "the strengthening of Christian unity" as part of our mission today. These two statements are reprinted with the permission of the Missionary Research Library, New

York, from the 10th edition (1973) of *Mission Handbook: North American Protestant Ministries Overseas*, edited by Edward R. Dayton and published by Missions Advanced Research and Communications Center in Monrovia, California.

ARTHUR F. GLASSER

Missionary work was born in the counsels of the triune God where it was decreed that, by the preaching of the Gospel to all people, there should be brought to eternal glory a great multitude which no man could number from every tribe, people and language.

—Confession of the Waldenses, 1573

There is a sense in which the mission of the Church is timeless. This arises from the nature of the Gospel, which is rooted, not in human thought, but in historical event. That event involved the sending by God of his Son, Jesus Christ, into the world to be its Lord and Savior. It climaxed in his death, burial and resurrection.

The Church has always stood in awe of the unique and unrepeatable significance of the one sacrifice by which the universe was reconciled to God. Inasmuch as this act of reconciliation presupposes estrangement, the Church has always understood Christ's cross to represent the enormity of man's sin: his unwillingness to submit to God and his violence against his brothers. The Church has also seen in that strange cross the act of substitution whereby one who knew no sin took to his innocency all human guilt and shame, and received in himself the righteous wrath of God that was mankind's due.

It is on the basis of the human condition and Christ's redemptive cross that the Church was given an unchanging mandate to proclaim the good news of forgiveness and restored relationship to God to the ends of the earth and to the end of time: "All men need the Gospel. For the human sickness there is one specific remedy, and this is it. There is no other. The Church cannot compromise on its missionary task without ceasing to be the Church. If it fails to see and accept this responsibility, it is changing the Gospel into something other than itself" (Neill, 1961:17).

The timeless dimension of mission means that the Church has an abiding apostolic role to fill. As God the Father sent his Son into the world, so the Son has sent and keeps sending the Church into the world. This means that the Church and every member of it is "in mission" and under the constraint of the Spirit to reach out to all men and proclaim by word and deed: "We are ambassadors for Christ, God making his appeal through us. We bessech you on behalf of Christ, be reconciled to God" (2 Cor. 5:20).

For more than sixty generations the Church, sometimes more and sometimes less, has spontaneously reached out from its local congregations with the Gospel. And, through planned expansion by means of para-church agencies such as missions, orders, and societies, it has surmounted geographical, linguistic, social and economic barriers to communicate the Gospel transculturally and bring new peoples to Christian obedience. True evangelism takes place wherever there is "the announcement of the good news of the intervention of God in history through Christ, with the intention of evoking the adherence of faith, conversion" (Maurier, 1968:233).

"Make disciples of all nations!" The emphasis is on converting peoples, not solely individuals. This means making disciples within the cultural context over which Christ desires to extend his Lordship. "Being a disciple (in this larger sense) does not signify 'anonymous' membership of a vague or uncertain sort. It signifies profession, obedience, and being taken into the light" (Schütte, 1972:43).

This task is still unfinished. Individuals, families, communities, whole peoples and cultures yet remain to be discipled. As Vatican II so succinctly put it, the Church still has a priority obligation, "for the Gospel message has not yet been heard, or scarcely so, by two billion human beings, and their number is increasing daily" (*Ad Gentes* 11:10).

There is a sense, however, in which performance of the mission of the Church is time-conditioned and culture-bound. It is especially so today. The Church must discern the times and be sensitive to the context in which God has placed it. It must make sure that its presentation of Christ is authentic and meaningful. This presupposes that God is moving in history and that his redemptive concern extends to the totality of the human condition. In these days of widespread exploitation and injustice the conversion process is affected by the socio-economic, political, cultural and human environment in which it occurs (Gutierrez, 1973:205). The Gospel calls not only to total communion with God but also to "the fullest brotherhood with all men." Hence, true conversion to Christ's Lordship must inevitably bring one into authentic solidarity with those who suffer from injustice. The Church must accompany its witness to the liberating Christ with prophetic protest against all that enslaves and with deep commitment to "the poor, the marginated and the exploited."

God would have his Church be a servant people in the midst of human need. Biblical Christianity keeps insisting that the most urgent problem of human life is sin—and this includes the evil that arises from the pressure of societal and environmental forces. Hence, mission today means not only going out into the world proclaiming a redemptive victory that was won in the distant past, but participating in the present victory of Christ. The Church in mission will be so energized by the presence and power of the Holy Spirit that the life and service of Jesus will be realized in every context in which it finds itself. Like its head, the Church will then deny itself the right to be neutral in the moral and social issues of the day (Mt. 5:10).

God would have his Church a servant people in the midst of human need. Only then can it authentically, by both spontaneous and planned outreach, embrace the task whose priority was reiterated at Bangkok 1973: "Each generation must evangelize its own generation. The concerns of Church growth and renewal are the chief, abiding and irreplaceable tasks of Christian mission."

Only a renewed Church can carry to completion the missionary mandate. And there is but one acid test that should be applied to all activities that claim to represent obedience in mission. Do they or do they not produce disciples of Jesus Christ?

TRACEY K. JONES, JR.

It may seem out of place to begin a brief statement on "What Is Mission Today?" with a reference to a recent book on *Power and Innocence* by Rollo May, the well-known psychiatrist. I do so, for the book provides a reminder of the human situation. The thesis of the book is that human violence, so prevalent today in all parts of the world, can be traced to individual and group feelings of powerlessness and the emotional condition of apathy that is the result of feelings of powerlessness. From a lifetime of study of disturbed persons and groups, Rollo May concludes that when persons and groups lose hope that they can determine the direction of their lives, they become dangerous to themselves and others. He takes seriously the demonic forces that affect human life. He is critical of Charles Reich's book *The Greening of America* in that Reich, he believes, does not face up to the dark side of human life where sin and alienation, like hungry leopards, stalk all our efforts. The way out of this climate of violence for Rollo May is to help individuals and groups to find in the very midst of the evil and darkness of personal and social life a "power" that can awaken in them hope and resourcefulness to determine their future. When this hope is recovered and concrete decisions are made in that direction, violent behavior, he contends, can be and is transformed into energy that works for constructive individual and social change.

Others would describe the human situation in different ways than Rollo May, but his perspective is essentially a biblical one. The mission of the Christian in the world today, as I see it, is to make the claim that the source of that "power" that delivers individuals and groups is found in the mystery of the incarnation, where God, in the fullness of time, decided to become a part of his human creation and, in the sharing of his life in Jesus Christ with human life, made possible a "power" that was not there before. We are not called to argue about this, but out of our own experience, in both personal and communal life, to witness to it. It is not required that we be successful in convincing others, but we are called to obedience to make our claim (Mt. 10:32-33). Everyone has a right to hear what we have to say. This does not mean we are not to listen to the claims made by men and women who affirm other faiths. We also have a right to hear what they have to say, but they have a right to hear us as well.

When we approach other people in religious dialogue, gentleness and reverence are essential attitudes of behavior. In 1 Peter 3:15 are the words: "Always be prepared to make a defense to anyone who calls you to account for the hope that is in you, but do it with gentleness and reverence." Too often in the past, Christians have lacked this Christ-like quality of respect and sensitivity to those who are not disciples of Jesus. With the end of Western domination of Asia, Africa and Latin America and the rise of religious pluralism on a global scale, it is my conviction that the most effective way to bring people to Jesus Christ will come in religious dialogue that is gentle and reverent in method and style.

The second thing I would say about "What is Mission Today?" concerns politics. The Bible has a great deal to say about God's concern for and identification with the poor, the captives and the oppressed. The record of both the Old and New Testaments speaks of this. It is the unmistakable theme of the Exodus story and also of the warnings and promises of the prophets. The same theme emerges in the sermon Jesus preached at Nazareth (Lk. 4:16-30) and in his description of one requirement for entrance into the kingdom of God (Mt. 25:31-46). An authentic task of mission today concerns the ways by which men and women can free themselves from oppressive systems that keep them poor, illiterate, subjugated and thwarted in their efforts to achieve for themselves the quality of life possible for them in their society. It is my conviction that Christians, both as individuals and churches, must be willing to use their social economic and political strength for the sake of disadvantaged people. When we all heard the good news that the American prisoners of war would be released from North Vietnam, it was apparent that this was possible only because of political decisions that rearranged the power balances. The same is true for the poor, oppressed minorities, and socially disadvantaged in every part of the world. There need not be agreement among Christians as to what particular political and social decision will help make possible economic and political deliverance of others, but it does seem to be important that there be agreement that carefully considered political action is, in certain situations, an authentic missionary responsibility.

I would add one further thought about "What Is Mission Today?" and that is the need for greater unity among Christians. Our Christian divisions, bitterness in theological debate and harshness with each other are not signs of "the first fruits" of the coming of the kingdom of God. John's Gospel (17:21) prays that Christians may "all be one" in love and trust, as a sign "that the world may believe that thou has sent me." Therefore, for me, the strengthening of Christian unity at the world, regional, national and local level, is a part of our mission today.

My three points about "What Is Mission Today?" are summarized in two sentences. The Christian mission today is a word of hope to all people that in a day when so many persons and groups feel powerless and apathetic and are therefore potentially dangerous to themselves and others, there is a way out of this sickness of our time. The signs of deliverance are seen in the lives of Christian men and women who, in their personal, community, national and international relationships, have shown that in the name of Jesus and in the power of the Holy Spirit they can determine in constructive ways the direction of their individual and group life, and that the "power" that they have found has transformed their lives which they desire to share with others, not that they want others to be like them, but that all who are willing to give themselves to this "power" can be transformed in such a way that they will please God, the Father of our Lord and Savior Jesus Christ.

SELECT BIBLIOGRAPHY

Gutierrez, Gustavo, *A Theology of Liberation* (Maryknoll, N.Y.: Orbis Books, 1973).

Maurier, Henri, *The Other Covenant: A Theology of Paganism* (Paramus, N.J.: Newman Press, 1968).

Neill, Stephen, *Christian Faith and Other Faiths* (Oxford: Oxford University Press, 1961).

Schütte, Johannes, "Why Engage in Mission Work?" in SEDOS, *Foundations of Mission Theology* (Maryknoll, N.Y.: Orbis Books, 1972).

Mission after Uppsala 1968

Johannes Aagaard

Since 1968, when the Fourth Assembly of the World Council of Churches met at Uppsala, Sweden, several significant developments have occurred in missiology. One of these is a critical re-thinking of the *missio Dei*—mission of God—concept which has dominated much mission theory, particulurly among Protestants, since the Willingen Conference in 1952. Johannes Aagaard, professor of missions and ecumenics at Aarhus University, Denmark, maintains that the "teaching on the *missio Dei* does not correspond to the general pattern of theological thinking today and . . . has become a hindrance in our efforts to respond to the developments in the modern world." He believes that *missiones Dei*—"the manifold ways in which God makes himself present"—is more appropriate theologically. It acknowledges a plurality of "missionary happenings" while maintaining a unity of purpose. This article is part of a longer essay which first appeared in *Ekumenisk Orientering*, "Missionary Studies XI" (Sigtuna, Sweden), August 1971. For further analysis of the years leading up to Uppsala 1968, see Dr. Aagaard's "Trends in Missiological Thinking During the Sixties," in *International Review of Mission* (Geneva), January 1973.

Introduction

The year 1968 is a decisive year in recent history. A radical change in the general attitude to political, social, cultural, philosophical and theological matters came into existence in 1968 and onward. First of all the collapse of the May revolt in Paris and the breakdown of the renewal in Czechoslovakia, but also the development in Vietnam and in Latin America together with the realization that the much-spoken-of "development program in

the Third World" remained a showpiece under the pressure of
continuing exploitation from the Western world, contributed to
this change in attitude.

The Assembly of the World Council of Churches in Uppsala
consequently took place in a setting which influenced the whole
Assembly in a way that could not have been foreseen.

The period up to the Assembly was characterized by a growing secular orientation of theology in general and of missionary
and ecumenical thinking in particular. The orientation toward
the secular and technological world with all its fascinating possibilities[1] was part of a general concentration in the churches on
the world as a secular and manageable reality.[2]

At Uppsala in the Assembly as a whole, but especially in
section II, a very important discussion took place on the nature
of mission today, a discussion which aroused considerable interest in all parts of the church and which has echoed since then in
misiology and ecumenics.[3]

Since 1968 the most typical trend everywhere has been "a
natural and necessary uncertainty." This is also the case theologically. The secular line of thinking up till 1968 developed into a
spiral, moving to and fro, adjusting itself and finding its way in a
hesitant and uncertain way, realizing the complicated nature of
the task. The world certainly had become much more difficult to
manage than before 1968, and the churches and missionary agencies found it very disturbing to respond to the situation in the
right way.

One has to admit that most of the discussions and studies in
that period seem to have evaded the issues in order not to face
the uncertainties, but to some degree a genuine and honest response can be found. A number of theologians have continued to
repeat the same things in spite of the new situations, but here
and there new and relevant voices can be heard.

A young Asian church leader and theologian recently
phrased his understanding of the situation in these words: "Scholars of missiology and ecumenics are in general not able to get out
of their pet traditional theories and open themselves to the new
realities of the world in which the world mission is placed. I am
sure there are exceptions—but very few. Most of them are im-
prisoned in juggling with certain traditional forms of words, and
incapable of even getting behind them to the ideas embodied in
these forms."

Experiencing the—at any rate partial—truth in such a statement, one is not surprised to find that the relevant books and ar-

ticles which illustrate the trends in missiology and ecumenics in recent years are as a whole not to be found under the headings "missiology and ecumenics," but under all other possible headings.

What is missionary and ecumenical can at any rate not be found just by looking to that which is done, said or written in the framework of missionary or ecumenical institutions and by missionary or ecumenical personnel. It is not that easy anymore. In the good old days missionary scholars could "consume their own smoke," i.e., construct a theory on what they or their missionary friends were doing.[4]

Today the important missionary work is often done by personnel and groupings which are not labeled "missionary" or registered as "missionary" institutions. At the same time a large part of the work of traditional "missionary" institutions and personnel is not missionary at all, but belongs rightly under the heading "inter-church aid" or "church cooperation," which is most certainly a necessary and interesting matter, but not mission.

One also has to accept the truth in the deadening statement that "studies and actions done only by 'ecumenical' agencies and personnel are per definition not ecumenical studies" (David Jenkins). "Ecumenical" can develop and has often developed into a new reduction of reality, a new "school" of thought, a new denominational approach. The word ecumenical, rightly understood, indicates on the one hand *a direction* (it happens for the world) and on the other hand *a dimension* (it happens with a genuine participation of the people of God).[5]

Understood in this way, missionary and ecumenical work are two edges of the same sword and cannot be considered in isolation from one another.

Missio Dei or Missiones Dei?

The concept "missionary" as an adjective has not yet made the distinction between "mission" and "missions" clear. By now we are all accustomed to "the gradual change in missionary thinking . . . where the term *missio* is less and less equated with the activities of missionaries and mission societies, while more and more attention is given to historical developments, to questions about history and eschatology, and to the acts of God, the *missio Dei* in history."[6] We are also accustomed to the idea that mission is "a dimension of the *being* of the church," not primarily "a series of recruiting actions in separate missionary enterprises."[7]

We are so accustomed by now to this thinking that some of us have started to disbelieve it. Personally my doubts were definitely confirmed when the small but significant "s" was deleted from the *International Review of Missions*.[8] This was done as an expression of the missionary task in the post-Uppsala period and as an attempt to make the *IRM* "more palatable to Asian, African and Latin American readers, for many of whom the old title must have been uncomfortably reminiscent of an era in which their continents were the only targets of the inexorable thrust of one-way missions from north to south, and an era in which mission was primarily the business of professional, dedicated expatriate Christians from the north rather than the primary business of all Christians, in every country and in every continent."[9]

The basis of the deletion, however, was first of all a theological one, the "growing consensus that the mission is *one* for the Church wherever it may be . . . that the mission of the Church is singular in that it issues from the one triune God and his intention for the salvation of all men. His commission to the Church is one, even though the ministries given to the Church for this mission, and the given responses of particular churches in particular situations to the commission, are manifold."[10]

"The commission is one—the ministries are manifold." In this statement we see our problem stated very clearly. For is *IRM* a review of the commission, or is it meant to be a review of the diverse ministries, the manifold missions? Of course we have to do away with "the one-way mission" concept; of course we have to operate on the basis of the one commission as well as on the basis of the one Church. But can we do that in any other way than by respecting the "s," the pluriformity of the whole missionary enterprise—in all continents and in all countries and including all Christians—but as distinct realities which are not identical with the total life of the Church?

One might dare the naughty question: Was the "s" in the title of the old magazine deleted exactly at the time when it was most relevant? Is *IRM* not by birth and upbringing the child of this "s," of the *missiones*, of the manifold ministries, of the diverse confrontations on the whole inhabited earth between Church and world? Should not the *IRM* in these days be the magazine for all experimenting groups and teams, the have-nots of the churches in their interplay with the have-nots of the world? Was it not a retrogressive step to fail to respond to the new situation in the late 1960's in which we had to deal with a new outburst of missions?

The concept of the one *missio Dei* no doubt was a logical consequence of the general theological thinking after the Second World War with its high tide in ecclesiological interests and with its emphasis on the one Gospel and the one Church. As an historian one can wonder, however, why this concept came in so relatively late and at the time—Willingen 1952—when ecclesiological domination was beginning to crumble.

I venture to propose that the well-established teaching on the *missio Dei* does not correspond to the general pattern of theological thinking today and that it has become a hindrance in our efforts to respond to the developments in the present world. I even dare to say that the concept as such is open to serious theological criticism.

When the *missio Dei* concept is tested by trinitarian thinking, the question arises: Is not the term *missiones Dei* the more genuine starting point? Already the many *missiones* by God—through the prophets, through his Son, through the Holy Spirit, through the apostles—suggest the need for a pluriform approach.[11] And the same thing is indicated when we consider the present *missiones* of God, the manifold ways in which God makes himself present in the Holy Spirit in our period of history.

When we operate from the concept of the one *missio Dei*, the reality of this *missio* easily disappears into a very lofty idea of a purely transcendant *missio* in which we only participate in a shadowy way through human signs and images. This often has as a consequence that missions are only understood as secular agencies pointing toward a reality beyond our human existence—or the other way around. This same concept can be used in such a way that everything we do is identified with the historical *missio* of God, unqualifiedly and indiscriminately. In this way all secular activities can get a type of divine sanction—and support—again indiscriminately and unqualifiedly.

In reaction to such tendencies, other groups of missiologists insist on defining mission in an exclusively churchy way. Secular activities as such are of course positive expressions of human responsibility, but mission as such is different and is only to be understood as an activity of the churches. They maintain that *missio Dei* is a salvatory concept, and salvation takes place only through the Church and its missions.

At the root of this discussion is found the monolithic concept of *missio Dei*. Both parties are arrested by the unity of this concept, and consequently for the one party all missionary activity is secular, while for the other party only the Church has a mission.

Starting from *the plurality of God's missions* to his world we can escape this dilemma. God has spoken to and acted in manifold ways with mankind, and God is still present and active in the world in a variety of missions to save and heal people from corruption and to renew the face of the earth. These missions are known as God's missions when the fruits of the Holy Spirit are manifested—those fruits which are "love, joy, peace, patience, kindness, goodness, fidelity, gentleness and self-control."[12] When the Spirit directs the course, these are signs and we are to believe (with Ambrose) that the Holy Spirit gives gifts which are not lesser than himself. Christians participate in God's missions to the world by being the Church for the world and by being this same world in which the signs of the activity of the Holy Spirit are seen. The Church as the people of God is recognizable for the world when the signs of the Spirit are seen together with the Gospel and the sacraments. However, we must understand that the Church as the extraordinary mission of God does not exclude, but presupposes, many ordinary missions of God.[13]

That God's missions to mankind are manifold belongs to the heart of the matter. Before Christ, God did not leave his creation alone, for the Holy Spirit was actively present in the development of the world through crises and catastrophes up to the present day. Outside the history of the incarnate Christ—where no confession to Christ is given because no Church has come into existence—the Spirit is there too, sent into the world and dragging mankind toward "love, joy, peace, patience, kindness, goodness, fidelity, gentleness and self-control," this harvest of the Spirit of which Christ is the first fruit.

Understanding these missions of the triune God in their relation to one another creates numerous difficulties in missiological thinking today. When the fundamental unity of the triune God is stressed, then the presence of Christ cannot be separated from the missions of the Spirit outside the churches. In this sense one has to accept that "Christ is already there" before the missionary arrives and before the explicit proclamation of the Gospel takes place. When the equally fundamental unity of the Gospel and the risen Christ is stressed, one has to accept that the missionary by nature is a "Christophorus" who brings Christ to the world. But certainly these two statements are both true and should not, as usually happens, be opposed to one another. For the unity of the triune God is a unity in *telos*, not a unitarian identification of God, Son and Holy Spirit. God has more than one *missio* to mankind, but they all have the same purpose.

When the plurality of the *missiones Dei* is stressed, one is not forgetting the divine nature of these missions, but one is probably not tempted to stress the transcendence of the mission as one-sidedly as has often been the case in the traditional *missio Dei* thinking. The *missiones Dei* are not just divine, they are theandric realities, God-human acts in history.

The *missiones* are most certainly not merely a number of human acts. They are not described adequately as "relative and dispensable" acts, as "historically determined answers of the churches to challenges in the past," as "transitory forms of obedience to the *missio Dei*."[14]

Certainly these *missiones* take place in secular and historically determined events, and no secular and historical event as such is God's mission. But in the whole realm of secular and historically determined events the *missiones Dei* take place as theandric realities which can be recognized only by the fruits of the Spirit. Theology should not be a supportive activity, but a critical one,[15] and this *krisis* has to take place in all the secular events. The fruits of the Spirit—and nothing else—are evidence of God's missionary presence. We are not so much going to point out as we are going to recognize that which happens before our eyes, confessing its meaning and participating in its fulfillment.

At any rate the *missiones Dei* definitely *are* happening, and the people of God are called into *God's happenings*. They take place everywhere, inside or outside the institutional churches, inside or outside the traditional missionary agencies. This is the surprising reality in which the nature of the Church as the community of the Spirit is tested and confirmed. The churches have no monopoly on God's salvation. They too have to prove their repentance by the fruits they bear. God can also today raise children for Abraham—and that means children by faith—from stones, or, in the words of Collin Morris, create "a body of Christ with honest politicians for saints, seekers after truth as priests, writers and artists and film-makers as preachers, and flower-children, civil rights marchers and crackpot advocates of total disarmament and world government as martyrs."[16]

As missiologists we represent a number of different schools of thought. We will never reach a general agreement on the nature of God's missions and their relationship to one another.

But I do think that we can appeal to a fundamental consensus. Most of us do agree that missiology is a part of eschatology and that missions are pneumatological realities and therefore that missions have a peculiar urgency as their nature. This eschatological and pneumatological urgency is an expression of the nature of the missions. They never become our missions; they remain God's missions. They take place when we do not plan them, and when we plan them they may even never happen.

From these missionary happenings we have to make our missiological and ecumenical interpretations. For missiologists and ecumenists the popular notion of action-research is the only possibility, if we do not work as antiquarians. We have to observe what happens and we have to participate in the happenings in order to know what missions are in these days and what it means to live an ecumenical life in a world like ours. Let me repeat: only by living in missionary situations, in which the world is real and surprising, can missionary and ecumenical theology be created.

NOTES

1. See *Experiments with Man*, ed. Hans-Ruedi Weber (New York: Friendship Press, 1969; WCC Studies No 6).

2. I have described the missiological part of this development in "Some Main Trends in Modern Protestant Missiology" *Studia Theologica* XIX, 1-2 (Oslo: Universitetsforlaget, 1965), pp. 238-259, and in "Some Main Trends in the Renewal of Roman Catholic Missiology," in *Challenge and Response* (Minneapolis: Augsburg Publishing House, 1966), pp. 116-144.

3. In *Drafts for Sections* (Geneva: WCC, 1968), the proposed draft is found on pp. 28ff with an important commentary on pp. 33ff. From Germany, "Kritische Bemerkungen" were presented to the section, and a group of Scandinavian missiologists presented "An Alternative Draft," but many more comments were given from all parts of the church. The final version of the text is found in *The Uppsala 68 Report* (WCC 1968), pp. 21ff. See also *IRM*, No. 230 (April 1969), pp. 145ff. and No. 231 (July 1969), pp. 354ff.

4. What is important for missiology and ecumenics today is often happening in very secular ways—in the newspapers, in press-services, in radio and TV, in associations for futurology, in youth and student groups, etc.

5. The principal studies of the World Council of Churches are listed on pp. 44ff. in *Study Encounter* VI, No. 1 (1970).

6. Mady A. Thung, in *Concept* (June 1970), p. 31.

7. *Ibid.*

8. The first issue without the "s" is April 1969.

9. Editorial in *IRM*, No. 230 (April 1969), p. 141.

10. *Ibid*, pp. 141-142. In *Planning for Mission* (1967²), pp. 37ff., Hoekendijk gives some "Notes on the Meaning of Mission(ary)" in which the *missio Dei* consensus is developed in detail.

11. *Drafts for Sections* (Uppsala 1968), p. 33; compare Galatians 4:4-6.

12. *The New English Bible*, Galatians 5:22.

13. N. A. Nissiotis, *Die Theologie der Ostkirche im ökumenischen Dialog* (Stuttgart, 1968); P. Evdokimov: *L'Ésprit Saint dans la tradition ortodoxe* (Paris, 1970).

14. *Drafts for Sections* (Uppsala 1968), p. 33.

15. Werner Simpfendörfer, *Offene Kirche, kritische Kirche* (Stuttgart: Kreuz Verlag, 1969).

16. *Include Me Out* (London 1968), p. 72.

Guidelines for a
New Theology of Mission

William B. Frazier, M.M.

"Can the Church be the same if the world is different?" Not if
the Church is going to realistically confront the world, says
Maryknoll Father William Frazier. There must be a fresh emphasis, he suggests, for redefining the Church and its mission.
This new emphasis is found in Vatican Council II's understanding of the Church as sign, in place of the former concept of the
Church as sanctuary ("a place of refuge situated in a hostile environment"). According to Fr. Frazier, the implications of this
new image of the Church, "far from threatening the relevance of
the Christian mission, actually reveal a new and brighter missionary challenge," and in this article, reprinted by permission
from the Winter 1967-68 issue of *Worldmission* (New York), he
discusses the implications for mission of the Church as sign.
William Frazier, M.M., has his S.T.D. degree from the Angeli-
cum in Rome and is professor of dogmatic theology at the
Maryknoll Seminary in Maryknoll, New York.

Current thinking about Christian mission is characterized
by a probing of the basic questions. Today we are occupied with
the very concept and purpose of mission in contrast to yesterday's concern with tactics and techniques. Walter Freytag put it
well when he said: "Formerly mission had problems; today it has
itself become a problem."

One of the best indicators of this new focus of mission
thinking is the reaction of distress and anxiety currently being
voiced by missionaries themselves, those actually laboring in the

field. No longer are they preoccupied with problems of personnel and finance; no longer is their thinking dominated by the difficulties of mission method and maintenance. Not that these perennial concerns have been settled but a new and more radical source of anguish has emerged. Today missionaries sense that the missionary enterprise itself may be in danger of foundering. What troubles them is not so much the manifold hardship of doing their job, but the far more debilitating uneasiness of wondering if they really have a job to do.

The situation is roughly analogous to the growing labor crisis in the United States where automation is gradually swelling the ranks of the jobless. Modern technology is discovering more than adequate substitutes for the productive energies of man. The result, of course, is that many are losing not only their livelihood, but also their identity as contributing members of society. A similar phenomenon seems to be occurring among those engaged in the missionary labors of the Church. For one thing, the missionary seems to be losing whatever identity he once may have had as a promoter of socio-economic development. Government organizations of the Peace Corps variety have stepped boldly and capably into the modern picture with monetary resources, personnel and techniques which can make the best efforts of missionaries look anemic by comparison. The prospect of losing his socio-economic leadership, however, is not a lethal blow to the missionary's confidence in himself and in his work, as long as he is able to find identity in the domain of the Spirit. The really distressing thing is that even here, where the missionary could always run to assure himself that he was needed, the unique importance of his contribution seems to be seriously challenged. For contemporary theology reminds us that the saving gift of grace does not wait upon the missionary efforts of the Church. What then is left for the missionary to do? Overshadowed in his socio-economic role by international welfare programs and compromised in his spiritual fatherhood by a non-Christian world already embraced by the Spirit, the missionary would seem to have been sent to the nations for no real purpose; he would seem to be headed for the ranks of the unemployed.

This problem, which currently dominates the agenda of missiology, has given body and direction to the presentation which follows. The burden will be to show that new departures in mission theory, far from threatening the relevance of the Christian mission, actually reveal a new and brighter missionary challenge.

A few words first of all about the crisis itself. Despite the insecurity and discomfort which accompany them, crises are usually occasions of progress. The reason, of course, is that progress simply does not happen until we have lost confidence to some degree in the status quo. There is every indication that missionaries are presently struggling with a crisis of this kind, a crisis of creativity, out of which, hopefully, a corrected sense of missionary identity may emerge. The soundest reason for optimism, of course, is that Vatican II has stimulated most of what is happening in the world of Catholic mission theory today. Paul VI admitted in his first encyclical that the Church had begun to question its own identity and was striving in council to gain a deeper self-awareness. What this means, of course, is that the crisis of mission is really a crisis of Church. Both are painful, but both enjoy the blessing of the Spirit.

We turn now to the theology of mission, and in particular to the developments of recent years. What is behind the new understanding of mission which is taking shape gradually but surely under the pressure of controversy? Like every other topic of theology today, thinking about mission is being profoundly influenced by the Church's new openness toward the world, that is, by the phenomenon of secularization. The human and the worldly are being taken more seriously and respectfully than ever before. The requirements of the next world are no longer being conceived in opposition to the genuine aspirations of the present one. Rigid barriers between sacred and secular realities are breaking down. Religious attitudes and values are being remodeled with the hope of stimulating Christians to greater respect for and participation in the secular order. The Church is learning to stand in awe before the goodness and nobility which thrive beyond its borders, and it has put aside the inclination to minimize these extra-ecclesial riches by relegating them to the merely natural order. The documents of Vatican II affirm, quite unashamedly, that the non-Christian world, to the very depths of the whole secular domain, is very much the dwelling place of the Spirit.

How is the Church to confront this newly discovered world, a world bathed in light rather than darkness, a world inviting confidence rather than distrust? Can the Church be the same if the world is different? Can the Church realistically confront such a world without redefining itself and its mission? These are the real questions which burdened the fathers of Vatican II and which inclined them to approve a new emphasis in the definition of Church. The fresh concept occurs for the first time in the opening paragraph of *Lumen Gentium:* "The Church is a kind of sacrament or sign," and again in paragraph 48 which asserts that the Church is "the universal sacrament of salvation." These declarations represent an epoch-making advance in the Church's self-understanding. They summarize very simply but very profoundly what the Church is meant to be in a "world come of age."

The tragedy is that the revolutionary implications of sign and sacrament as expressions of Church are simply not coming through. Many Christians are aware that these terms are being used repeatedly and emphatically with reference to the Church, but relatively few seem to realize what difference this makes. The reason is not that these terms are so nebulous in themselves, nor that theologians have failed to explain them. The main reason is that sign and sacrament represent a new departure in thinking about the Church and can only be understood when placed in contrast with a former way of thinking. To speak of the Church as sign and sacrament is not only to assume a new point of view, but to put aside an old one. Until the older view is recalled and clarified, the newer one is bound to remain ambiguous. "The human mind," as Bergson observed, "is so constructed that it cannot begin to understand the new until it has done everything in its power to relate it to the old."

What is the concept of Church which Vatican II attempted to correct with its emphasis on sign? Admittedly, there is no one term which represents the former concept of Church as well as sign represents the current one, but there is a term which conveys rather well the kind of siege mentality that more or less dominated the Church's self-image prior to Vatican II. That term is sanctuary. The pre-conciliar Church seems to have understood itself as a kind of sanctuary of salvation. Implicit in the Council's definition of the Church as sign is an admission that sign-thinking has replaced sanctuary-thinking in matters of ecclesiology. Accordingly, the full meaning of sign as applied to the Church can be appreciated only by careful reflection on what distinguishes a sign from a sanctuary.

A sanctuary is a place of refuge situated in a hostile environment, which justifies its existence by bringing men into its premises in order to protect and nourish them. For a long time, the Church conceived itself more or less in this way, as a kind of sacred vessel or receptacle possessed of saving resources not available, or at least not readily available, beyond its visible circumference. The mission of this Church was to extend its unique riches to all men by laboring to contain all men. In principle, if not in fact, Vatican II brought an end to this manner of conceiving the Church, not by explicitly rejecting it, but by preferring to speak of the Church as a sign. For sign is a term and a concept which runs counter to the major premises of sanctuary-thinking, and in so doing offers a radically new starting point for reflection on the Church and its mission. Unlike a sanctuary, a sign is meant to point beyond itself and to have its impact outside itself. Unlike a sanctuary, a sign is not an enclosure, but a disclosure. A sign performs its function not by containing, but by communicating; not by annexation, but by representation. In relation to their respective environments, sign is a humble image, sanctuary a haughty one; sign is an image of service, sanctuary an image of separation; a sign is cooperative, a sanctuary is competitive; a sanctuary finds within itself any action which is really important, a sign points beyond itself to where the action is. In a word, the main improvement of sign over sanctuary as an image of the Church is the quality of openness to its environment which, in application to the Church, means openness to the world.

Failure to take account of sign and sanctuary as competing images of the Church explains much of the distress and confusion associated with the new theology of mission. On the other hand, once this competition is recognized it can serve as a helpful instrument for probing the new theology itself and for resolving many of the problems which it raises.

As indicated earlier, current thinking about the nature of

mission has been profoundly influenced by the process of secularization, through which the Church is developing a more optimistic attitude toward the world. By far the most striking example of this new optimism is the growing theological consensus that salvation is as open and available to those outside the visible Church as it is to those within. Theologically, it is becoming more and more difficult to hold that Christians have a better or easier chance to be saved than non-Christians. The main reason is that there is really no other way of taking seriously the biblical affirmation that God is the "Savior of all men" (1 Tim. 4, 10). And, incidentally, there is really no other way of taking the world seriously either. We stand distant enough from the origins of Christianity to know that the visible Church has not succeeded and very likely will not succeed in bringing the majority of men to the waters of baptism. There are other indications too, such as the New Testament's awareness of a world of faith beyond the borders of Israel, and Augustine's impression that those really inside the Church and those really outside are often very difficult to distinguish. Data like these support the Vatican Council's own vigorous affirmation about the availability of saving grace for all non-Christians who "sincerely seek God and . . . do his will as it is known to them." Surely, these last were not meant to be a minority group in heaven.

Here, then, is the nub of the contemporary crisis of mission: the conflict between the accessibility of salvation outside the visible Church and traditional missionary aims. If membership in the Church does not make it possible or at least easier to be saved, then what meaning can the Church and its mission possess? In fact, there may be no meaning or great meaning, depending on how Church and mission are defined. If, in the given circumstances, the Church is conceived as a sanctuary and its mission as a membership drive, there is simply no way of preserving significance for either of these realities. A sanctuary is needed only when salvation is impossible or at least imperfect outside its walls. Accordingly, sanctuary-thinking, as applied to Church and mission, is thoroughly incompatible with the growing theological emphasis on the universal availability of salvation. The only way of preserving the identity of the Christian mission in a world already caressed and cultivated by the Spirit is to break through the common sanctuary pattern of Church with the more appropriate imagery of sign.

Sign is an ideal term for defining a Church newly conscious of the manifold workings of grace and salvation beyond its own visible limits, that is, in the so-called secular world. This is because sign is an agreeable kind of image which allows for cooperation with other forces and factors toward the realization of a common goal. Implicit in the very idea of sign is a readiness to serve an objective larger and more important than itself. And this is precisely what is demanded of the Church once it has come to realize the enormous spiritual potential of the world which surrounds it. The mission of such a Church is not co-extensive with the mission of God; rather, the mission of God is the all-embracing power of salvation at work always and everywhere, whereas the mission of the Church has its own special role to play within that broader process. Just what that role is becomes clear as we delve further into the implications of the Church as sign.

Very simply, the function of a sign is to represent or testify to something which otherwise would remain hidden or obscure. Such is the essential missionary task of the Church. The Church is a community formed to witness on a universal scale to the saving love of God which embraces all men. Strictly speaking, nothing more than this can be demanded of a successful missionary undertaking. The Church fulfills its mission in any given locality and becomes the privileged instrument of the risen Savior by its efforts to lend flesh and bones to the ideal of Christian love. The missionary aim of the Church is not to bring men the gift of salvation, but to acclaim and accommodate the saving mystery already at work in them.

Understanding the essence of mission in this way amounts to a departure from what has long been regarded as the primary goal of evangelization, namely, individual conversion. No one will deny that conversion, as a turning to God from sin, is necessary for salvation. Rather, what seems to be minimized by conceiving mission in terms of sign is the importance of conversion to the Church. The topic has become a sensitive one and is frequently overlaid with emotion and misunderstanding. Accordingly, special care must be exerted to clarify the issues involved.

One thing is certain: a sanctuary-Church, by its very definition, is obliged to look upon conversion as a maximum priority. Among the most important signs of its vitality will be its size and its rate of expansion. A sanctuary-Church is essentially a converting Church. It is just as evident, however, that the Church as a sign is not essentially a converting Church. A sign preoccupies itself with exposure, rather than expansion. This is not to say that expansion is unimportant, but that it is a subordinate concern. The Church as sign is interested primarily in perfecting its loving service of men, not as a kind of bait offered to lead unbelievers to baptism, but simply as a testimony to the presence of God's saving love in the world. Witness is not for the sake of conversions, but conversions for the sake of witness. The rule of expansion for a witnessing Church, then, is simply the need to give the sign of salvation indigenous roots in every human situation. Beyond this it is useless to probe as to how little or how large the Church is meant to be. The important thing is that the Church understand and faithfully pursue its call to raise the sign of salvation in the world.

The current secular trend in mission theology requires that the Church become thoroughly rooted in the human condition and obedient to the demands of development, peace and unity in the world. As a sanctuary, the Church could concentrate legitimately on providing its members with the sacraments and the Word of God, and its non-members with appropriate inducements to partake of these riches. But if the Church is a sign, its energies will be centered not only on its own sacramental life, but on the paschal mystery at work in the events of secular life and time. So conceived, the Church will not be content to take care of itself, but will actively shoulder the whole range of human problems in testimony to the saving concern of God. Aware that a dis-incarnate Gospel will not reach the ears of men, the Church will strive to proclaim the good news first and foremost in the idiom of action.

A further requirement of the secular emphasis in mission is that the so-called secular wing of the Church, the laity, enter fully and responsibly into the missionary enterprise. The people of God have been given the command to carry the Gospel to the ends of the earth. Only as a witnessing community comprised of priests, laity and religious can the Church portray the mystery of salvation in all its fullness.

Lastly, the new mission of the Church must be a mission of sharing and exchange with all peoples and cultures, an ecumenical venture in the broadest sense of the term. Dialogue must be the ruling theme rather than unilateral imposition. This attitude arises, not out of a sense of politeness or fair play, but as a direct consequence of the realization that the grace of Christ always precedes the Christian mission. Accordingly, the Church is sent to the nations, not only to enrich, but to be enriched. The world has a mission to the Church as well as the Church to the world. This means, of course, that missionary adaptation is much more than a question of expediency or technique. For only by clothing itself with the cultures of the world is the Church able to recognize the depths of its own catholicity.

As indicated earlier, the major stumbling block of the new theology of mission is its insistent recognition of the non-Christian world as a normal locus of God's saving action. This is difficult for Christians to accept because they have long since learned to be comfortable with the idea that salvation, at least in its full and proper sense, is a Christian prerogative. Non-Christians have, in fact, been relegated to an inferior position in the eyes of God. The result is that Christians tend to be rather possessive and status-conscious in matters pertaining to salvation. Catholics seem particularly susceptible to this way of thinking because of the climate of caste and privilege which they experience within the Church. The Catholic laity, for example, have occupied for centuries a state of spiritual inferiority within the Christian community due to a theology which restricted the possibility of Christian perfection to those who embraced the evangelical counsels. Accustomed as they are, then, to accepting higher and lower states of perfection within the Church itself, Catholics are unlikely to see anything incongruous about the rather precarious status of salvation traditionally assigned to non-Christians. If there are first- and second-class Christians within the Church, there will be little difficulty in finding a still lower class for non-Christians. Under the impetus of Vatican II, however, the whole question of the so-called privileged states of perfection has been brought under re-examination. The *Dogmat-*

ic Constitution on the Church affirms unequivocally that every Christian, by reason of his baptism, is called to perfect holiness. This clarification was received with enthusiasm, of course, by married Catholics and others who have embraced vocations in the world. Members of religious communities, on the other hand, were immediately confronted with a crisis of identity, not unlike the one currently preoccupying the thoughts of missionaries. If religious vows are not a means of achieving a special degree of holiness, why bother with them? If one can attain equal perfection in a worldly occupation, why go to the trouble of entering a religious order? Over the years, the validation of religious life in the Church has developed at the expense of denying full Christian status to non-religious. The theology of religious vocation seems to have developed its own brand of sanctuary-thinking in order to justify the existence of the religious life. Only in the life of the vows, it was argued, could one acquire the protection and nourishment necessary for mature Christian existence. The walls of the religious sanctuary, so to speak, would repel the weakness and hard-heartedness inevitably attached to life in the world. It is significant that theology is currently offering a solution to the crisis of religious vocation in much the same terms as are being used to address the crisis of mission. Religious life is no longer being defended as a sanctuary, but as a sign of perfection.

While all Christians are called to perfect holiness, they are called to manifest this holiness in different ways, some through marriage and life in the world, others through the life of the counsels. Religious life is not a more perfect state of life than life in the world, but it is a better sign of one aspect of the life which all Christians must live, namely, the mystery of transcendence. Christians living in the world, on the other hand, are better able to portray the incarnational aspect of the Christian vocation. The validity of the religious life, then, does not depend on a depreciation of the lay vocation; each state of life serves the other in manifesting the riches of Christian holiness. When Catholics become more accustomed to the advantages of sign over sanctuary thinking within the Church itself, and when they have fully accepted the new classless Catholicism which is emerging, they will be much more ready than they are now to apply the same principles to their relations with non-Christians. Just as the religious life can justify itself without making second-class Christians out of non-religious, so also can the Christian mission justify itself without diminishing the salvational status of non-Christians. Non-Christians do not need membership in the visible Church in order to be saved; they do need the Church to arrive at a deeper awareness of the saving mystery by which they are continually embraced. All men stand equal before the saving invitation of God; the Church is meant to stand out only as an unambiguous sign of the hidden depths and eventual term of a salvation which never ceases to be offered.

Once the idea of sign is substituted for sanctuary as a working image of the Church, the crisis of mission assumes new proportions. It is no longer a matter of wondering if the Church as mission really has a job to do, but of wondering if the job it has to do is really being done. The real crisis of mission today is the Church's failure to function consistently in the world as a relevant sign of God's redeeming love, a failure to be present and active in today's version of the human conflict, a hesitancy to take sides, a refusal to speak out. The failure of the Christian mission today is not a failure to convert the world to the Church, but a failure to convert the Church to the world. This failure is due in great part to the persistent influence of sanctuary-thinking on the formation of missionary attitudes. There is, in fact, a subtle correlation between sanctuary-thinking and irrelevancy in the Church today. As indicated earlier, sanctuary-thinking turns the Church in upon itself and away from the world and its problems. Retaining, increasing and nourishing its members are its chief preoccupations. Individual conversion and salvation are top priorities. Needless to say, a gigantic institutional structure and enormous monetary reserves are required to keep such an operation going. As long as the Church labors under this kind of self-image it will experience a dilemma between the need to retain its membership and the need to espouse unpopular social causes. A sanctuary-Church will always be preoccupied with numbers, for a sanctuary is simply a failure if it does not keep most people inside. The Church as a sign, on the other hand, is free to concentrate its energies on the demands of relevancy. For as long as a sign is communicating, it doesn't have to apologize for being small. If the Church is to emerge successfully from the crisis of relevancy in which it is now engaged, it will be through a gradual awakening to the fact that the world, and not the Church, is the focal point of God's saving action, and that the Christian mission is a joining in that activity in the world. Christians have not been called to the Church for their own sakes, but for the sake of others—to serve as a sign and instrument of God's universal saving purpose.

The secularization of mission theology which is taking place under the impetus of Vatican II represents a milestone in the course of mission history. Never before have missionary aims and energies been so thoroughly re-examined. The results, as we have seen, are a new terminology and a new awareness of the essential missionary task. But there are also some ambiguities.

The first of these is the misunderstanding sometimes engendered by the idea of secularization itself. To secularize mission theology does not mean to divest it of its connection with God; quite the contrary, the whole movement of secularization as a Christian phenomenon is to recognize the saving action of God in situations where it has not been recognized before—that is, in the domain of the secular, as secular. To secularize is not to belittle the influence of God, but to broaden it; it is to affirm that secular realities, as such, are God-intended, God-given and God-blessed.

A related misconception is that the secularization of mission leads to an uncritical optimism about the non-Christian world and the whole secular order. Such is not the case. Secularization implies the universal availability of salvation; it does not imply that all men are actually saved. Sensitivity to the profound spiritual values of the secular world does not excuse the Church from judging the world and its enterprises in the light of the Gospel. As a matter of fact, the Church simply cannot function as the prophetic sign it is meant to be unless it is willing to criticize deviations from the Christian ideal, no matter where they occur.

Another criticism often leveled at a secularized concept of mission is that it seems to reduce the Church to an elite corps of practicing Christians who are ready to involve themselves seriously in the task of being a sign to the nations. This would seem to exclude the little man from the Church, the man of minimal Christian inclinations, the backslider. Such is not the case, however. If the Church is to be a realistic sign of God's activity in all men, it should be expected to reveal not only the triumph of grace, but also a full cross-section of the struggle and failure which all men experience in trying to find their way to God.

Finally, there is a complaint that the secularization of mission theology has reduced the urgency of the missionary task. This is true. The urgency of mission is much greater when it is linked to the prospect of damnation for all who die outside the Church. Supplying men with the necessary means of salvation is a more urgent undertaking than simply manifesting and serving the salvation already at work in them. But in another sense, the challenge of the new mission is far brighter than that of the old. Early missionary efforts, based on a rigid connection between salvation and baptism, for all their urgency, were severely limited in scope and impact. The missionary was really able to help only those who decided to enter the Church; his labors really made sense only if they ended at the font of baptism. In the new mission, however, there are no such limitations. For the mission of the Church as sign is a mission to all men, and even especially to those who will never bear the Christian name. Moreover, no legitimate effort of the missionary need be in vain, for the new mission contributes to a broader saving venture.

In conclusion, a word about the law of progress and growth which seems to be at work in the theology of mission. It is the same law which is constantly recurring in the Scriptures—the law of time and history and experience. The development of the old Israel into the new was not according to a clear-cut ideal or pattern which the chosen people first understood and then reduced to practice. Quite the contrary, Israel responded to the call of God like Abraham, "without knowing where he was to go" (Heb. 11:8). Only in the course of living their vocation did the people of God gradually discover what their vocation really was. Israel never solved its own crisis of identity until it solved its hesitancy to move into the future and to take instruction from the hard facts of history. A similar law has long been at work in the Church's struggle to identify the nature of its missionary task. The Church has learned about its mission from the events of history as well as from the sources of revelation. Like Israel, the Church has matured in its understanding of mission through the pedagogy of time and events, and particularly through a deepened awareness of the world. The new missiology is a milestone in the continuing journey of the Church toward full availability as an instrument of the Savior-God. As the Church moves into the future, not always knowing where it is to go, new missionary objectives will emerge and better missiologies will be devised. Through this experience the Church will come to recognize a hidden pattern which has been present all the time, namely that the purpose of mission is to discover the purpose of mission.

The Present Crisis in Mission

José Míguez-Bonino

Many Christians today are confused and concerned by all the talk about a "crisis" in the Christian world mission. What is the nature of the crisis? What caused it? And what does it require of us? In this speech given in the United States, Dr. José Míguez-Bonino—an Argentine Methodist theologian who for nine years was president of the Union Theological Seminary in Buenos Aires—says that conditions in the Third World today "call into question not only mission as such, but the theology which has undergirded it, the Church which has supported it, and even the message that it has proclaimed." He sees the crisis as "God's call to repentance, to conversion, and to obedience . . . the time for a new birth for the Church." The test of renewal in mission, he says, will be "our ability to proclaim Jesus Christ as the liberator." Dr. Míguez—the only Latin American Protestant observer at the Second Vatican Council—is now dean of graduate studies at the Higher Institute of Theological Studies in Buenos Aires. His address is reprinted, with permission, from the November 12, 1971 issue of *The Church Herald* (Grand Rapids, Michigan), the official magazine of the Reformed Church in America.

The problem of the mission enterprise is very real today. I say this because I am deeply concerned about what happens to all of us when we discover the sickness of the missionary enterprise into which you have poured so much money, people, love, and hopes, and to which we in the younger churches owe our very existence as Christians and as churches.

The depth of the crisis is indicated by the fact that the amount of money given for missionary work is decreasing in most large denominations. If it is not in others, it is because some churches are usually a few years late in being hit by the crisis. The number of those who choose missionary vocations follows this same trend. The uncertainty and confusion among many missionaries who return home early is also widely known. Mission boards engage in self-examination and reorganization, sometimes revealing more insecurity than functionality. Criticism from overseas churches and secular specialists becomes sharper and sharper.

All of this has been amply documented. We cannot hide the fact that we don't quite believe in what we have been doing and are doing in missions. The crisis can be described in a variety of ways. It is partly connected with upheavals in theological thought. There have always been conflicts in interpretation in theological thought, but they used to be restricted to the academic world. Now they have broken into the mass media and seem to erode the certainty without which a person cannot commit himself or his resources to a cause.

The growth of the younger churches, on the other hand, has also had an impact. To some extent, the missionary enterprise has lost its adventure of pioneering and has become bureaucratic. The basic fact, though, to which all the other factors are related, is this—and the crisis we face hinges on it: we have discovered that the missionary enterprise of the last one hundred and fifty years is closely related to and interwoven with the expansion of the economic, political, and cultural influence of the Anglo-Saxon world. We from the Third World call this expansion neocolonialism or imperialism. It has been related to the idea of Manifest Destiny, civilizing enterprise, the white man's burden, and many other slogans.

Whatever the name, however, certain things are clear. First, this is the process through which the world has been and increasingly is being divided into the affluent northern world, and the impoverished so-called Third World. Second, this constantly deteriorating situation is no longer accepted by the Third World. Whatever the cost, two-thirds of the population of the world is committed to a struggle to the death for their own liberation, which means for us the elimination of what we understand to be imperialistic aggression. Third, consciously or unconsciously, and mostly unconsciously, the missionary enterprise has been related to the routes of expansion, the channels of penetration, the slogans, the cultural patterns of this process of expansion and domination. Fourth, Christians in both the sending and the receiving countries are increasingly aware of and concerned with this fact, which results in remorse, uncertainty, loss of confidence, and crises in identity for many missionaries and national church leaders, both here and overseas.

All this seems to call into question not only mission as such, but the theology which has undergirded it, the Church which has supported it, and even the message that it has proclaimed. This is, I submit, our real problem. What can we do now? We could try to apply all sorts of qualifications, distinctions, exceptions, and corrections to these facts. I think you have been given some of these qualifications. Theologians and historians are usually clever in doing this. And we could conclude that perhaps things are not really that bad. Or we could try to introduce a number of modifications without coming to terms with the basic issue. We could start adding to our work all sorts of social action projects, development goals, and humanitarian motivations, until we have replaced the mission of the Church by a sort of mixture of welfare state, Rotary Club, and debating society. I hope you will not take this role either. The mission of the Church can be only one thing, and that one thing has to be rooted in Jesus Christ alone. All activities must be centered on this one thing.

It is precisely at this point that I think that the present crisis must be our point of departure. We must not try to go around it, or over it; we must go through it. This crisis is God's call to repentance, to conversion, and to obedience. It is the way to a renewal of all our churches. It is the opportunity for a deeper understanding of the Gospel. It is the possibility of bringing to the obedience of the Gospel areas of life and thought which so far have been held captive by the world. In a word, I think this is the time for a new birth for the Church.

The Struggle for a New Society

On my continent, Latin America, the people involved in the struggle for a new society and new men evoke only one name more often than that of Che Guevara. It is the name of Jesus Christ. You find it in protest songs, in books, in declarations, and in poetry. The exaltation of Christ is as common as the condemnation of the Church. Our revolutionaries appeal from the Church to Christ. It would be all too easy to point out theological heresies, exegetical errors, and confusions in their interpretation. These corrections have to be made. But more and more Christians, and even theologians, are beginning to see that in their sometimes strange and even blasphemous insistence on identifying Jesus Christ and the fight for liberation, they are true prophets. The Holy Spirit is calling all of us to repentance, understanding, and obedience. It is at this point that our faith will be tested, our ability to proclaim Jesus Christ as the liberator. The Redeemer asks that we commit ourselves totally to him as he leads our people through the Jordan to a new life and a new society out of the slavery of Egypt; to shape the life, the worship, the service of our churches according to this. Our ability to see this as our confession of faith today will be the test of our faith in Jesus Christ. Our blindness, our half-hearted commitment, or our reluctance to this commitment will be our denial of Jesus Christ.

Faith and unbelief mark the ways for us before the call of Christ, the liberator. There is no third possibility. "He who is not with me is against me." We believe that this identification of Jesus Christ with the struggle for liberation means for us Christians both assuming as our own and criticizing from the inside the concrete struggle for the emancipation from Western, and mainly but not exclusively, American economic, political, and cultural domination and from internal oppression and injustice. It means participating completely in this struggle and criticizing it from the inside.

Second, it means dialogue with the groups and ideologies which are pioneering in this struggle. We cannot accept them as they are, but we cannot remain in some sort of other-world reality, outside the struggle. Actually, there is no such reality. An area free of political and ideological commitment is a false paradise which does not exist. Certainly we are now conscious of the fact that the Church always plays a role in society; it has always done so, in favor of one group or another; it has always thrown its weight on one side of the struggle or on the other side. Perhaps for the first time we can now bring this fact into the open, see clearly what the alternatives are, and try to shape our choices according to the Gospel. We can now see that we will either support the continuation of oppression or the struggle for liberation. We will support one or the other by the way we teach, worship, preach, use our money, speak, or remain silent. There is no third possibility. Perhaps our fathers will be excused at the judgment because they did not see this clearly. But we will have to give an account for our decision.

I fully agree with those who insist that evangelism, person-to-person witness to the Gospel, and social action (I would prefer to speak of the struggle for justice) must not be played against each other. But I don't think that this says enough, particularly because I sense that there is a tendency to think that evangelism can remain unaffected, can carry on business as usual, without forgetting social action, but without being fundamentally changed. This, it seems to me, is to be a deadly misunderatanding. The real problem is that the alliance of missions and Western capitalistic expansion has distorted the Gospel beyond recognition, and that evangelism, prayer, worship, and personal devotions have been held captive to an individualistic, other-worldly, success-crazy, legalistic destruction of the Gospel. Evangelism, prayer, worship, and private devotions do not have to be abandoned. They have to be converted to Christ. What happens when somebody is converted to Christ? He must know that he is not going into some sort of secluded soul fellowship, but that he is called to obedience to the one who said, "The Spirit of the Lord is upon me, because he has anointed me to preach good news to the poor. He has sent me to proclaim release to the captives and recovering of sight to the blind, to set at liberty those who are oppressed, to proclaim the acceptable year of the Lord." This is the Christ of the Gospel and there is no other Christ to be converted to.

We pray to the God who wants righteousness and mercy, to

the God who puts down the mighty from their thrones and raises up the poor and the downtrodden; this is the God of the Bible to whom we say, "Thy will be done." And there is no other God. You say that Jesus loves you. But who is this Jesus who loves you? The Jesus who had compassion on the people. But he was no sentimental flower boy. The Jesus who loves you is the Jesus who threw the merchants from the temple, who rebuked the Pharisees, and who was nailed to the cross as a subversive.

This is the only Jesus there is. Preaching another Christ, worshiping another God, is preaching and worshiping an idol. We must have evangelism; we must have person-to-person witness to Christ, to the Christ of the Gospel; we must have prayer and devotion to the God of the prophets. This is the God, this is the Christ we are called to worship and proclaim. We could go on talking about resurrection, about life everlasting, about heaven and hell. There is nothing that we cannot bring into this new perspective. But there is a need to convert everything we do to the Gospel of Jesus Christ.

A Struggle for Liberation

Now I have been speaking about "us." Who is "us"? I was speaking primarily of a growing number of Christians, both Catholic and Protestant in Latin America, but I think this has to do with all Christians everywhere. Perhaps I should stop now because it is not for me to say what this may mean for the mission of the Church in this country. On the other hand, in Christ, I have the privilege, indeed the duty, to take your questions and needs and struggles as my own. I trust that you will believe me that I do this, to the best of my knowledge, in real love and humility.

I am also aware that precisely when we are called to reject a form of mission which has been too closely allied with the Anglo-Saxon culture, I am calling you to participate in a form of mission which is closely related to the Third World struggle for liberation. I dare to do it, first, because I think that liberation is not only our problem, but also your problem, and second, because you cannot be neutral. Your Church, your money, your people will either reinforce the pattern of domination and exploitation, or participate in this struggle for liberation. Perhaps our grandchildren will have to correct our errors one day, but if we cannot remain neutral today, what are the hope and future of the American Christian mission overseas in the light of all this?

Now I offer a challenge. In the tenth chapter of the Book of Acts, we read the dramatic story of the first Gentile convert, Cornelius. It could also be called the conversion of Peter. God invites Peter in a dream to eat unclean animals—unclean from a Jewish point of view. Peter refuses. He is still wondering about the dream when he is invited to go to the house of a Roman to preach the Gospel there. Somewhat reluctantly, he does it. The Holy Spirit is poured out on the Roman household and Peter finds himself baptizing this Gentile into the Church.

A few days later, he has difficulty explaining to the brethren in Jerusalem what he has done. Finally, he is driven to a rather curious apology. "It is clear," he says, "that God gave the Gentiles the same gift he gave us. Who was I, then, to try to stop God?" In fact, as Peter says, "I couldn't help it. It was God's fault, not mine. After all, what could I do? He is the boss."

Just like Peter, we all know what worked in missions. You sent a missionary, who went from house to house, gathered the people, and preached the Gospel. Some were converted, then instructed and baptized and gathered into a church, and there they learned to behave as Christians, adopt civilized habits, abandon drink, polygamy, and other vices, learn honesty and responsibility, and in turn work for the conversion of other people. God has indeed worked in this way, and we must be thankful for it. But when he starts doing strange things, we are invited to sit with unclean people. Revolutionaries, politicians, scientists, and educationists will speak of a number of things which we are not used to—political-economic structures, systems of production, international relations—and we are called to speak in the name of Jesus Christ to these people on some of their issues. Even more, God seems to be pushing us to work with them.

To be quite honest, we are taken aback, and are afraid. But again and again we find a genuine openness for the Gospel, a passionate commitment for justice and real human life in which we cannot but see the work of the Spirit. We cannot quite understand it or explain what is happening; we cannot give any other but Peter's explanation, "Who am I to try to stop God?"

The Struggle against a System

Then there is the cost, and the cost for the American churches is very heavy. I wish I could spare myself and you the harshness of what I am going to say, but I don't think I can. The struggle which we are called to join, which I am calling you to join, pitches us against the policies and interests of this country, at least against the policies and interests that dominate this country. It is not merely this or that exceptional economic concern or military program that we have to resist; it is an entire system that concerns local tyranny in our own Third World in foreign interests, economic exploitation, military repression, and cultural brainwashing, to perpetrate oppression. Many of you and many of us are knowingly or unknowingly part of that system.

Is the Church ready to pay the cost of joining this struggle? Again, we must decide. We know now that the alternative is to accept and reinforce, or refuse and attack. The Church has usually conformed to the cause and interest pursued by the society in which it was found. At times it has dared to say no to certain things in it—vice, corruption, slavery. Perhaps this is the first time since the third century that the Church is offered the challenge to set itself against the whole structure of an evil world —and the world is evil as the New Testament says—and say "no" in the name of Jesus Christ.

For too long the Church has been seen smoothly accompanying the life of society. For too many people the Gospel and the American way of life have been synonymous. Private foreign investment, cultural influence, and foreign aid have too often been seen as closely allied to mission. Anyone who starts questioning this alliance cannot expect a cordial welcome. The prestige, the respectability, the financial resources, the influence of a Church which would dare to take this way are in grave danger. For us in a repressive society in the Third World, the cost may be more dramatic. For you, in an apparently permissive society, it may be spiritually much more painful.

The biblical story of the rich young ruler comes to mind again and again as I think about the challenge facing the American Church. It is not merely a question of selling and giving. It is the willingness to risk the things on which one could count. It is so natural that the rich young ruler went away sad, with a heavy heart. And not even the Lord, who loved him, precisely *because* he loved him, was able to accept him unless he was willing to pay the cost.

Historians will not be surprised if the American Church chooses to remain on the side of its society and follow in its trends. What historians will find difficult to explain is why so many Christian leaders, missionaries, mission boards, pastors, laymen, and young people in America have begun to act out of character. I could now begin quoting names and stories, strange stories of pastors who will risk their pulpit, of Church administrators who will say things that will undoubtedly harm the budgets, of synods and conventions taking sides on issues that will bring them reproach and accusations, of missionaries who are warned and threatened by the embassy of their own country— these stories will one day be told as a chapter of the Book of Acts of the Spirit. And at that time the Church will be proud of them. And it will also tell the story of the many who went away sad because they were very rich. The cost was too much for them and the Lord did not keep them by his side.

The Tasks of Our Mission

Finally, there are the tasks of mission. We are called to accept the challenge and to pay the cost. But this never happens in a void, in a vacuum. It is always related to concrete tasks. Christian faith and, consequently, Christian mission are never mere declaration. They are to be caught in God's action. To become witnesses to Jesus Christ, the liberator, in the struggle for the liberation of man and the transformation of society, is to be called to concrete tasks. We have the task of thinking together about the road to liberation.

In this thinking together we have to ask some questions: What is the concrete meaning of the new quality of human life which we are seeking? What are the values for which we strive? How can we witness to the value of the life of every person in the midst of the struggle to change structures and systems? These are the questions raised in the process of liberation, the questions which we must answer as Christians engaged in that process. As Christians we share the privilege of sharing together in thinking about what liberation means personally and collectively.

There are the tasks of sharing personnel, funds, and influence. Liberation is a costly enterprise. It does not just happen, particularly not when immense sums of money, technical know-how, and propaganda are being used for the perpetration of oppression and slavery. Liberation has a concrete meaning in missionary relations. We need to develop a discipline for sharing, particularly for sharing financial resources and personnel. We in the younger churches have to learn the discipline of freedom to accept and freedom to refuse, to place resources at the service of mission rather than to have mission patterned by resources.

To Learn True Sharing

You have to learn to renounce resources as a means of domination. In order to do this you must learn to lose control over what you give. Our temptation is that of the poor—the temptation to sell ourselves. Your temptation is that of the rich—to become masters. Both are sins against God and against men. There is a long way for all of us to go to learn true sharing.

There is much discussion going on in missionary circles as to whether we need short-term or lifelong missionaries, whether we need ministers or specialists in technical areas of development, whether we need people for institutions or for pioneering. What we really need is the ability for the struggle for liberation. The strategy of the struggle changes from place to place and from moment to moment. Here we need a minister and there a technician; now a person for a month, another for three months, and another for life.

The worst danger for mission at this time is reductionism.

In reductionism we try to tie God down to one form of work—personal or social, institutional or spontaneous, intellectual or practical. God's strategy is always many-sided and unpredictable. He defines for us the direction in which he is moving and invites us to follow him. But he goes as he wills and he refuses to give us job descriptions valid for all. He defines the job in the situation. What he demands is availability and obedience.

For us in the younger churches integrity is of the essence. We cannot permit ourselves to forget integrity or our own responsibility before God and before men. We cannot for the love of our brethren or for the love of God let anybody or anything stand in the way of our taking on our own shoulders our responsibility. If, in order to do that, we must say to you, our friends, "Stay home," we will do so because before God we have this grave responsibility of our integrity.

For us the most important thing is not whether we will fight with the Americans or without the Americans. It is whether or not we will fight for the liberation of our people, individually and politically. And if American churches are ready to join us in this struggle, let them be welcome. We will work with them, we will think with them, we will plan with them, we will receive their missionaries, we will use, together with them, their resources as our own resources in freedom.

If on the other hand, they want to impose on us a way of understanding in witnessing to Christ that is not related to our struggle, to what we feel is the call of God to us, we will have to tell them, "Stay home, go home; we must do our task before God and take our responsibility alone." This is the main issue, not whether the missionaries will stay at home or go abroad. It is in this respect that I speak of thinking together, sharing, and being available.

I will end with an old-fashioned evangelistic story, the story of the man who came to the minister because he was a drunkard and wanted to change. The minister said, "You just have to stop drinking, that's all." And then the man began to bargain and asked whether he could have at least one drink a day, before going to bed, or just to get up his spirits in the morning. The minister kept saying, "You have to stop drinking altogether." Finally, the man said, "Preacher, if I stop drinking, I will die."

"Then go and die and come back afterward," said the preacher.

This is my message for missions: Go and die and come back afterward. I think there is no other message for missions today than the message that Christ gave to one man a long time ago, "You must be born anew."

Mission '70—
More a Venture Than Ever

Hans Jochen Margull

After examining four traditional views of mission, a seminar at
the University of Hamburg, Germany, concluded that none was
"theologically or sociologically concrete enough," and an attempt was made to develop a new and more adequate view, starting with the ecumenical concept of the "signs of shalom." Dr.
Hans Jochen Margull, professor of missions at Hamburg, reports on the results of that effort and says that in his own view
"one of our tasks today is to accept a plurality of views of mission, and therefore a plurality of forms of missionary activity."
Professor Margull, a student of the late Walter Freytag, has
served on the staff of the World Council of Churches and as a
visiting professor at Union Theological Seminary, Tokyo. He is
the author of *Hope in Action: The Church's Task in the World*,
published by Muhlenberg Press in 1962. This article first appeared in *Der Überblick* in September 1970 and is reprinted with
the permission of Dienste in Übersee, Stuttgart, Germany. It
was translated from the German by the World Council of
Churches' translations section and first appeared in English in
the January 1971 *International Review of Mission* (Geneva).

In line with the contemporary trend, a cautious and tentative title, "Introduction to the Understanding of Mission," was
chosen for the seminar which took place in the summer term of
1970 in the Missions Academy of Hamburg University. It was
open to the whole university and attended by about fifty students
—a surprisingly large number. They included Asian, African and
Latin American students, some missionary candidates, a handful

of pastors, but mostly students of theology, among them a fairly sizable socialistic core-group.

The question in my mind as I prepared for this seminar, and obviously in the mind of the students when the discussion began, was: Are the traditional views of mission still tenable in the present year, 1970, and for the immediate future? Or, how tenable are they? We began by examining four views of mission which may be regarded as being (or at least as once having been) representative and theologically constructive:

1. Walter Freytag's view of mission is essentially the view taken by German evangelical missionary societies and is found, for example, in his 1950 address on "The Meaning and Purpose of the Christian Mission." In this view, mission is the venture of witnessing to Jesus Christ in the time between his first and second coming and consists in "the gathering of the community which waits for the Lord who will come." This gathering, however, which reaches out to the ends of the earth, is not an end in itself. The point of it is "that the message of the Lord who is to come goes through all nations as a witness to the day on which only the children of the kingdom shall escape destruction. In that sense the Christian mission is a witness of the kingdom which has come to that which is still to come."[1]

2. The view of mission in the *Decree on the Missionary Activity of the Church* of the Second Vatican Council, published in 1965 under the title *Ad Gentes*, defines the purpose of Catholic missions thus:

> The specific purpose of this missionary activity is evangelization and the planting of the Church among those people and groups where it has not yet taken root (n. 6). Through this activity that plan of God is thus fulfilled whereby the whole human race is to form one people of God, coalesce into one body of Christ, and be built up into one temple of the Holy Spirit. Since it concerns brotherly concord, this design surely corresponds with the inmost wishes of all men (n. 7). In the course of history it unfolds the mission of Christ himself (n. 5).

3. The view of mission found in Tillich's 1954 essay on

"Missions and World History"[2] represents also the approach of certain historians of religion and systematic theologians, but is also in the same direction as the thesis of Karl Rahner concerning "anonymous Christians" and the "implicit Christianity" of all men. According to Tillich, mission must be viewed as an attempt "to transform the latent Church, in its hiddenness under the forms of paganism, Judaism and humanism, into its manifestation."

4. The view of mission worked out in ecumenical discussion, especially on the basis of the theses of Hans Hoekendijk, is characteristic of the approach of those who are concerned with the practical historical effects of missions and of Christianity in general, with the conviction that faith is historically conditioned, with present social challenges and the problem of the goal of history. It can be summed up thus: "We regard our mission(s) as movements which participate in God's mission (*missio Dei*) to gather up all things in Christ—and so we are led to set up a variety of signs of the *shalom* of God in the world." According to Hoekendijk, whose use of the term *shalom* is an attempt at a concretization of the concept of the kingdom of God, this term is "a secularized concept taken out of the religious sphere (= salvation guaranteed to those who have strictly performed the prescribed rites) and commonly used to indicate all aspects of the restored and cured human condition: righteousness, truth, fellowship, communication, peace, etc. (cf. Ps. 85)." *Shalom* is in fact the Old Testament term for peace and wholeness. In Hoekendijk's view *shalom* is "a social happening, an event in interhuman relations," and as such "the fullest summary of all the gifts of the messianic era." In the discussion on this approach of Hoekendijk the following attempt at concrete illustration was proposed: "Today we find examples of the setting up of '*signs of shalom*,' among many other movements, some of which take place, quite without notice, in the Freedom Movement in the USA, in the *Aktion Sühnezeichen* in Germany, in the presence of worker-priests in France, in the venture of interconfessional groups in Holland, in the industrial missions of England or America, in the work at Riesi in Sicily, in the Telephone Samaritans, in the involvement of academies and lay institutes, in many sorts of service for peace."[3]

*The Question of Contemporary
Contexts and Challenges*

Our seminar took the view that these four concepts of mission, which in one way or another influence over 105,000 missionaries and the older and younger churches they serve, were neither theologically nor sociologically concrete enough. Even ecumenical statements formulated as recently as 1965 proved out of date or unusable in their present form. The seminar soon dismissed the four documents presented to it. In the present situation and in face of the worldwide challenges for revolutionary change, it was convinced that it must find in its own way what to concentrate on in the present moment and what to prepare for.

A starting point seemed possible in the ecumenical concept of the "signs of shalom." In order to be concrete and also to test out the historical and theological possibilities of the "signs of shalom" line of thought, we focused discussion on the following areas, each of which was taken up by a study group:

—signs of *shalom* in the face of world hunger;
—signs of *shalom* in our relations with the revolutionary situations in Latin America;
—signs of *shalom* in relation to the racial situation in Southern Africa;
—signs of *shalom* in a suburban German parish;
—signs of *shalom* in internal church situations.

The seminar thus worked over ground already covered in ecumenical discussion by the Structure of the Missionary Congregation study (1962-67). At that time, and again in the seminar, one could not take the easy way of simply and even docilely adopting accepted views of mission and then going on to discuss questions about applying them with "theological consistency." Rather, in each particular situation one had to deal with the theological question of what was to be done and what aspect of the faith was to be emphasized. The definition of mission was thus to be in terms of the situations to which it was directed. This is not without its dangers, but it was in fact the way the first Christians arrived at mission and a theology of mission. In their effort to understand missionary activity in present contexts and in the face of contemporary challenges, the study groups at the Hamburg seminar found themselves plunged into passionate and, for many, liberating discussions but also into lively arguments about formulating objectives which must be pinpointed here and now.

Lest there be any doubt about the integrity of the participants and the vigor of their faith in the light of human need, and also in the belief that they spoke for many others, I quote here some of their objectives:

Mission Viewed as Advocacy

—"Advocacy is on the side of justice; mission must go beyond acts of mercy to acts of justice."

—"Wrong is not merely to be contested case by case; the causes of injustice, violence, social inequality, etc., must be tracked down and exposed."

—"The global structures of power and economic systems—for example, those which intensify the inequality between North and South—must be made plain."

—"This involves, among other things, more stress on ethics in educating public opinion in the rich countries of the North so as to prepare them to accept economic disadvantages and genuine partnership in trade."

—"In certain circumstances churches have to recommend development service rather than military service."

—"Churches can also find themselves in situations where they must support certain revolutionary liberation movements."

—"In every case, aid must not be reserved for Christians and people willing to become Christians; as a life for others, missionary activity is for the benefit of all."

—"Mission is necessarily concerned with increased freedom for all men because it came into being as a call to the liberty of the children of God. It must therefore always include advocates who oppose every denial, diminution or mockery of freedom."

*Mission Viewed as Participation
in the Development of Humanity*

—The complacency of existing societies must be shattered, not
strengthened. To this end, social (political) needs must be effectively dramatized.
—To this end, Christians will also in certain circumstances have
to work for the socialization of land.
—Racism must be opposed and missionary activity in areas of
acute racial conflict must focus all available resources on set-
tling this conflict.

*Changes Required in the Church
and in Christian Countries
If Such Aims Are To Be Achieved*

—An example must be given in self-discipline—for example, in
self-taxation.
—The redistribution of wealth will be necessary on a wide scale.
For example, it is already proposed that Church funds be
made available for sociological studies of the activities of German firms in development countries.
—The redistribution of Church workers will also be necessary on
a wide scale. Old parishes can in great measure look after
themselves. In the area of the younger churches, missionary
personnel should be withdrawn from non-indigenous upper
class congregations.

So much for contemporary needs suggested spontaneously
by the seminar and regarded by it as sample priorities in answer
to the question of the aim of missionary activity in this present
time.

Who Changes the Structures?

Following this discussion, conducted among themselves by
members of the seminar as is today right and proper, I in-

troduced the question as to who is not merely prepared but actually in a position to do these things, or to do them in this way. What I had in mind was not the number of people or congregations but their quality. I was thinking of people who, in my view, needed themselves to have experienced a process of change in order to be able to initiate change in quite concrete ways, i.e., with humanity and a genuine concern for people. I pointed out that the ordinary theological word for this was conversion.

In describing the discussion which followed, I should like to refer to a statement which admittedly only came into my hands just after the seminar had ended, but which brought out what its members sensed in my question. In the annual report for 1970 of the Hermannsburg Mission occurs the following pregnant statement: "To bring about a fundamental change in the whole social and political structure of the people and nations of the Third World, the financial aid given by both secular and Church development programs is not enough. There must be a complete change in outlook and a process of transformation embracing and permeating the whole man, i.e., regeneration in the form of a transfer of allegiance to Jesus Christ."

The question about conversion remained unanswered—for several old and familiar reasons but also because of some new considerations which have to be accepted. Our scientific development has shown us that the problem of conversion is a problem of the social context and the psychological pattern within which conversion takes place, since it is also a problem of the theological statement in which the call to conversion is clothed. What was clear was that the history of missions contains an impressive number of conversions directly or indirectly connected with often radical changes of social structures.

It was also clear, however, that the history of missions includes conversions which not only did not result in social change but actually consolidated the social *status quo* through, for example, the individual's escape from the world, or the ghetto-like existence of the converted. The decisive thing about this two-way possibility was the social aspect, apart from its success or failure, whether it was intended or not even envisaged. This much was clear, then: an historical study of conversion cannot look at the phenomenon of conversion apart from its social context, not even as an individual process to be then included in a social process.

It would be wrong, therefore, to interpret the Hermanns-burg thesis as follows, though this may well be its own self-interpretation: First, the conversion of a few people or a number, and then, through these people, a change of the social structures. Rather, these must both be part of a single process, as is evident from those cases where missionary history was successful: conversion takes place and is achieved in interaction with existing traditional structures of society and in overcoming them. The change of heart and mind brings with it a change in religious and social ties and therefore a change of structures. From this standpoint it is easy to understand the view of contemporary theological students that their individual renewal can only take place in and with the renewal they must try to bring about in society, and this because, under pressure from their society, they can only think of themselves in social terms.

A student of this description (and also the teacher who interprets students in this way) is more like a member of a tribal society than a European missionary of the individualistic nineteenth century. In other words, the question of conversion is inseparable from the question of the change of structures; indeed, only the call to change the structures and a serious start in this direction bring about the experience of the need for and the possibility of conversion. This presupposes, of course, that the God who presses change on us can also be known and recognized in the pressure to change the social structures.

Feedback

Along with many other questions, there remains the question whether such thinking, or the line which this thinking takes, can be introduced into a concept of mission which is still dominated by the view expressed in the writings of Walter Freytag or in the *Decree on the Missionary Activity of the Church* of the Second Vatican Council.

Here we all need wisdom—or perhaps we should say, concreteness. In the seminar, the feedback took the form of an emphatic reference to the past history and present situation of the younger churches. Anyone who takes part or even thinks of taking part in mission has to take seriously the heritage in which the younger churches stand. It is certainly easier to understand the present, but even here the situation must be taken fully into account. There is always more in it than the definition, and it is stronger than the definition. The latter must always be subject to correction.

My own view is that one of our tasks today is to accept a plurality of views of mission, and therefore a plurality of forms of missionary activity, provided they can be broadly justified. Missionary history itself suggests this course, for it has itself never been limited to one concept of mission. The present also suggests this course, characterized as it is by a host of varied situations. The challenge of alternatives, the need for which is felt particularly in responsible missionary circles, can also be accompanied by a pluralistic attitude. If nothing else, it at least makes it possible for people, whose only form of variety has been to say the same things in different ways, to listen to some new questions.

Among the questions needing to be asked are those of the kind we have touched on in this report of an intensive seminar discussion. They need to be asked not simply because of their character and quality, which in any case must speak for themselves, but in virtue of a factor which played a part in producing them. The core-group of socialist students, who must have had something in mind when registering for this course, brought into the discussion the challenge of Marxism. This at once introduced into the deliberations a partner who increasingly challenges the Christian tradition and contemporary Christendom, and whom we can no longer evade, least of all in the Third World. To try out on this partner something of the meaning of mission could, contrary to traditional views, help to make our mission more concrete and in doing so ultimately help the people for the sake of whom mission exists. This seminar was a beginning.

NOTES

1. *International Review of Missions*, Vol. XXXIX, No. 154, April 1950, pp. 158-159.

2. Gerald H. Anderson ed. *The Theology of the Christian Mission* (New York: McGraw-Hill, 1961).

3. *Planning For Mission*, ed. Thomas Wieser (New York: US Conference for the World Council of Churches, 1966), pp. 43 and 51-52.

The Orthodox Church and Mission: Past and Present Perspectives

John Meyendorff

While the ecumenical movement has brought about greater understanding and appreciation of many aspects in the life and faith of the Orthodox Church by those in other Christian traditions, there is not generally a clear conception of the Orthodox perspective on mission. Therefore, at an Anglican-Orthodox Consultation held in New York on April 21, 1972, this paper was delivered by Fr. John Meyendorff, professor of patristics and Church history at St. Vladimir's Seminary (Russian Orthodox), in which he gave an Orthodox reaction to recent developments in the theology of mission and spoke about the theological and practical issues involved in the Orthodox Church's mission in the West, and particularly in America. Orthodoxy, he says, "would readily agree that mission belongs to the very nature of the Church." The Orthodox would disagree, however, "with the 'secularist' interpretation of mission" and also "with the ecclesiastical presuppositions . . . behind the integration of mission into the structure of ecumenical organizations." Fr. Meyendorff is editor of *St. Vladimir's Theological Quarterly* (Crestwood, Tuckahoe, New York) in which his essay appeared in 1972, volume 16, number 2.

Developments in the Theology of Mission

Until recently, Christian mission was generally understood in a fairly simple way: it consisted of an organized and institutionalized effort to expand the membership of the various Christian Churches and denominations among those who did not belong to them. Throughout the nineteenth century, most Protestants—not to speak of the Roman Catholics and the Orthodox—took for granted that the denomination to which they belonged was indeed the "true Church," and that it was fully legitimate to proselytize everywhere among non-Christians, as well as among members of other Christian groups.

Such a simple and straightforward conception of the Christian mission led, on the practical level, to two consequences of major importance:

(1) Direct competition between Christian missionaries in the so-called "mission lands," i.e., primarily the countries of Africa and Asia where Western European countries extended their colonial empires and where missions thus became possible. This competition constituted a serious handicap to the progress of Christianity: the "younger churches," being nothing but branches of European church organizations, became bound by post-Reformation theological and institutional categories, and were obliged to import the white man's factionalism, adding it to their own racial and tribal divisions.

(2) Protestant and Roman Catholic proselytism extended to the Christian East, especially the Middle East and India. Totally unsuccessful among Moslems, Western missionaries justified their assignments to Middle Eastern countries by turning toward the economically and intellectually "underdeveloped" masses of Eastern Christians, Orthodox or Monophysite. As a defensive reaction against this proselytism—which actually started in the seventeenth and eighteenth centuries with the active support of Western diplomats and money—Ecumenical Patriarch Cyril V issued his well-known synodal decision in 1755, declaring the invalidity of all sacraments performed by Western Christians and, therefore, requiring the reception of converts through baptism.[1] This decision superseded the earlier practice of accepting the Western converts through chrismation, as required by the Council of 1484. It was accepted in the standard Greek canonical collection known as *Pedalion*, or *Rudder*, and is considered as binding by some Orthodox conservative circles, especially in Greece.

One should also note that active proselytism among Orthodox was also widely practiced by Western Churches on the American continent. It remains active even today on the part of conservative-fundamentalist groups—for example, among the Alaskan natives.

At the time of the big missionary expansion of the Western European churches in the nineteenth century, the Church of Russia was the only one in the Orthodox world able to engage in a similar undertaking. It did so on the territory of the Russian European and Asian empire, but also beyond it. The mission to Japan was most successful, under the leadership of the recently canonized St. Nicholas Kasatkin (d. 1913), and missionary activity was not interrupted in Alaska after its sale to the United States in 1867, or in other parts of the American continent. This Russian missionary activity was not restricted to non-Christians, but also welcomed Roman Catholics and Protestants. As is well known, most Orthodox communities of Slavic background in the United States are of "Uniate" origin. These Russian missions followed the principles accepted in Byzantine times, i.e., they were based on a liturgy translated into the various vernacular languages. Thus, the Orthodox liturgy was celebrated in dozens of Asian dialects; Scripture was also translated.[2]

As is well known, it is among the Protestant missionaries that the idea of an "ecumenical movement," which would stop missionary competition and make possible a unified Christian witness to the world, took its initial shape. It was based upon the realization by the theologians that unity and mission are inseparable in the New Testament's understanding of the Church. Being practical men, those responsible for the various missionary boards and organizations also understood what could be gained by cooperation and sharing of resources.

This missionary impulse was a constant element in the ecumenical thinking of the first half of this century. It culminated in the merger of the World Council of Churches and the International Missionary Council at the Assembly in New Delhi (1961).

Since that time, the "turbulent 60's" brought a radical change in prevailing ideas about mission, and therefore of the ecumenical movement itself as well. The idea that there was a "Christian world" sending missionaries to evangelize the "pagans" was discarded totally and replaced with a new global theology of mission which, on the one hand, properly assumed that the Church's mission could not be restricted to some geographical areas or mission lands at a time when the entire world had become "secular," and, on the other hand (and less properly), also proclaimed a "secular understanding of Christianity." Christian mission was now identified with involvement in those historical processes which were presumed to be "progressive," i.e., promoting a better human life. Christians were called to abandon their traditional concentration on Scripture and worship and to "listen to the world." "The secular" was defined as a source of continuous revelation, and the mission of the Church was to consist in helping those causes and ideologies which were struggling for "peace" and "justice." The major problem in the newly prevailing understanding of mission was that it practically excluded any concept of "peace" and "justice" except the "secular" ones, that it followed the fads and utopias of current sociological trends, and that it betrayed the *basic content* of the Christian Gospel, which is about eternal life, resurrection, and the kingdom of God, i.e., realities impossible to define in sociological, "secular," or political terms.[3] The culminating point for the progress of these ideas on mission was the Conference on Church and Society (Geneva, 1966) and the Fourth Assembly of the WCC (Uppsala, 1968). Since Uppsala, militant secularism seems to be subsiding, with the "secular world" itself (whatever that term means) seeming to be more receptive to irrational pentecostalism and emotional religious revivalism than to the dry utopias of political activists.

Through its involvement with the various ecumenical agencies, the Orthodox Church was in constant touch with these developments in the Christian idea of mission. One should honestly recognize that so far it has had a rather negligible influence upon the outcome of the various debates on mission. Perhaps history will show, however, that the serene immutability of Orthodox worship, the sort of passive immunity which has been shown so far by the mass of the Orthodox people (the contradictory attitudes of a few "professional ecumenists" notwithstanding) to theological fads and slogans, will prove to have been ultimately an effective witness—something deeper and greater than conservatism for conservatism's sake. It is clear that the Orthodox understanding of the Christian Gospel and of the Church is very difficult to reconcile with either the pre-New Delhi or post-New Delhi prevailing concepts of mission.

The Orthodox would, of course, readily agree that (1) mission belongs to the very nature of the Church, which is called "apostolic" both because it carries on the apostolic faith and because it is being sent into the world, as the apostles were, to witness to Christ's resurrection, (2) mission cannot be reduced only to preaching the Gospel—it implies service, i.e., witness through deeds, as well as words.

These two points imply that a Church which ceases to be missionary, which limits itself to an introverted self-sustaining existence or, even worse, places ethnic, racial, political, social, or geographic limitations upon the message of Christ, ceases to be authentically "the Church of Christ." Also, since Christ was "anointed to preach the good news to the poor" and "sent to proclaim release to the captives" and "to set at liberty those who are oppressed" (Lk. 4:18), it is clear that his Church must do the same.

However, the Orthodox cannot but disagree with the ecclesiological presuppositions which would be behind the integration of mission into the structure of ecumenical organizations, such as the World Council of Churches, because these are associations of *divided* Christians. The Orthodox hold the Orthodox Church to be the one undivided (i.e., theologically and biblically *indivisible*) Church, and consider any association of divided "Churches" as nothing but an *ad hoc* attempt to work for the unity of Christians, or as a means of cooperation in fields where cooperation is possible, including some forms of proclamation of the Christian Gospel to the world. But *mission*, in its ultimate theological meaning, is an expression of the *Church itself.* It cannot grow out of a divided Christendom, but only from the one Church, and leads to conversion to this one Church.

The Orthodox will disagree also, obviously, with the "secularist" interpretation of mission. The goal of mission is an acceptance of the Gospel, which *liberates* from the determinism of secular categories, i.e., "the world." The Johannine text, which has always served as the basis of the "missionary" dimension in ecumenism—"that they may all be one; even as thou, Father, art in me, and I in thee, that they also may be in us, so that the world may believe that thou hast sent me" (Jn. 17:21)—speaks of a *divine* unity which is also to become the unity of men, and which is something which the world "cannot give." This is precisely the reason why true unity of Christians is realized not in common action, nor even in common witness to those outside, but in the *closed* sacramental mystery of the *Eucharist.* It is only because the Eucharist is an eschatological event, an anticipated advent of the kingdom to come and a fullness of divine presence, that it is also unifying. This is also why any form of inter-"communion"—i.e., eucharistic communion between Christians who are divided in faith and in ultimate ecclesial commitment— necessarily *reduces* the Eucharist to a form of human fellowship, distinct from the union in the kingdom of God which is the Eucharist's ultimate meaning.

I personally believe that there is general agreement among the Orthodox on the positions described above. However, for a variety of non-theological reasons, the Orthodox have failed to act with sufficient consistency and logic. For example, they accepted the integration of the World Council of Churches and the International Missionary Council in New Delhi (1961), even if several of them voted against it at the Assembly. The reason for such an accommodating spirit was that since the Russian Revolution the Orthodox Church has had very little possibility to engage in an organized missionary effort, the hierarchies of the various Orthodox Churches did not feel any practical threat on this point from the proposed integration. On the other hand, many Middle Eastern prelates were happy with the idea of having Protestant missionaries somehow controlled through an organization of which the Orthodox themselves were members.

Similarly, one can certainly say that the Orthodox reaction against the "secularized" concept of mission would have been stronger if the tragic situation of the Moscow patriarchate did not compel it to participation in the various "progressive" organizations of the Western world, which are considered to be useful by the Soviet government, provided they are silent about the defects of Soviet society and vocal only in criticizing the West.

These and other practical considerations are hardly conducive to a consistent Orthodox witness. I believe, however, that it is our particular responsibility, as Orthodox Christians of the West, to make a truly positive and useful contribution to the current theological debate in world Christendom about the nature of mission.

Orthodox Mission: East and West

Until the beginning of this century, the Orthodox Church was closely associated with the national tradition of those East European countries which were part of what historians recently labeled the "Byzantine Commonwealth":[4] Greece, Bulgaria, Serbia, Romania, and Russia. From Byzantium they all inherited a social system which implied the alliance between Church and State. On the other hand, the traditional Byzantine missionary approach, immortalized by Sts. Cyril and Methodius in the ninth century, consisted of translating both Scripture and liturgy into the vernacular. This led to the creation of Christian nations which integrated Christianity deep into their ethnic and cultural experience. New Orthodox ethnic-religious groups continued to appear until our own times: in Poland, in Czechoslovakia, and in Albania, as well as in Asia, where Russian missions were in progress.

Since nineteenth-century nationalism was a fundamentally *secular* phenomenon, the Orthodox world, in adopting it, passed through its own peculiar experience of "secularism": the Church often became directly involved in causes which the particular ethnic group considered as "just," even at the expense of the national interest of others. Examples of ecclesiastical nationalism are numerous and shameful.

In spite of it all, however, the *framework* of national life was still largely determined by Orthodox Church tradition. The mission of the Church was understood clearly as a preservation and expansion of that tradition, alongside of the national and social life of the various so-called "Orthodox nations." The mission of the Church developed, as part of a "Christian civilization," a social and personal ethos which had itself been shaped by Orthodox Christianity.

This situation was not without ambiguity because it frequently led to confusion between Church and civilization, religion and nation. It was radically changed, however, by the Russian Revolution and the establishment of Communist states in countries of Eastern Europe. Driven into a ghetto, administratively persecuted, prevented by law from exercising any influence on society, the Church struggled for survival as a closed worshiping community. The historical future of the Orthodox Church, as a world communion, depends upon the result of that struggle.

But the Russian Revolution also resulted in a dispersion of Orthodox Christians throughout the world, and this dispersion gave a totally new dimension to Orthodox mission. In this new "diaspora" were many theologians and intellectuals who, especially in Western Europe, contributed much to the Orthodox witness in the ecumenical movement.

In terms of numbers, however, it is in America that the Orthodox presence is most sizable. Most Orthodox communities here were founded not by political anti-Communist emigrés, but by immigrants from Central and Eastern Europe, as well as from Greece and the Middle East. They came here in the nineteenth century of their own free will and in order to build a new permanent life for themselves and their children. Thus, for the first time since the Great Schism and the Reformation, Orthodox Christians were permanently sharing a country, a language, and a culture with their Roman Catholic, Anglican, and Protestant brethren.

The role of the "churches" in shaping American society is, of course, well known. Denominations coincided with the ethnic and economic *strata* to which the various groups belonged.[5] On the other hand—and this is especially true of the Orthodox—church-belonging signified token-faithfulness to the old country and served as a tool of ethnic identification and fellowship. As distinct from classical European confessionalism, the "denominationalism" of America was not doctrine-oriented. It never excluded forms of "non-denominational" religious experience—revivalistic, pentecostal, pantheistic, deistic, or national. But the American religious scene was also rich in "sectarian" phenomena, reacting against broad denominationalism through exclusiveness, fanaticism, and bigotry. The Orthodox Church could accept neither the "denominational" nor the "sectarian" patterns of American religion for itself. It claimed to be the true "Catholic" Church, excluding ecclesiological relativism, but also assuming the responsibility and the mission of "catholicity." This sense of responsibility and mission—which clearly distinguishes "the Church" from a "sect"—implies openness to everything true and good anywhere. Thus, by establishing itself permanently in America, the Orthodox Church was confronted with the difficult challenge of remaining true to its catholic self-understanding in a pluralistic society, without becoming either a denomination or a sect.

The original diocese established on the American continent in Alaska in 1840 was canonically dependent upon the Russian Holy Synod in St. Petersburg. It remained ecclesiastically under Russia after the sale of Alaska to the United States in 1867, when it extended its jurisdiction and activities to the entire continent, its center being transferred first to San Francisco (1872), then to New York (1903). A major particularity of that diocese was that it was always multi-ethnic and multi-lingual. Immigrants from the Russian Empire proper constituted a very small minority in its midst. It always called itself a "mission," i.e., a mission first to the natives of Alaska, who had their native clergy and worshiped in their own tongues, and second to the Slavic "Uniate" immigrants from Austria-Hungary, who returned to Orthodoxy in hundreds of thousands, once they were established in America. The diocese also welcomed into its midst Orthodox immigrants from all countries. An Arab, Raphael Awaweeny, was consecrated auxiliary bishop in New York. In 1905, Archbishop Tikhon presented to the Holy Synod of St. Petersburg a report containing a proposal for an independent American Church, which would, however, recognize the identity of the various ethnic groups.[6]

Without idealizing the picture (for, indeed, there were inconsistencies and shortcomings), one can say that the policies of that original Orthodox diocese of America were at that time faithful, at least in intention, to the truly catholic aspect of the Church's mission. It was only after the Russian Revolution that the Orthodox mission in America disintegrated. New waves of immigrants organized themselves ecclesiastically on a purely ethnic basis, in spite of a few prophetic voices, like that of Ecumenical Patriarch Meletios Metaxakis, who spoke of the establishment of an "American Orthodox Church" in his enthronement address in 1921.[7]

Indeed, overcoming ethnic divisions and acting truly as one Church is the pre-condition for a meaningful Orthodox witness in the West, especially in America. But the ultimate problem lies on an even deeper level: Is Orthodoxy intrinsically the "Eastern" form of Christianity? Or, conversely, is Christianity fundamentally and culturally inseparable from the East? An affirmative answer to the latter question would imply that to be a Western Christian or a Western Orthodox is, to say the least, a great handicap in one's spiritual progress, for true Christianity and "the West" are actually incompatible. Those among the Orthodox who adopt that position and rationalize it in terms of practical behavior reduce Orthodoxy to the sectarian pattern of American religion: one simply *cannot* be both Orthodox and American, but one has to become—at least culturally and spiritually—a Greek or a Russian. However, quite often this identification of Orthodoxy with Eastern cultural or ethnic patterns also leads to a practical "denominationalism." Some people believe that since one cannot reasonably expect to have Western Christians transformed into Greeks or Russians, one should try to co-exist with them peacefully, sharing the common interdenominational deism of American religion. This corresponds to the so-called "unity without union" pattern in ecumenism. Thus, paradoxically, ethnicity naturally allies itself either with "sectarianism" or with "denominationalism," because it constitutes, first of all, a negation of the catholicity of the Church.

Thus, a definition of the Orthodox mission in the West today requires, first of all, a clear understanding of what catholicity means, what is implied by a truly *catholic Church life*—which is more than a conceptual definition of the third "attribute" of the Church.

It should be understood, first of all, that catholicity does not imply bland cosmopolitanism—a renunciation of the cultural diversities, identities, and peculiar "talents" of nations, civilizations, or ethnic groups. The Cyrillo-Methodian pattern of creating national churches, without imposing upon them external linguistic conformity, was a direct application in the field of mission of the miracle of Pentecost, and therefore the best possible witness to catholicity.

Yet once Christianized, nations, languages, and cultures accept the common criterion of catholicity and cease to be mutually exclusive. The Byzantine Orthodox hymnography for the day of Pentecost is entirely built on the biblical theme of the opposition between the story of the tower of Babel ("the tongues divide men from each other") and the miracle of the tongues in the upper room ("the *same* Spirit" speaks in the languages of all nations). Catholicity therefore implies comprehensiveness: not indifference and individualism, but a comprehensiveness built upon the universality of redemption. The Orthodox claim of being the "Catholic" Church involves the Church's mission to the world, a world which has been redeemed by Christ in its entire wholeness. The Church, therefore, cannot be "Eastern" or "Western" in its very nature if it is to remain the Church of Christ.

There is a fundamental sense, however, in which the New Testament revelation implies history and geography: the incarnation took place in history and the establishment of the Church involved concrete people—Jews and Greeks—who belonged to the civilization of their own time. They were not twentieth-century Americans. The historical uniqueness of the Christ-event presupposes that no other moment of history but the time of Jesus of Nazareth was "the fullness of time" described and explained in the writings of the New Testament. It also presupposes that the incarnate Son of God was the Jewish Messiah, and that the universality of life and salvation was to be revealed nowhere else but in Jerusalem. Also, if one holds a belief in tradition, one accepts that the Church, as the new temple and the vehicle of the Spirit, has taken the right options and given the right definitions of doctrine throughout its history. These definitions are also historically and geographically qualified. Our task today is then to remain *consistent* to these options and definitions of the past, even when we are called to develop them, or to take totally new options relevant for the issues of our own time.

There is an important sense, therefore, in which our mission today as Orthodox Christians cannot be uprooted from the tradition of Eastern Christianity, where the fullness of the Christian tradition has been carried through centuries of history, the tradition of the Greek Fathers in particular. But a true sense of our mission must also recognize that catholic tradition has had in the past expressions other than the Greek or the Russian, and that any reduction of Christian truth to a particular historic form presupposes a reduction of catholicity itself. The Greek Fathers expressed holy tradition not because they were Greek, but because they lived the Church's catholicity, which was also lived by others and should be relived anew by us in the twentieth century.

It is not my purpose in this paper to attempt a definition of the "Christian West" from the point of view of Orthodox ecclesiology, and this does not seem to be the main point when one is concerned with Christian mission in a country like America, which can hardly be considered a Christian country anymore. America challenges the Orthodox Church with problems which it never had to face before, and this challenge is, frequently, a challenge to the Christian faith itself. I believe that Orthodox tradition is particularly explicit on some fundamentals which our society—and particularly American society—could discover to be directly relevant, such as a Trinitarian view of God, a "theocentric" understanding of man, and an ecclesiology based on communion, rather than on authority.[8] If only Orthodox mission and witness could be more consistent than they practically are with these fundamentals of the Orthodox faith! Orthodoxy could assume a crucial responsibility in reshaping Western Christianity at a moment when the secular activism of the 60's is subsiding and when people are more ready than before to understand the language of prayer, of contemplation, and of experience, and may thus become concerned again with the truth for its own sake. On the other hand, one can say that an American Orthodox Church, invested with freedom and dynamism learned in the West, can have a "mission" to the mother churches of the Orthodox East, where freedom does not exist and dynamism is impaired by law or custom.

NOTES

1. The texts relative to that decision can be found in J. D. Mansi, *Sacrorum Conciliorum Nova et Amplissima Collectio*, ed., L. Petit, Vol. 38, cols. 576-640.

2. It is useless to refer here to the very extensive literature available in Russian on the Orthodox Missions; easily accessible general surveys are available in E. Smirnoff, *Russian Orthodox Mission* (London, 1903), S. Bolshakoff, *The Foreign Missions of the Russian Orthodox Church* (London, 1943), and also in J. Glazik, *Die russisch-orthodoxe Heidenmission seit Peter dem Grossen* (Münster-Westf., 1954) and *Die Islammission der russisch-orthodoxen Kirche* (Münster-Westf., 1959).

3. I have given a brief critique of those trends in a talk delivered to the WCC Commission on Faith and Order, Louvain, 1971, and published in *St. Vladimir's Theological Quarterly*, 15:4 (1971), pp. 163-177.

4. Dimitri Obolensky, *The Byzantine Commonwealth: Eastern Europe 500-1453*, (New York: Praeger, 1971).

5. It is sufficient to refer here to R. H. Niebuhr's classic, *The Social Sources of Denominationalism* (New York: Meridian Books, 1957).

6. English text of the main passage of the report in *St. Vladimir's Seminary Quarterly*, 5:1/2 (1961), pp. 114-115.

7. An extract of the address in English in *St. Vladimir's Seminary Quarterly, ibid.*, p. 114.

8. See our article on "Orthodox Theology Today," *St. Vladimir's Theological Quarterly*, 13:1/2 (1969), pp. 77-92.

*II: The Message and
   Goals of Mission*

Is There a Missionary Message?

Charles W. Forman
and Gregory Baum, O.S.A.

What should be the attitude and approach of the Christian to
persons of other faiths? Should the missionary message aim to
convert persons to saving faith in Jesus Christ? Charles W. Forman, professor of missions at Yale Divinity School and a former
missionary to India, believes that while the missionary must be
open, humble and respectful in dialogue with others, nevertheless
"the primary thing about the missionary is that he does have a
message." That message concerns what it means "to live by
God's grace which in Christ has plumbed the depths of our
human history." The missionary's primary concern, in Forman's
view, is that persons should have an opportunity to hear the message and respond to it with an assurance of trust and acceptance.
Gregory Baum, O.S.A., in reply to Forman, maintains that the
aim of the missionary message is not to convert people to Christ,
but rather "to free people for a saving contact with the best of
their own religious traditions." Father Baum, who comes from a
Jewish family, edits *The Ecumenist*. He discusses why—in his
view—"the Christian Church cannot go on repeating the absolute claims of New Testament and ancient Church teaching," but
must instead "create theological space for the great world religions." These two articles are reprinted from the March-April
1973 issue of *The Ecumenist*, a journal for promoting Christian
unity, published in New York by Paulist Press in collaboration
with the Institute of Christian Thought at St. Michael's College
in the University of Toronto, where Father Baum, a Canadian
citizen, teaches theology.

CHARLES W. FORMAN

A recent issue of *The Ecumenist* (July-August 1972) carried, by fortunate coincidence, two articles dealing with contemporary issues of Christian missions. The first, by Gregory Baum, was aimed explicitly at Christian-Jewish relations but moved on to the wider questions of inter-religious relations generally and the attitude which Christians should adopt toward the followers of other faiths. The second article, by Eldon R. Hay, represented a reconsideration of the work of Christian missions as a whole. Both articles contain much of value and deserve the most serious consideration. Yet both seem, to my mind, to suffer from some crucial omissions and it is these which I would like to discuss at the present time.

Ideology

Father Baum's article, "The Jews, Faith and Ideology," takes its inception from a clear analysis of the many ways in which ideology can warp our perspective in life. We have, as he points out, an unconscious tendency to create world-views and values which legitimate our role in the world and protect us against competing groups. Ideology provides a defense for our prejudices, our superstitions, our positions of power or our fear of life. Father Baum applies this analysis only to those who have power and are oppressors. This is the customary application, from Marx on down, of the concept of ideology. But it is necessary to note that ideology can afflict the powerless and the oppressed as well. They can create world-views and values which protect their role, establish themselves against competing groups, and defend their prejudices, superstitions or fears. They can produce systems of thought in which they depict themselves as true humanity and teach that all power should belong to them.

There is no doubt that the oppressed have relatively more truth in their ideologies. They stand outside the established system, and therefore, instead of being inclined to hide or justify its evils as the oppressors are, their interest is in revealing and attacking those evils. All human systems fall under divine judgment and they are instruments of that judgment. But the mixture of falsehood with their truth becomes apparent when they come to power and establish their own system with its own, different types of oppression.

This point with regard to ideologies needs to be made in relation to religion, which is the central concern of Father Baum's article. As he says, ideologies operate effectively in the religious realm, defending our prejudices, our positions of power and our fear of life. They encourage us to create a separate religious community and then to protect it. "In subtle ways at first," he says, "and then more drastically we shall speak of ourselves as the measure of humanity and of others as below the norm." Christians should be quick to recognize these operations of ideology, for the Bible repeatedly lays bare the pretenses by which men consciously or unconsciously protect themselves, revealing that their decency is composed of only a covering of "filthy rags." The modern sociological and economic disclosure of ever fresh bases for ideological distortion illustrates in new ways the New Testament's conviction of the insidiousness of human self-justification and the resistance in man against a trusting surrender to God and an acceptance of justification by God's grace.

As Father Baum fails to apply the ideological analysis to the oppressed along with oppressors, he does not seem fully to universalize the role of ideology in the religious realm. Though the human capacity for self-justification is unlimited and universal, he believes it is "possible, thanks to God's powerful Word, to be delivered from these ideological elements and to be open to the truth." Do we not have to admit, on the contrary, that all of us continue, to a greater or lesser degree, to use our ideas to protect our status or role and to defend our fears of life? Though the Word of God which exposes our pretenses acts as a liberating force in our lives, none of us is fully open to the truth. This is to say, in more traditional terms, that we all are still sinners and have to rely finally on God's grace rather than our own righteousness. That grace has been extended to us in costly fashion in Jesus Christ and we do not outgrow our need of it.

The suggestion in this article that we can transcend the human condition, be delivered from ideology and live in true

friendship and solidarity with our fellow men gives rise, not un-
expectedly, to a new, more subtle ideology wherein certain men
who have presumably done this are singled out as the measure of
humanity. "They find it easy to be friends across the boundaries," "they know that they belong together," and they "never
think that anyone should change from one religion to another."
Here are the seeds of another "we-group" speaking of outsiders
as below the norm, instead of recognizing that the outsiders are
just like us. The outsiders are indeed sinners, but sinners whom
God loves and values—like ourselves.

Final Allegiance

Perhaps it is this failure to universalize the human predicament which leads the author to deny the need for any change of
religious allegiance. He deplores the idea that "members of the
world religions become Christian" and believes rather that the
struggle for liberation from ideology should be carried on by all
men "in their own particular traditions." No doubt we have in
the past been too quick to call for a change of religion, but this
proposal may go too far in the other direction. It is not for us to
consign other men to staying in their own traditions or to leaving
them. This is a question for them rather than us to decide. It is
for us to make clear the astonishing news that God is to be
trusted—despite our fears—and we are not to be trusted—
despite our wishes. If men can sense what it is to live by God's
grace which in Christ has plumbed the depths of our human history rather than remaining aloof as a lovely idea, then they can
decide whether they are to live by that light within their own
traditions or can only give final allegiance to Christ.

Father Baum's concern is that all men should work toward
ridding themselves of ideological limitations, certainly a goal on
which we should all agree. But he says nothing about a basic
trust and assurance that is offered to those to whom ideological
limitations still apply, i.e., to all men. The recognition of the
grounds for that trust and assurance might lead to a much more
open attitude toward changes of religious allegiance.

Some different yet related problems arise in connection with the second article I have mentioned, the one by Eldon R. Hay, entitled "The Christian Missionary—Vanishing Species?" Professor Hay is rightly repelled by the self-righteousness, past and present, that has characterized much Christian missionary activity. He feels that to continue to proclaim the unilateral message of a uniquely saving truth, hoping to convert men, is to fall back into that self-righteousness and to neglect what we have come to know of other men's faith and dignity. He reminds us of the evidences of God's redemptive activity which are to be seen in the goodness, the grace, the kindness, the humility and the humanity of the followers of other religions. He believes God's mission to transform men and make them whole can be carried forward through any and all faiths, though it is far from complete in any one of them.

Accordingly, Professor Hay sees the proper role of the Christian missionary to be one of "mutual sharing and concern and responsibility among men of faith—whereby the other may be changed, whereby I may be changed." Religious plurality is to be welcomed by the missionary since his own understanding of God's mission is so partial. The Christian should help Muslims, Hindus or Buddhists solve their own problems, humbly, genuinely, openly, with respect for those traditions and a willingness to learn.

The Christian Mission

Most of this is deeply true and sheds much light on the direction that should be taken by Christian missions. The dialogical approach to other men which is recommended, with its emphasis on listening and trying to understand as well as speaking and trying to be understood, is surely more congenial to a truly Christian mission than is an insensitive, one-sided proclamation which denies the dignity and integrity of other men before God. But what Eldon Hay neglects is the element of proclamation or, in more acceptable terminology, sharing, which is part of the Christian missionary's role in a sensitive, open dialogue. Professor Hay seems indeed to have his own type of Christian convictions which he could share. He speaks of God as the power which penetrates the abyss of our existence, illumining our dark-ness and challenging it, making our sins but mistakes in his transforming goodness, assuring us that life is trustworthy and the universe is friendly. Looking over these convictions, one has the impression that here is a lot of good news which men have not commonly recognized. Couched in rather philosophical terms, there is found here the religious message that God can be trusted ("life is trustworthy"), that he loves us ("the universe is friendly") and forgives and redeems us ("makes our sins but mis-takes in his transforming goodness"). This message has the dia-lectical effect of both transforming our lives by removing the need for our destructive self-assertiveness and at the same time granting us an assurance by which to live when we recognize the all-too-little-transformed quality of our lives.

One wonders then why Eldon Hay deprecates any "unilater-al message of a uniquely saving truth." One has the feeling that he is setting forth just such a truth. Once the faithfulness and forgiveness of God have been recognized, any other grounds for our salvation appear unnecessary and also seem inevitably to imply that we must save ourselves by some kind of ultimate human achievement which would belie the very reliance on God's grace which we have recognized. We should indeed, as he says, be aware of our need for change and be ready to change in the course of any dialogue with other faiths. There are surely many ways in which other faiths will show us our need for repentance and improvement. But the very readiness to change is based on an acknowledgment of our present sins and shortcomings and of the wider trustworthiness, friendliness and love within which we stand, within which we are not condemned and cast out but ac-cepted and encouraged. The grounds for change are not to be abandoned in the dialogue or we will lose our readiness to change and will slip into the usual attitudes of self-vindication. The message which the Christian missionary carries requires by its very nature that he be humble, open, respectful of others and of their integrity of conviction, but the primary thing about the missionary is that he does have a message which requires all this. When we talk about his attitudes and neglect his message, we are trying to put up a structure without its foundations.

Both these articles have much to say by way of encouragement for human betterment, humanization, etc., but they appear all too silent about the grounds for that encouragement and also about our hopes when we discover how pitifully little betterment and humanization we have achieved. Yet it is from those grounds and those hopes that the Christian mission springs. We need to be refreshed by them continually as we explore how the Christian should live in a world of religious pluralism.

GREGORY BAUM, O.S.A.

Professor Charles W. Forman's article "Is There a Missionary Message?" raises the important issues about the Church's mission, vehemently discussed in Christian theology today. They deserve the greatest attention. For if the Church loses its sense of mission, the Christian community turns in on itself and slowly dies. Charles Forman has defended the classical concept of mission: the Church has received a message of salvation and its mission consists in preaching this message to all men so that they may be converted and saved. He supposes that God desires all men to be Christians. He is critical of two articles, published in *The Ecumenist*, which question whether it is God's will today that people leave their religion to become Christians. While the authors of these articles strongly affirm the Church's mission, they propose that the aim of the missionary message is to free people for a saving contact with the best of their own religious traditions.

In this response to Charles Forman's article, I wish to examine in greater detail the role of ideology in religion.

Ideology and Utopia

In my article criticized by Charles Forman, "The Jews, Faith, and Ideology," I had made a great deal of the ideological deformation of truth that takes place, unconsciously for the main part, in a community that affirms itself with vigor, tries to triumph over others, and wants to defend its power and privileges. I suggested that over the centuries the Christian message has become tainted with ideology and that for this reason it was the special task of the Church today to purify its own self-understanding from these ideological trends. I suggested that the preaching of the Christian message to convert members of other religions to Christianity was today a hidden form of aggression, a disguised attempt to triumph over other religious cultures, and hence not in keeping with the Church's self-understanding in the present age.

Charles Forman agrees with the theory that religions are strongly affected by ideological trends. He agrees that the unconscious self-interest of a religious community finds expression in its religious message and thus deforms the truth that is uttered. Such an ideological tainting of the truth belongs to the sinful human condition: it affects, according to Professor Forman, not only the dominant group that seeks to preserve its power but also the dominated group that affirms itself against the pressure of history. All groups are in need of repentance. All groups, including the Christian Church, must purify their self-expressions from the ideological overtones. After the Church has found repentance, after it has removed all claims of power from its proclamation, Charles Forman holds, it must in all humility confess that the truth it utters is God's saving Word addressed to all men, calling them to become Christians.

At this point, following Karl Mannheim, I wish to introduce the distinction between ideology and utopia. The interest-laden utterance of the dominant group is called ideology, while the interest-laden utterance of the dominated group coming to self-realization is called utopia. Ideologies are sets of symbols and images that defend and reinforce the dominant values of society, affirm the inherited power structures, and hence promote the stability of the present system. Utopias, on the other hand, are sets of symbols that weaken and undermine the dominant ideals of society, present the inherited power structures as threatened by God's judgment or their own inner contradictions, and thus encourage the hope that the present system approaches its breaking point. Both ideologies and utopias modify the truth for the sake of social interest, but since the social functions of the two are so different, they should be carefully distinguished.

The meaning of a sentence or symbol is quite different depending on whether it is proposed by the dominant group or by a dominated group. "We Shall Overcome!" was a powerful utopian song. It was sung by people without power. If the same words were uttered by the government and its police force, their meaning would be quite different; it would announce that these men with access to power were ready to reinforce their authority. In the first setting "we shall overcome" is the language of survival and self-identity; in the second setting, it would be the language of power and domination. It would be quite misplaced to call both groups to repentance and ask them to abandon their threatening language; such a call to universal repentance would simply confirm the present power relation.

"Black is beautiful" is a utopian slogan. It is survival language. To affirm "white is beautiful" in the United States today would be an ideological utterance; it would be an attempt to neutralize the trend among the blacks toward self-recovery and affirmation in the community. It would be power language. Similarly, a strongly nationalistic self-affirmation of the Mexican Americans in Texas and California fulfills a utopian role; its aim is to create the new self-confidence necessary to struggle for self-identity and survival. If the same nationalistic self-affirmation were made by the silent majority in the United States, its political and social meaning would be entirely different. It would be a language of power and domination.

We conclude that unless we examine the socio-political background of the message and the symbols adopted by a community of men, we are unable to understand its meaning. One and the same sentence may be survival language in one context and power language in another. I propose that the exclusivist claims of the New Testament, and the proclamation of the early Church that apart from its message there is no salvation, were survival language. The trusting surrender to Jesus Christ as source of salvation, experienced in a small threatened community within a hostile Roman Empire, surrounded by competing religious groups, demanded the language of survival and self-identity. However, when the Christian Church became the religion of the Roman Empire and later identified itself with Western society, the same doctrinal statements acquired a different meaning. The Church's exclusivist claims became a language of power and domination.

Utopian language changes its character when uttered from a position of success. After the successful establishment of a formerly unprotected community in power, the utopian language acquires an ideological meaning. By repeating the same message, something else is being announced. If the original message is to be repeated in the new situation of success and authority, it must be reformulated. The absolutes of the utopian language must be relativized by the powerful group, lest it leave no room for other groups on God's earth. It is my view, therefore, that the Christian Church cannot go on repeating the absolute claims of New Testament and ancient Church teaching without becoming unfaithful to their original meaning.

Truth and Power

It is important to recall at this point that religious language and religious symbols have a powerful social effect quite apart from the inwardness associated with them. Charles Forman puts great emphasis on the humility of the ideal Christian. He is justified by faith, not by his achievements. Yet quite apart from personal intentions, exclusivist language and symbols adopted by a community in a position of power will give rise to certain social sentiments and customs, bring forth structures of exclusion, eventually create laws keeping the outsiders in a subservient position, and in the long run provoke social action that is unjust and gravely harmful to them. The Church's theological view of Judaism is the classical example of this process. Because the Church regarded itself as superseding Judaism and left no theological space for the Jewish religion before God, it created a language of exclusion, then social sentiments of discrimination, eventually a legislation that kept the Jews in a subordinate position, and in the long run a social attitude that repeatedly broke out in aggression and unjust practices. Feelings of love and humility are quite powerless against the objective power exercised by language and symbols in the creation of society. I must conclude, therefore, that if the Christian Church is unable to leave theological room for other religions, in particular for Judaism, then it will inevitably legitimate the present hegemony of the West over the other parts of the world and keep on nourishing the so-called Christian world with dreams of unity under a single authority. An imperialism built into religious language and symbols will never be neutralized by faith, hope and charity.

Charles Forman puts great emphasis on the priority of faith and the inwardness of religion. While this stress is important in some contexts, in connection with the Church's mission it could easily encourage an ideological trend. It is conceivable that at the time when Israel was oppressed in the land of bondage, the taskmasters who ruled over them were sensitive, humble and inward men who exercised their rule with distaste and repentance. They met in prayer groups where they regretted the sinful condition of their country. They did not trust in their own works but in the goodness offered to them by life itself. It is conceivable that the Israelites were much less inward. They were angry, impatient, and coarse. The social situation had made them into braggarts who boasted of their own achievements. Their frustration made them so foolish that they even trusted in their own efforts. The gentle taskmasters may well have recommended greater inwardness to the Israelites. It was wrong of them to dream of a new society, for since mankind is inevitably sinful this new society would soon be as unjust and harmful as the present one. What the Israelites should believe, instead, is that the universe is friendly, that life is trustworthy, and that the sins which men commit will not be held against them. We realize, of course, that this is not the biblical story. God was at that point not interested in the state of soul of the Egyptians; he wanted them to abandon political power and let his people go. I conclude that if a dominant religious or secular group is able to persuade the dominated groups that what really counts is faith and humility, then it will be able to protect the existing power relation and preserve its position of dominance.

I conclude that today the Christian theologian must create theological space for the great world religions. As a utopian statement, as a language of survival and self-identity, the ancient Christian message is as valid as ever. But when uttered from a position of cultural dominance, from which we cannot separate ourselves by repentance and good will, it contains a bent toward spiritual imperialism with devastating effects on the human family. This bent cannot be overcome by a grudging acceptance of religious pluralism. A rethinking of our theological tradition is necessary. Theologians must examine the possibility that the Church's missionary message exercises its salvational power where people in fact are, in their own cultural environment, enabling them to cling more faithfully to the best of their religious tradition and live the full personal and social implications of their religion more authentically.

Salvation Today:
A Theological Approach

Yoshinobu Kumazawa

The tendency to distort the Christian message of salvation is familiar to students of Western Church history. It should come as no surprise, therefore, that the "younger churches" are experiencing similar problems—partly as theological spillover from the West and partly as response to indigenous socio-political pressures. In this essay, Yoshinobu Kumazawa describes the Protestant theological experience in Japan, both of distortions or "splits" in the concept of salvation and also of current efforts at correction. Kumazawa, who is professor of systematic theology at Tokyo Union Theological Seminary, sees essentially three concepts of salvation that have competed and dominated during this century: the existential, the social, and the eschatological. He also notes that each stage of theological progress has been accompanied by social retrogression. What is needed, he says, is an integration of the understandings of salvation to bring out "the con-temporal truth of the event of Jesus Christ." Dr. Kumazawa was born in New York and was dedicated to the Christian life at Riverside Church by Dr. Harry Emerson Fosdick. After spending his boyhood in the United States and China, his family returned to Japan. He later studied under Emil Brunner at Zürich and received his doctorate from Heidelberg University. In 1973-74 he was the Henry Luce Visiting Professor at Union Theological Seminary, New York. Some of the themes in this essay, which first appeared in *Japanese Religions* (Kyoto) in July 1972, are developed further by Dr. Kumazawa in his chapter "Japan: Where Theology Seeks To Integrate Text and Context," in *Asian Voices in Christian Theology*, edited by Gerald H. Anderson (Nashville: Abingdon Press, 1974).

I

WHY SALVATION "TODAY"?

When one tries to discuss the problem of "salvation today," it is almost inevitable for him to meet with the criticism that salvation as the basic content of the Christian Gospel belongs to the eternal dimension which is not only a matter of today but of yesterday and tomorrow also. Theological discussion of the topic "salvation today" should therefore first make clear why it tries to take up the subject from the temporal aspect and not from the supra-temporal aspect.

One often quotes Hebrews 13:8 when one stresses the supra-temporal character of salvation: "Jesus Christ is the same yesterday, today, and forever." Alexander C. Purdy's exegesis of this passage points up a typical misunderstanding. In connection with verse 7, he comments as follows: "They are gone, but Jesus Christ is timeless" (*Interpreter's Bible*, Vol. II, p. 755). Here "the same" (*ho auton*) of our text is interpreted as "timeless" and we see that the Hebrew concept of God or deity is put into the supra-temporal dimension which is a Greek idea. The Greeks made a sharp distinction between "time" and "eternity," which is timeless and unchangeable. Truth belongs not to changeable time, but to unchangeable eternity. It is quite evident that the truth is understood as "timeless truth," and gods who belong to the realm of truth are also timeless.

Such a timeless truth or timeless God is, however, quite strange from the biblical concept of truth or God. According to the Bible, God or truth which belongs to God is not timeless, but "historical." The biblical concept of God neither excludes time nor confines itself to the realm of the timeless. It is the historical God who created heaven and earth. As St. Augustine described in his *Confessions*, he is even the creator of "time" itself. He is the Lord of time and history who leads his people out of Egypt. And this historical concept of God became decisive in the event of Jesus Christ, in which eternity became time. Time and eternity cannot be separated in this event.

The biblical concept of God is clearly expressed in such passages as Exodus 3:7. God who called Moses told him that he who called Moses in that moment was the God who called his forefathers. "I am the God of your forefathers, the God of Abraham, the God of Isaac, the God of Jacob." If we take up, for instance, Isaac as the key person here, Abraham belongs to the dimension of the "past" and Jacob belongs to the dimension of the "future." The God of Abraham, Isaac and Jacob means that he is the God of the past, the present and the future. This means that he is the God of history. He was present as the Lord with Abraham, is present with Isaac as the Lord and will be present with Jacob as the Lord. It might therefore be better to express the unchangeability of God with an historical term such as "contemporaneity" rather than "eternity," which is easily misunderstood as philosophical timelessness. God in the Bible is unchangeably with us in this time as the Lord of all history. He is not merely beyond time, but also with time, contemporaneously.

The words "Jesus Christ is the same yesterday, today and forever," therefore, do not mean that he is timeless truth but that he is historical truth, always contemporaneously with us as the Lord in the past, present and forever. This very character of the biblical truth gives us the theological motivation to take up such a theme as salvation "today." Salvation as God's act is not timeless truth but historical truth, unchangeable historical truth which is always contemporaneous. The understanding of salvation which is lacking in this point of view will inevitably be abstract. Salvation today tries to recover an historical reality in an understanding of salvation which will overcome static quietism. Salvation today aims to make the historical dynamism in the concept of salvation clear.

II

SPLITS IN THE CONCEPT OF "SALVATION"
IN JAPANESE CHRISTIANITY

Japanese Christians, like Christians elsewhere, are seeking a way to recover historical dynamism in the concept of salvation. Looking back on the history of Japanese Protestantism since 1859, we cannot help noticing that there have been splits in the concept of salvation. Some took salvation solely as an existential matter, while others took it as a social problem, and still others strongly criticized the latter from an eschatological point of view.

Split between Existential and Social Understanding

The history of Japanese Protestantism since its beginning in 1859 might be characterized as "theological progress" and "social retrogression."

Japanese Protestantism had, in its beginning stage in the early part of the Meiji period, a very naive monotheistic faith. It was necessary for those Christians to stress monotheism in the midst of the pantheistic-pluralistic faith of the native Shinto religion of Japan. But this concern for a monotheistic God has been greatly broadened in the realm of Christology since the famous controversy between the two Christian leaders Masahisa Uemura and Danjo Ebina in 1901 and 1902. Uemura summarized the differences between Ebina and himself by saying, "Mr. Ebina does not believe in the deity of Christ; he denies him worship, and says that Christianity is not centered in Christ himself. We believe in his deity. We believe that he is God-made-man. We believe in Christ's omnipresence and immanence. We worship him and pray to him. Mr. Ebina looks up to Christ only as a teacher. We do that, but believe him also to be Savior" (M. Uemura, "Discussing the Difference between Him and Me," *Fukuin Shimpo*, No. 342, Jan. 15, 1902). As a result the Evangelical Alliance decided to exclude those who did not believe in the deity of Christ and therefore excluded Ebina at the Fourteenth General Assembly in 1902.

Such a Christological concern was succeeded in the Taisho and early Showa periods (1912-1930), first by the theology of Tokutaro Takakura, and then by the influence of dialectical theology. It is not my intent to follow the details of these developments, but it may be significant to notice that dialectical theology exclusively concentrated on the theology of Karl Barth after his debate on natural theology with Emil Brunner in 1934. Japanese theology accepted the ideas of Karl Barth solely because of his strict Christological concern. The development of Japanese theology from the naive concern for the concept of a monotheistic God to such a strict Christological concern as Barth's might be considered "theological progress" in Japanese Christianity. Christ is now understood as exclusively the only salvation of my sinful being.

On the other hand, however, a "social retrogression" can clearly be traced parallel to such "theological progress." As we already noticed, this theological progress toward a strict Christological concern began in 1901 with the Uemura-Ebina debate. This was the same year that the first socialist party in Japan, the Socialist-Democratic Party, was ordered to disband on the same day as its establishment. Although their numbers were not great, Protestant Christians had a strong impact on Japanese society in the early and middle Meiji era. This Socialist-Democratic Party was founded by six socialist leaders among whom were five Protestant Christians. Around 1903 the shift of leadership concerns from Christian to materialistic ones within the socialist movement took place and became more and more pronounced after the Russo-Japanese War in 1904/5. After the victory in the Russo-Japanese War, Japanese society experienced the rise of capitalism for the first time in its history. During this trend the Japanese church became more and more the church of middle-class people and lost the social impact which it had before. The Japanese church became the church of the bourgeoisie.

The prosperity of Japanese society after the victory in the First World War did not continue very long and post-war panic took place in 1918. At this time concerns for the common people took leadership in the socialist movement once more. Toyohiko Kagawa led a strike for the rights of 30,000 workers in 1921 and founded the Japan Farmers' Association. Leaders of the Socialist People's Party, the Japan Laborers' and Farmers' Party, the Japan Farmers' Party and the Japan Labor Federation were all Christians. The Japan Christian Federation published a Social Creed with fifteen articles in 1928, and the Kingdom of God Movement, which was based on this Social Creed, was established in 1929. This development in the later Taisho and early Showa periods could not be carried to a wider extent because of the rise of Japanese nationalism after the Manchurian Incident in 1931. Not only because of this change in the social situation, but also because of the severe criticism of liberal tendencies in the Japanese church, it was scarcely possible for Christian social concerns to develop theologically. Here we cannot help noticing that theological progress always seemed to happen at the expense of social retrogression. In other words, we would like to emphasize the split between the purely theological and the social understanding of salvation. This purely theological understanding of salvation can be denoted in Japan by this Christological concern which was tightly connected with the personal conviction that Christ alone was exclusively and existentially one's own Savior. We may therefore signify such a split in the understanding of salvation as the split between a personal or existential understanding and a social understanding.

Split between Social and Eschatological Understanding

The split between the personal or the existential understanding and the social understanding of salvation has also caused a keen split between the social and the eschatological understanding of salvation in Japan which became more and more evident with the introduction of dialectical theology around 1930 in the early Showa period.

Toyohiko Kagawa, who appeared as a leader of the labor movement at the end of the Taisho period, became a champion of social Christianity in Japan within the Kingdom of God Movement, which was established in 1929 after the Social Creed was declared by the Japan Christian Federation in 1928. The central idea of Kagawa's theology was the redemptive love of Christ which should be realized in social economics. "Economic movements are essentially the same as the movements of love" (T. Kagawa, *Love the Law of Life*, 1929, p. 200).

Kagawa, however, was not the only leading theologian in this period. Tokutaro Takakura, who was in a sense the theological successor of Masahisa Uemura, wrote *Evangelical Christianity* in 1927. The understanding of salvation of these two leading theologians had just the opposite emphases. Takakura, who was strongly influenced by Scottish theologians such as Forsyth, Denny and Mozley as well as German and Swiss theologians such as Barth, Brunner and Gogarten, severely criticized the liberal tendencies of Social Christianity in Japan. He said: "The realization of the kingdom of God is not a progressive matter but a redemptive and creative one" (*Evangelical Christianity*, 1947, p. 40). Takakura was thus "eschatological," while Kagawa was "evolutionary." The former put stress on the transcendental, the latter on the immanent. Takakura tended to be more and more individualistic, while Kagawa was open to social problems.

Such a split between the social and eschatological understanding of salvation can also be traced in the development of Japanese Christianity after the introduction of dialectical theology. Social Christianity in the early Showa period around 1930 became more and more radical in the Student Christian Movement, which was also influenced by Marxism. Enkichi Kan, who was the leading theologian in the SCM Movement at that time and who drastically changed his position to Barthian theology afterward, discussed his convictions as follows: "Salvation of the individual is possible only when he finds his place in the society founded on God. He can be saved only when he takes his share in building up the God-centered society as begun by Jesus" ("Social Christianity," in *Student World*, Vol. 26, 1933, p. 230). God, according to his idea, is immanent "life power," which should be developed in history by building up an ideal society. "In terms of the temporal relation of the kingdom endeavor, it is clear that in Kan's mind, as well as in the thoughts of others during this period, the kingdom was to be realized on earth in history. The sources of the period are silent as regards eschatology in the sense of the intervention of God as the transcendent Lord of history at the end of time to bring his kingdom into reality" (C. H. Germany, *Protestant Theologies in Modern Japan: A History of Dominant Theological Currents 1920-1960,* 1965, pp. 76f.).

Dialectical theology was introduced with strong criticism against the immanent tendency in Social Christianity, and it expressed itself in a clearly transcendental and eschatological tone. As we have already mentioned, after the Barth-Brunner-Debate on natural theology in 1934, Barthian theology became the theology in Japan. This development might be understood as theological progress in a sense, but at the same time one cannot help feeling the irony of history that this took place at the very moment when Japanese nationalism began its imperialistic invasion of China which caused the Manchurian incident in 1931 and drove Japan into World War II. Barthian theology with its strong eschatological tone got rid of liberal and immanent Social Christianity right in the midst of the social situation characterized by enthusiastic oppression of all kinds of socialistic ideas. The Summer School of the Student YMCA, which was dominated by SCM students, was disrupted in 1932 not directly by the intervention of the police but by the fear of such an intervention. Dialectical theology put stress on the authority of God over against anthropocentric liberalism but at the same time went along with the authority of the state without any criticism against it. Japan was subsequently driven into the war by this nationalism, and the Japanese church, led by the eschatological theology of Karl Barth, never tried to be the confessing church. Here we see more vividly the problem mentioned above. The more theological progress one may notice, the more social retrogression one may have to acknowledge.

The Problem Today

The situation of Japanese Christianity after World War II is essentially the same as before. Needless to say, post-war Christianity had to be critical of the way of life and thinking of the Japanese church during the war. In other words it could not help recognizing that a deeper social dimension should be rediscovered in the understanding of salvation. This led post-war Japanese Christianity to the revival of the social understanding of salvation by good deeds. However, this special emphasis on the social understanding of salvation is causing a problematic situation in the theological sense today. For instance, in Japanese Christian thinking today there is a radical separation of Jesus from Christ. Christ is seen as only a product of the theology of Paul, who was the promoter of a religious movement within the Roman Empire. He never tried to protest the authority of the state; on the contrary, he was given Roman citizenship and was guaranteed by the state. His activities were solely within the institution and not against it. Pauline theology is, therefore, the theology of compromise, which could never be the starting point of the anti-institutional movement that post-war Japanese Christianity needed to overcome its failure during the war. Not only Paul but the whole development of Christianity in the Book of Acts and afterward had to be denied because of its compromise with the state. All the Christological dogmas, formation of the institutional Church, canonization of the Bible, etc., were severely criticized from this point of view. However, Jesus, who was not the Christ of Pauline theology, did not compromise with the authority of the state. On the contrary, he was crucified by the Roman Empire. He had fought until the last moment against the state and therefore became the hero of the anti-institutional movement.

With such a separation of Jesus from Christ, atonement as the work of Christ was also denied. It was felt that the crystallization of religious ideology only provides a good excuse for doing nothing against the state. Today justification by faith alone is criticized from the same point of view, and instead justification by work—needless to say, by anti-institutional work—is being stressed. It may become quite clear in such arguments that the reality of human sin or of my very sinful being totally drops out of the discussion. Atonement does not have any reality and is treated as a form of abstract religious ideology, because one's sinful being has lost reality for him completely. One may have full rights only when one tries to rediscover the social understanding of salvation. But if one does it by losing an existential understanding of one's own sin and salvation, one may encounter the same split between the social and existential understanding of salvation.

The lack of existential understanding in the ideas of such radicals necessarily leads to an optimism that one can or at least should realize social justice within this given historical situation. Social understanding of salvation is easily identified with the realization of a social reform program or revolution, which loses the eschatological perspective of salvation. It seems to be very difficult for radical activists to wait with hope. One cannot wait anymore and is driven to action. In a sense, salvation is action, but action without eschatological hope easily tends to nihilistic action. The split between the social and the eschatological understanding of salvation is therefore evident.

The main feature of post-war Christianity in Japan is, as we have seen, the revival of the social understanding of salvation. The existential and eschatological understandings of salvation were once emphasized at the cost of the social understanding. Now, to the contrary, in post-war Japan, social understanding is being emphasized at the cost of the existential and the eschatological understandings of salvation. This is nothing but a continuation of the same split that existed in Japan before the war, and the situation is essentially not at all changed. It is clear that we have to be cautious not to take up only one aspect of the understanding of salvation when we discuss salvation "today." Our task is not to insist upon one aspect exclusively, but to find a way to integrate these three understandings of salvation.

III
THE WAY TO INTEGRATION

Each of these, the existential, social and eschatological understanding of salvation, has its own rights to be maintained, and what is most urgent today for the theological understanding of salvation is not to insist upon any one of these exclusively, but to discover a way to integrate our understandings and develop a more inclusive theology.

Going back to our observation in the first part of this article, we tried to make clear that we are not dealing with a timeless truth but an historical truth which was crystallized in the fact of Jesus Christ. This is, so to speak, not a supra-temporal but a con-temporal truth, which we can deal with here and now in a given historical situation. Here we find not only salvation "today," but also the very point of the integration of the "salvation" itself. The whole work of God, the *missio Dei*, is crystallized in this con-temporal truth in the event of Jesus Christ.

Here the *missio Dei* is understood as the work of the triune God who has communion within his own essence as Father, Son and Holy Spirit. Trinity means that God has relation between Father, Son and Holy Spirit within his being itself. His "being" is "relation" and his essence is *koinonia.* His work of creation as the Father means that he created us so that we may join in his *koinonia.* In other words, the work of creation is an invitation to his *koinonia*, which is the essence of the triune God. Man, however, as the crown of creation did not accept this invitation, but tried to stay outside God's fellowship by falling into sin. God the Son did not give up his will of inviting man into his fellowship, and he expressed it in the most radical way by his redeeming work. Moreover, through God the Holy Spirit he expressed his will to accomplish this invitation. The end of his whole work of salvation, namely, the fulfillment of the kingdom of God, is simply the fulfillment of this invitation to the fellowship, which is the very essence of the triune God. The whole work of God can therefore be described as a circle which starts from God and ends at God. This whole work of God, which starts from and is oriented to God, is the *missio Dei* and is accomplished by the other half of the circle, the *promissio Dei.* This work of divine economy can scarcely be understood by us as limited creatures, but in the con-temporal event of Jesus Christ we are given the key to open the mystery of the whole economy of God. In the event of Jesus Christ the whole work from God to God is crystallized in his pre-existence, incarnation, death, resurrection and ascension, which is a circle starting from God and ending at God, revealing the divine economy. This Jesus Christ, the *missio* as well as the *promissio Dei*, gives us the basis of our being, the aim of history and the common mission of the people of God. Here we are given the point of integration of the different understandings of salvation. Accordingly, we may understand salvation as follows.

Salvation as Faith

This means that Jesus Christ is "the basis of our being." The understanding of salvation today which seeks to make the con-temporal truth of the Gospel clear always has to answer the question: "Where is Christ today?" The biblical answer to this question is very clear. Christ, the Savior, is always with those who need him, namely with those who can never exist as being with any other basis. He is with me here and now as the real basis of my existence, and "there is no salvation in anyone else at all, for there is no other name under heaven granted to men, by which we may receive salvation" (Acts 4:12). Here is the basis on which we can establish our identity, and salvation can be understood existentially as a matter of my faith.

Salvation as Love

Christ "is" with us, but he also "precedes" us and asks us to follow him. Christ as the *missio Dei* is sent into the world and clearly reveals to us that even this world which is fallen into sin is not the world of the devil but the world of God who created it and loves it. This means that Christ, who precedes each individual as well as the Church, shows us that those who are outside the Christian Church are also under his Lordship and are not our enemies but our neighbors whom we are asked by our Lord, who is also their Lord, to love. This "preceding Lord" has two aspects. He precedes individuals as well as the Church and shows us the aim of history toward which we are expected to work. In this he is *promissio Dei*. He is also *missio Dei* who is sent into this world, and this dual character brings out the social understanding of salvation. Christ will be seen as the *promissio Dei* as soon as one becomes aware that he is the *missio Dei* for him. He is sent to me as my salvation, but he is also sent to the whole world as the salvation of all, and here the existential understanding of salvation is not to be separated from the social understanding. Christ, who is the *missio Dei* to the world, is at the same time the *promissio Dei* which we are expected to follow in the work of loving our neighbors. Salvation as love is therefore gift as well as task, and Christ is at the same time the "basis" of our being and the "aim" of history. Existential understanding and social understanding are quite inseparable here. The former deals with the "basis," while the latter deals with the "aim," and the tension between these two motivates the work of love.

Salvation as Hope

This tension between "basis" and "aim," or the *missio* and the *promissio Dei*, will bring out the eschatological way of living.

We already have seen that this will motivate the work of love, but more precisely this is love which develops out of hope. The task of love will be accomplished in the consummation of the kingdom of God, which will be brought about by Jesus Christ. He, therefore, is the hope in which we see that the social understanding and the eschatological understanding of salvation are quite inseparable. God calls his people who live in this hope and are ready to participate in his work of love. The unity of the Church will be realized only in this "common mission" of the people of God. It seems to me very significant that the Faith and Order Conference of WCC at Louvain in 1971 took up the theme "The Unity of the Church and the Unity of Mankind." The classical faith and order theme of the unity of the Church is here taken up within the wider context of all mankind. The unity of the Church is the "first fruit" of the unity of all mankind, and here we see again that the eschatological hope for the unity of the Church is inseparable from the task of love for all mankind. In other words, salvation as hope in the *promissio Dei* will combine the eschatological and the social understanding of salvation.

Thus salvation today is the con-temporal truth of the event of Jesus Christ who is *missio* and *promissio Dei*, where one can find the point of integration of the existential, social and eschatological understandings of salvation.

What Is the
Christian Message?

Hans Küng

Mission as effective proclamation requires a clear and concise
statement of the substance and uniqueness of the Christian message. In one phrase, the message is Jesus Christ. But what is the
message of and about Jesus Christ which is the good news of the
Gospel? Hans Küng, a theologian at Tübingen University, says
that the Christian message is this: "In the light and power of
Jesus we are able, in the world of today, to live, to act, to suffer,
and to die in a truly human way, because we are totally dependent on God and totally committed to our fellow human beings."
The phrases "in the light and power of Jesus" and "in the world
of today" are crucial, and Professor Küng elaborates on their
meaning. The Christian message, he says, will transform the
world. This is the Christian hope, based on the promise of Jesus
Christ who is the ground of that hope. Among Father Küng's
numerous published works are his books *The Church, Infallible?
Justification*, and *Truthfulness: The Future of the Church*. This
article is reprinted, with permission, from the December 1970
issue of *Japan Missionary Bulletin* (Tokyo).

I

As Christians, as the Church, we must know what we want,
for ourselves, for other human beings, for the world. It is not
enough to know what we know. We cannot afford theories which
are irrelevant to practice or formulations of the Christian message which have nothing to do with human life. We must learn to

do the truth, to translate our programs into action. When a Marxist is asked what he wants, he can give the answer in different ways: world revolution, the dictatorship of the proletariat, the new man, the classless society. To the same question, the Christian can give different answers: faith and conversion, justification, freedom, love, life in the spirit, the new man, the kingdom of God. Different formulas can be used—by the Marxist as well as by the Christian, in the New Testament as well as in the Church of today—but the message, the program, the goal, the heart of the matter, is, in the final analysis, unique. Otherwise people would go in different directions and there would be no community. If these various formulas we use are authentic, they must reflect a single message, a single program, a single substance.

And what is this message? What is it that holds the twenty-seven books of the New Testament together? What is the thread of unity which runs through twenty centuries of Christian history and preaching? It is Jesus Christ. The Christian message can be expressed in these words: Jesus is the Christ. Only the man who can appeal to Marx is a real Marxist. In a far more radical sense, only he is a Christian, only this is a Christian church, who can appeal to Christ, or even better, who is a follower of Jesus Christ.

We have heard what this meant in the New Testament, particularly for Paul. And we have heard that the content of the Christian message must be formulated anew for today. We are going to make the almost rash attempt to outline in a few pages how this Christian message can be formulated for today. It is not our intention to give a summary of the Christian faith. We will try to state simply what is necessary today, with a view to the needs of the future and with the awareness of our continual dependence on the original Christian event.

One can think of different ways of formulating the one Christian message. The following one seems to me to be particularly suited to the needs of today. The Christian message is this: *In the light and power of Jesus we are able, in the world of today, to live, to act, to suffer, and to die in a truly human way, because we are totally dependent on God and totally committed to our fellow human beings.* This brief formulation is intelligible enough but needs considerable elaboration.

What does this phrase *in the light and power of Jesus* mean? What did Jesus want? Jesus preached neither theories nor laws; he did not even preach himself. He preached the *kingdom of God.* He certainly did not belong to the priestly establishment (the Saducees); he was a "layman," surprisingly enough unmarried, and he proclaimed not simply the dominion over the world which God had exercised from the beginning, but the future, eschatological kingdom of God. He was no political revolutionary (Zealot); he did not proclaim a national religious-political theocracy, but the immediate, unrestricted dominion of God himself over the world.

He was not an ascetic (an Essene or member of the Qumran community); he did not believe in a divine judgment which would exercise vengeance over the children of this world, the children of darkness; he rather proclaimed the good news of God's grace precisely for the sinners and those who were without God.

He was, finally, not a pious moralist (a Pharisee); he did not appeal to the Scriptures and he had no use for casuistry. In his view the kingdom of God would come about not through faithful fulfillment of the law but simply through God's own gracious act which expects of man his confident acceptance and commitment of himself in faith and love.

Thus Jesus does not conform to any pattern; his life was a provocation to both liberals and conservatives; he was nearer to God than the priests, freer in respect to the world than the ascetics, more "moral" than the moralists, more revolutionary than the revolutionaries. As such he proclaimed the *will of God* as the supreme and immediate norm. And what is the will of God? For Jesus the answer is clear: *the good of men.*

For this reason Jesus, who in general lived in accordance with the requirements of the law, had no hesitation, in individual cases, in acting against its prescriptions. Rituals are not taboo; only the pure of heart are really pure in the eyes of God. He did not emphasize fasting but let himself be mocked as an "eater and drinker." He had no anxiety about Sabbath observance; man is the measure of both the Sabbath and the law.

For this reason he denied, in scandalous manner, the absolute claims of sanctified traditions and institutions. He denied the absolute claims of the law, because the law is there for the sake of men. He denied the absolute claims of the temple, because reconciliations and the daily service of one's fellow man take priority over worship.

For this reason he preaches a love which, while allowing man to be both pious and reasonable, really proves itself by the fact that it excludes no one, not even the enemy, and is prepared to commit itself totally and absolutely. Such a love transforms society by transforming the individual.

For this reason Jesus identifies himself, to the annoyance of the pious, with all of the "poor devils": the heretics and schismatics (Samaritans), the immoral (prostitutes and adulterers), the politically compromised (tax collectors and collaborators), those rejected and neglected by society (the lepers, the sick, the needy), in general, the common people, who either don't know the law, or, at any rate, do not live in accordance with it.

For this reason he even dares to proclaim not God's punishment for violation of the law, but rather his gratuitous forgiveness. He speaks this forgiving word personally to men and in so doing makes it possible for them to undergo a real conversion, to forgive one another.

This is truly the good news (the Gospel) of grace, hope, freedom, love and joy; it is a Gospel convincingly lived by the one who proclaims it, accompanied in a striking way by charismatic healings of the sick and of those possessed—eschatological "signals" for the coming of the kingdom of God, an event which touches man in his very physical nature. In Jesus' life there was no split between theory and practice; his very life was an unheard-of challenge for the entire religious-social system (the law) and its representatives. With what *authority* does he do this? This is the question put by friend and foe alike. Instead of preaching the unconditional fulfillment of the law, he claims a remarkable freedom for God and man. In the final analysis, isn't he preaching another God—a God who is on the side of the sinners rather than of the pious? Doesn't he make himself greater than Moses (the law), greater than Solomon (the temple) and greater than Jonah (the prophets)? How can this man, of humble origins and not backed by any institution or party, speak and act with such authority? How can he make the claims he makes? Is it because of the unique immediacy of his presence with God, because he is at the same time there for God and in God's place? Jesus' very person was a sign to the times he lived in and a call for decision. His preaching and conduct sealed his fate; a life and death conflict seemed unavoidable. Did the guardians of the law, of morality and of the religious order have any other choice than to liquidate this man who had no use for the law or the God whom the law proclaimed, and who led the people astray? The death of one man is preferable to the death of many. Jesus is arrested but he sticks to his position. He is examined by the Jews as one who despised the law and the temple; he is condemned to death by the Romans as a political rebel. The Jews made use of the Romans, but they themselves were used by the law. The law killed him—and Paul will later on draw the radical consequences of this fact for the freedom of the Christian. Jesus died between two condemned criminals, formally identified with sinners, abandoned by the very one whose nearness he had proclaimed in his words, in his deeds, in his very person. This man was abandoned by God and his failure seems manifest; he died, and the God whom he proclaimed died with him.

Was his death the end of everything? Obviously not. It is a fact of world history that the movement which took its origin from Jesus really began only after his death. What is the source of this movement? If we look beyond the legendary elements and contradictory traditions, we are left with the testimony on which the first witnesses all agree. They saw that their faith was grounded on something that really happened: *the one who was crucified lives!* The fact of this new life is the decisive element, not its how, when and where. Jesus, who was abandoned by God, lives with God. He has been given new life. He is the victor. His message, his way of life, his person, are justified. His way was the right one.

Now for the first time, in the light of his new life and through the experience of his Spirit, the disciples see clearly that God—and it was, after all, the real God—was with him from the beginning. They see that in his very person he took his stand for God and man, then and now. They see that the cross is not the event in which God rejected him, but the salvific event par excellence. They see that through the cross the kingdom of God has broken into history—the kingdom of reconciliation, freedom, justice, love and peace. In virtue of this fact the person of Jesus receives a unique meaning for all who turn confidently to him in faith: Jesus is the Christ, anointed and sent by God, God's final revelation, his incarnate Word. Titles and conceptions current in his contemporary world are applied to him and receive their definitive meaning through him. (They deal particularly with his pre- and post-existence.) And now for the first time the Church is formed—a community of believers united in their confession of him. This Church bears his name and is borne by his Spirit, the Holy Spirit.

The Jesus who preached has become the Jesus who is preached; he who brought the message has become the content of the message. Jesus Christ in his life and death is the sum and the substance of the message of the kingdom of God. He himself is the key to the meaning of history, he himself is the Christian message, he it is that sets Christianity apart.

II

What does this mean *in the world of today*? Christians are no less committed than others to the humanistic ideal. But they see man and God, they see humanity, freedom, love, life, justice and peace from the standpoint of Jesus. They cannot forget that all of these values have been bought at the price of death. They cannot forget that for them this Jesus who lives is identical with the crucified one. The cross is not merely an example and model but the source and power of faith; it is the element which radically distinguishes Christian faith and the Lord who is the object of this faith from other religions and their gods. It is the element which distinguishes faith from unbelief and superstition. The path to new life and freedom leads through the cross. The cross of Christ as the cross of Jesus of Nazareth was never a timeless myth or a profound symbol; it was a hard, cruel, historical fact. No human being, no Jew or pagan at the time of Jesus and in the world in which Christianity appeared would ever have thought of connecting the shameful way in which slaves and political rebels were put to death with a religious ideal. "We proclaim Christ—yes, Christ nailed to the cross; and though this is a stumbling block to the Jews and folly to the Greeks, yet to those who have heard his call . . . he is the power of God and the wisdom of God" (1 Cor. 1:23ff.).

It is here that faith always encounters the challenge to live out the *following of Christ*, to recognize the cross as a sign, not of cramped self-abasement, but of liberating hope. Faith is challenged to see the cross as a sign of God's presence in his very absence, as a sign of life through death. The following of Christ does not imply imitation. It means to act in a way analogous to, correlative with, Christ's way of acting. We do not live in the times of Jesus. We live in our own day and age, in our own place, and with our own problems. The message of Jesus Christ must always be translated. When the Christian *in the world of today* takes his own cross upon himself in faith and confidence in the crucified Christ, he is able, in virtue of the hope inspired by the crucified Christ, not merely to *act*, but also to *suffer*, not merely to *live* but also to *die*. And even at the point where pure reason must throw up its hands, when one is caught in the web of meaningless suffering and guilt, he can see a meaning, because he knows that even there he is *absolutely dependent on God*. The message of the cross takes man's insecurity and anxiety, darkness, estrangement and guilt seriously. Man does not have to play the hero. The message of the cross says simply: God is there in man's insecurity, anxiety, darkness, loneliness, estrangement and guilt. Man does not know how to help himself, but God is always there to help him. God is for man and God will make man triumph over every situation which threatens him, over his abandonment and over his guilt. The message of the cross is not one of repression but one of liberation: the liberation of man through the divine forgiveness, reconciliation and salvation he has received. The cross frees him for life, meaning, love, thankfulness and hope.

Faith in the crucified Christ bestows on man peace with God and with himself, but it by no means ignores the problems of the world. This faith does not make justice superfluous, nor does it want to do away with power in human society. But faith in the crucified one takes both power and justice into itself, denies the absolute claims of both, and in so doing makes man *truly human* because he is truly committed to his fellow man. It makes man into one who is *totally committed to his fellow human beings who need him*, his neighbor. Faith in the crucified Christ permits a man to be so free in the realm of justice that he is able, for the sake of his neighbor, not to insist on his own rights; he is able to go two miles with the man who has forced him to go one. Faith in the crucified one makes it possible for man, involved in the struggle for power, to use the power which is his not for himself but for his neighbor, to give not only his coat but his cloak as well. The Christian message, embodied in the Sermon on the Mount and backed up by Jesus' life and death, does not intend to establish a new law or legal order. Its intention is to free man from law. The Christian message aims at a state of things which is, in itself, too much to ask of either bourgeois or Marxist society, and yet a state of things which is of absolute importance, not only for the human life of individuals, but for that of human society, of all the races, classes and even churches into which man is divided. This message aims at a state of things where, instead of calculating one another's guilt, men are able to forgive one another; where, instead of defending their own positions, men are able to be unconditionally reconciled; where, instead of continually insisting on their own rights, men embrace the higher justice of love; where, instead of engaging in the merciless struggle for power, men search for the peace which surpasses all understanding. Such a message does not function as an opiate and dull man's awareness of the needs of the world. Far more radically than other programs, it turns his attention to this world, directs him to change the world, wherever men are oppressed by those who hold power, wherever persons are sacrificed to institutions, wherever freedom is sacrificed to the established order, wherever justice is threatened by power.

The Church as the community of those who believe in Christ must commit itself actively to bringing about this state of things in its preaching and action. Above all, the Church must bring about this state of things in itself by effecting a bond of union and love between those who are separated by barriers of culture, race, sex, money, or class. In this way the Christian mes-

sage can have now an impact on human society, and bring finally, as a gift of the Holy Spirit, the kingdom, the kingdom of perfect justice, unsurpassable freedom, unspoken love, universal
reconciliation and eternal peace. This kingdom can only come
about as the gift of God; it calls upon man to be active, but
man's activity will never bring it about, either through the
progress of bourgeois society or through the achievements of
classless socialist society. Thus the Christian message makes it
possible for man to be active, to take the initiative, in society, in
the scientific and economic worlds, in politics, law and culture;
and the Christian message makes it possible for him to remain
committed even when it seems that no progress is being made,
where neither social evolution nor socialist revolution is able to
triumph over the tensions and contradictions of man's existence
in society. The Christian message makes it possible for man not
to despair, even when he is caught in a situation where justice,
freedom and peace are totally absent. The Christian message
makes it possible for him to hope against hope; it makes possible
a love which includes one's enemy; it makes it possible for man
to persevere in his attempts to humanize himself and society even
where man's inhumanity to man is the rule.

Jesus, as the crucified and living Christ, is the Christian
message with all these consequences. *He* is the message, not ab-
stractly but quite concretely; not theoretically but very practically; not at the periphery, but in its very center; not simply as a
fact but quite consciously as a program. Jesus is in his very person this concrete program of world transformation—he and he
alone: not Socrates, not Buddha, not Moses, not Mohammed,
not Marx, not Freud.

III

What is the Christian message? We are now in a position to
better understand the brief formula proposed at the beginning.
The Christian message is: *In the light and power of Jesus we are
able in the world of today, to live, to act, to suffer and to die in a
truly human way, because we are totally dependent on God and
totally committed to our fellow human beings.*

This same brief formulation can be expressed in other ways, either in more cosmological or more theological terms.

In more cosmological terms we could say: In the light and power of Jesus we can remain free from the powers of the world (enslavement to economic, scientific or political principles), free from the idols of the world (persons), and free from false gods of the world (possessions, pleasure, power); through our faith in God we neither fall prey to the world nor do we regard it as an enemy, but we are alive to the world in the confidence that history has a meaning, that at some time in the future the world will be reconciled.

The same thought can be put theologically: In the light and power of Jesus in the world of today we can call upon God as our Father; he is the mystery of love which embraces all men, frees them of guilt and manifests itself as ultimately triumphant over sin and death.

We have come to the end. Can the Christian message transform the world? It *has* transformed the world. That is an historical fact. But it has not transformed the world deeply enough— and this is the fault of Christianity.

But the Christian message will transform the world. This is our hope and Jesus Christ himself is the ground of that hope. "Behold, *I* am making all things new" (Rev. 21:5).

III: The Missionary

Missionary Commitment

Pope Paul VI

In his message on Mission Sunday in October 1972, Pope Paul VI addressed himself to some of the problems faced by those in missionary service today. This is an excerpt from that statement.

We wish to state the problem clearly. Local personnel are being called upon to take an ever increasing part in the evangelization of their own people. Also, personnel coming from other churches genuinely desire to be of service and consequently must continue in their missionary commitment. It is not merely a question of balance: the common cause of God's kingdom associates both ranks of evangelical messengers closely together so that they may collaborate closely with one another. Such collaboration is necessary and most certainly fruitful. We do not mean merely a working relationship but, rather, harmonious coordination which should be the expression of ecclesial communion.

Missionary, Go Home . . . Or Stay

Federico Pagura

At a meeting between Costa Ricans and missionaries to discuss issues of missionary work and relationships, Bishop Federico Pagura of the United Methodist Church read a brief statement expressing his concerns about the context of missionary service in Latin America today. That statement has been widely published in Latin America as well as in other parts of the world. It has been translated from the Spanish by William J. Nottingham and is reprinted here from *The Christian Century* (Chicago), April 11, 1973. Federico Pagura, an Argentine, was bishop of the United Methodist Church of Panama and Costa Rica from 1968-72. After completing his term as bishop, he returned to Argentina to serve as superintendent for the Mendoza district of his church. Well known as a poet, author and hymn writer, Pagura did graduate study at the School of Theology in Claremont, California, and is president of CELADEC (Latin American Commission on Christian Education).

Missionary, go home . . . or stay.

If you are not able to separate the eternal Word of the Gospel from the cultural molds in which you carried it to these lands and taught it with genuine abnegation: Missionary, go home.

If you are not able to identify with the events, anxieties, and aspirations of those peoples prematurely aged by an unequal struggle which seems to have neither termination nor hope: Missionary, go home.

If your allegiance and fidelity to your nation of origin are stronger than loyalty and obedience to Jesus Christ who came "to put down the mighty and lift up the lowly" (Lk. 1:52): Missionary, go home.

If you are not able to love and respect as equals those whom once you came to evangelize as "the lost": Missionary, go home.

If you are not able to rejoice at the entry of new peoples and churches upon a new stage of maturity, independence, and responsibility, even at the price of committing errors like those which you and your compatriots committed also in the past: Missionary, go home.

For it is time to go home.

But if you are ready to bear the risks and pains of this hour of birth which our American peoples are experiencing, even denying yourself, if you begin to celebrate with them the happiness of sensing that the Gospel is not only proclamation and affirmation of a distant hope but of a hope and liberation which are already transforming history, if you are ready to give more of your time, your values, your life in the service of these peoples who are awaking, then:

STAY! There is much to do; hands and blood are lacking for an undertaking so immense in which Christ is the protagonist and pioneer.

What Makes a Missionary?
Toward Crucified Mind,
Not Crusading Mind

Kosuke Koyama

An encouraging aspect of the missionary situation today is the increasing number of missionaries being sent by Third World churches to the Third World as well as to Europe and North America. As Third World missionaries and mission agencies wrestle with the crucial issues in missiology, they bring a vital perspective to the discussion. At a consultation on "Missionary Service in Asia Today," convened by the Methodist Church in cooperation with the East Asia Christian Conference at Kuala Lumpur, Malaysia in 1971, Dr. Kosuke Koyama addressed the assembled missionaries, national church leaders and Western mission board representatives on "What Makes a Missionary?" He defines a missionary as "anyone who increases by participation the concretization of the love of God in history." A missionary, he says, is always in process of becoming; therefore growth and nurture are important aspects in the making of a missionary. Dr. Koyama, who has a Th.D. from Princeton Theological Seminary, was a Japanese Kyodan missionary to the Church of Christ in Thailand from 1960 to 1968, teaching at Thailand Theological Seminary in Chiengmai. From 1968-74 he was executive director of the Association of Theological Schools in Southeast Asia, dean of the Southeast Asia Graduate School of Theology and editor of the *South East Asia Journal of Theology*, with headquarters in Singapore. He is now senior lecturer in phenomenology of religion at the University of Otago in Dunedin, New Zealand. His speech was first published in the report of the consultation, *Missionary Service in Asia Today*.

This paper has four sections: (1) a reflection on the complexity of human and historical realities; (2) an attempt to give some working summary of God's saving act in history; (3) the study of the mode of communication of God's saving act in history—communicator-communication; (4) "What makes a missionary?"—discussed in the light of the foregoing discussions.

I

One of the important things which theological seminaries did not teach me while I was a student, and that later I had to find out myself, was a simple fact that to meet and to know a Hindu is more interesting and more rewarding than to know Hinduism, a Buddhist more than Buddhism, a Marxist more than Marxism, a revolutionary more than revolution, a missionary more than missiology, wife more than wife-logy, Jesus Christ more than Christology.

My life is being lived basically within the constant interaction of five living persons (my family). If I were living in the interaction of five "logies," my life would be much easier! But I am afraid it would be much less colorful. I speak, I shout, I spank (children, not wife), I laugh, I think, I eat. In all these doings I am forced to feel and realize the difference between "I" and "I-logy" and children and children-logy. Personal encounter (human community) is pregnant with unpredictable possibilities. The living person who confronts me defies the best possible definition of him. He is far more mysterious and complicated than I can possibly delineate even with the help of Freud, Marx, Dostoevski and Heidegger. (It involves difficult intellectual research to locate "timely help" in these giant thinkers.) I look at missionaries. I am one of them. I find that missionary is indeed more "mysterious" than missiology. Missiology I can tame, but missionary I cannot. That "man is made in the image of God" may sound simple. But the living person who stands in front of me is a staggering anthropological, sociological and historical complexity. Permit me to make some clumsy remarks. Missiology does not sweat, thirst, complain, cry, laugh (and practice family planning). But missionary does! He is a *full* person whether he likes it or not.

I am sorry that I did not realize this simple distinction much earlier. I should say, to be more precise, that I am sorry I have not personally appropriated and experienced in my whole existence this simple distinction and what it means. If I had, it would have contributed greatly to the manner of appreciating other persons when I came to meet them. Is it perhaps possible—what a terrible possibility!—that study of theology did this to me? Certainly, has not "theology" inflated my language and thought? And has this particular inflation kept me from real contact with real man? Isn't it true that theology is more manageable than God himself? Isn't it true that wife-logy is more tranquil than wife in person? While I was in Thailand I studied Buddhism. What a wonderful time I had in the quiet library of Thailand Theological Seminary as I went undisturbed through the pages of the Buddhist Canons. Thanks to some knowledge of the library-Buddhism, I began to say a few sensible words about Buddhism. But when I realized the difference between library-Buddhism and street-Buddhists, my library-Buddha was paralyzed. Library-Buddha and street-Buddhists are, of course, related. In fact, I felt quite often that the street-Buddhists should study more about library-Buddhism. Yet, it is the street-Buddhists who are the brothers whom I see, with whom I speak and with whom I live. To love them *as they are* in all their complexity—and not just to live anthropological, sociological, theological "formulations" of the brothers—is the command of God whom we have not seen (1 Jn. 4:20).

That particular inflation can be brought down to dependable proportions only by way of loving the brothers as they are seen by us. I began as hard as I could to examine the relationship between "the idea of man walking in the idea of history" and "the living person in the concrete historical situation." Perhaps here is an unemployed man. He has to live with devastating awareness that his community does not need him. He has no income. He is a Thai. He is walking in the street of Bangkok with an empty stomach. The sun is mercilessly beating down on him. He is bitter about his lot. In his tired head he schemes this or that in order to get a scanty meal. He has had only three years of formal education. I observe him. I may even produce a book about him as voluminous as Gunnar Myrdal's *Asian Drama*, yet I am afraid that he may elude my best definition of him. He is a living person. A person is a "monstrous" complexity. He exercises freedom.

Let me insert one paragraph here for illustration. I realized one day that an almost insignificant thing about me has a complicated historical background. Start with an easy one: Why do I have miserable English pronounciation? It is because my father, my grandfather, my great-grandfather and all the way back to my first known ancestor who was a mountain bandit (some 200 years ago) and even beyond, spoke the Japanese language. The fact that I find it difficult to distinguish the *a* sound and *u* sound ("flash toilet, please") does not derive from my private short-comings, but from the historical chain of Japanese ears and tongues. I would make the same point about my liking to eat raw fish: tuna, trout, octopus, squid. Yet I do not enjoy raw oyster. It is because the community from which I derive my sense of taste did not appreciate raw oyster. Why do I have this or that particular (mysterious?) type of emotion, psychological reaction, sense of value? Why is there in me that which is suspicious of activism? Why do I have my secret appreciation of "hara-kiri"? Why is there pantheistic emotion within me even though I reject it theologically? Why do I appreciate the Gospel in this or that way? Why do I see three Koyamas or perhaps five Koyamas within one Koyama? Which Koyama is the Koyama who is now speaking? There must be some complicated personal and historical answer to all these questions.

The realization of the complexity of human existence has concurred with the realization of the complexity of history. A person is as complicated as history. History is as complicated as a person. Appreciation of this correlation—you may think it is not so inspiring—became a point of new departure for my missionary thinking. As I began to appreciate the complexity of history, I began to see the hidden value of history. History became, as it were, personal. And my personal life became, as it were, historical. I realized a strange thing. The appreciation of the complexity of man and history suddenly opened my eyes to a more meaningful appreciation of love of God in history. The greater the appreciation of the complexity of man and history, the greater became my appreciation of the love of God. Emotionally, at one point—and this may sound irrational and perhaps ridiculous—I felt the love of God in the fact that my tongue fails to say "flush toilet" and my stomach naturally accepts rice and unnaturally accepts hamburger.

The theological statement "God in history" is a stupendous assertion when we stop to think about what it means. In all fantastic complexities—complexities of Egypt, Assyria, Babylon, Persia, Rome—"God experiences history." "Are you not like the Ethiopians to me, O people of Israel?" says the Lord. "Did I not bring up Israel from the land of Egypt, and the Philistines from Caphtor and the Syrians from Kir?" (Am. 9:7).

Isaiah speaks of God's absolute might over the complexity of history:

> In that day the Lord will whistle for the fly which is at the sources of the streams of Egypt, and for the bee which is in the land of Assyria. And they will all come and settle in the steep ravines, and in the clefts of the rocks, and on all the thornbushes, and on all the pastures. In that day the Lord will shave with a razor which is hired beyond the River— with the king of Assyria—the head and the hair of the feet, and it will sweep away the beard also (Is. 7:18-20).

Look at the man called Zacchaeus. He was a tax collector. He must have heard about the famed rabbi from Nazareth and wanted to take a good look at him. We know why he went up to the tree. His calculation was right. Being a director of a tax office, he must have had a trained sense of estimation. When Jesus came, he stopped and looked at him. "Hurry down, Zacchaeus," Jesus said, "for I must stay in your house today" (Lk. 19:5). Zacchaeus nearly dropped dead by surprise. That was *all* Jesus said. But see what that word of "hotel-arrangement" did to that man. It was a declaration of acceptance. What happened was like the breath of God "breathed into his nostrils" (Gen. 2:7). He changed. The old Zacchaeus discontinued. Listen to his confession of faith in the language of a tax collector: "Listen, sir! I will give half my belongings to the poor; and if I have cheated anyone, I will pay him back four times as much" (Lk. 19:8). This is the only language he knew to express the change which took place in the depths of his spiritual life. What was it that happened? Jesus explained it for us: "Salvation has come to his house today" (Lk. 19:9). What happened was salvation. He was emancipated into a new relationship with his neighbors.

What a fascinating and unpredictable story! Is this a simple story—just that Jesus accepted Zacchaeus and Zacchaeus changed? Is it as simple as that? Perhaps. But why the simple acceptance of Jesus—"hotel-arrangement"—produced a spiritual revolution within this man has a complicated history.

One day some years ago I met a missionary couple from the West in Bangkok International Airport. They had just arrived in Bangkok. There they expressed the view that Thai Buddhism is a manifestation of demons! How simple! Thirty million people in the Buddhistic tradition of seven hundred years were brushed aside in one second. The remark betrayed super-arrogance and super-ignorance. More than this, I heard that the Peoples' Republic of China with her seven hundred million are all "atheistic," therefore "not saved," and even positively the enemy of the Gospel! This calamity of super-arrogance and super-ignorance derives from inability to appreciate the complexity of the living man in the living history. Here is a case of an extreme "inflation." Inability to meet man produces tragically a superficial grasp and appreciation of history. "Human failure," as it were, results in "historical failure." That which is human is historical, and that which is historical is human. God comes to us "humanly and historically." "The Word became a human being and lived among us" (Jn. 1:14). "We write to you about the Word of life, which has existed from the beginning of the world. We have heard it, and we have seen it with our eyes; yes, we have seen it, and our hands have touched it" (1 Jn. 1:1). This expresses the ultimate coming of God to man who lives in his historical and human complexities.

II

Let me go to the second stage of this paper. My aim so far has been to bring out what that distinction between a living real person and "logy" is, however, the danger of "inflation" when we fail to appreciate the complexities of man and history. Now, the historical and human coming of God—I admit this is an awkward expression, but I trust you understand what I mean—is the coming of Jesus Christ. In the coming of God in Jesus Christ we see God's resolution to come to man to save man. He comes with his good intention. "God was truly in Christ, reconciling the world to himself" (2 Cor. 5:19). God's saving will is most movingly described in one of the parables of Jesus. When the younger son returned, the father in the parable says: "Let us eat and make merry; for this my son was dead, and is alive again; he was lost, and is found" (Lk. 15:24). Here God's experience of history is summarized. He is deeply involved in the history of "dead-alive-lost-found." God's presence in the historical and anthropological process of dead-alive-lost-found must be the primary concern of man. In the confession of faith the order of dead-alive-lost-found not alive-dead-found-lost is central.

Let us listen to the Deuteronomic "Apostles' Creed" which summarizes the whole theology of the Pentateuch:

> My father was a homeless Aramaean who went down to Egypt with a small company and lived there until they became a great, powerful, and numerous nation. But the Egyptians ill-treated us, humiliated us and imposed cruel slavery upon us. Then we cried to the Lord the God of our fathers for help, and he listened to us and saw our humiliation, our hardship and distress; and so the Lord brought us out of Egypt with a strong hand and outstretched arm, with terrifying deeds, and with signs and portents. He brought us to this place and gave us this land, a land flowing with milk and honey. And now I have brought the first fruits of the soil which thou, O Lord, has given me" (Dt. 26:5-10).

This experience of emancipation from imprisonment-dead-alive-lost-found has decided the character of the biblical faith. In the historical experience of dead-alive-lost-found, Israel and the Church saw "a strong hand and outstretched arm." It is the content of the apostolic witness. "A strong hand and outstretched arm" reaches its ultimate form in the incarnation of the Son. "We have beheld his glory" (Jn. 1:14). The God is the God who involves himself in the historical and human drama of dead-alive-lost-found. And what does this "dead" mean in Asia today? What does this "alive" mean? What does "lost" mean? What does "found" mean? We must ask these questions in the midst of historical and human complexities. And *there* God becomes real to us. There? Yes. There only! God's presence is not what one may call "general presence." He visits us in our "specific" time and place of complexity. Love is the mind that tries to understand specific needs of this man and that man, this community and that community. That "God is love" is not a general statement applicable to the general overall situation. He is "specifically" love.

"And the Lord God made for Adam and for his wife garments of skins, and clothed them" (Gen. 3:21). This is the way the theologians of the Pentateuch express God's "specific" act of love.

III

But how do we *communicate* this saving truth of God which I have summarized in a clumsy way—"God in history of dead-alive-lost-found"—to our neighbor? Communicate? Yes. Communicate that novel "idea" of "God in history of dead-alive-lost-found." Well, if what we are asked to do is to communicate an idea, it does not involve too much difficulty. One can, perhaps, communicate it just as one would communicate the state of the Hong Kong housing situation to Japanese visitors. What should be communicated is, however, something more than an idea. It is the communication of life, history, hope and love. Here the simple word "communication" suddenly assumes a profound and mysterious dimension. Communication becomes difficult and *costly* in the sense of demanding tremendous spiritual energy and commitment. God who involves himself in the history of salvation process of dead-alive-lost-found is the God who says, "Your problem is my problem." He commits himself: "Behold, he who keeps Israel will neither slumber nor sleep" (Ps. 121:4). He does not sleep—not because he is "neurotic," but because he is the "keeper." He gives himself. Now, how do we communicate such a reality of God to our neighbors who are different from "neighbor-logy," real living neighbors who are in the human and his-torical complexity?

This communication is made possible through the medium of the communicator—a living person. The only way to establish this communication is through the communicator himself. It is not through "communication-logy" that one can communicate God who says "your problem is my problem," but through the life of the communicator. The "message" and the "messenger" must become one! If the message is incarnated in the messenger and produces, as it were, a message-ful person, then through this message-ful person the message will be communicated. The mes-sage here is no longer an "idea" but an "event." Incarnational communication is the way by which God's event is eventfully communicated. Communicator is more fundamental than com-munication! In the life and person of Abraham, God sends his message to the nations. God's message is incarnated (personal-ized) in Abraham. I am not saying that "one who has seen Abraham has seen the Father." The ultimate and complete unity of message (the world) and person took place only in the person of Jesus Christ. What I am saying is that Abraham became a communicator by the initiative of God. Since God decided to make him his communicator, Abraham, in his acts of obedience and disobedience, in his scheming of tricking others and being tricked, in his believing and doubting, becomes the "walking message" for the nations. As soon as Abraham steps in the promised land, he is beset by famine. What a disappointing promised land! He goes down to Egypt. Upon entering Egypt, he plans certain strategy because his wife is "very beautiful." He accepts Sarah's advice to have an heir. In all these events he remains a communicator. It is not a matter of how well (skillful-ly) he communicates the mind of God. It is a matter of simply remaining a communicator. Abraham is not assigned to the task of communication. He was called to be a communicator.

Jeremiah's "trouble" begins with God's decision to make him his communicator: "Before I formed you in the womb I knew you, and before you were born I consecrated you; I ap-pointed you a prophet to the nations" (Jer. 1:5).

Jeremiah tries to refuse this appointment. But in his refusal he is already acting and living as a communicator. He was ap-pointed before he was formed in the womb: "My anguish, my anguish! I writhe in pain! Oh, the walls of my heart! My heart is beating wildly; I cannot keep silent; for I hear the sound of the trumpet, the alarm of war" (Jer. 4:19).

The impending danger from the north is internalized in Jeremiah. History's crisis is incarnated to "the walls of my heart." His heart beats wildly since history's heart beats wildly. His total personality cries out under the pressure of "being a communicator":

O Lord, thou hast deceived me, and I was deceived; thou art stronger than I, and thou hast prevailed. I have become a laughing stock all the day; everyone mocks me. . . . If I say, "I will not mention him, or speak any more in his name," there is in my heart as it were a burning fire shut up in my bones, and I am weary with holding it in, and I cannot (Jer. 20:7-9).

This is not an ordinary lament. These are the words that indicate the destiny of the communicator. In this interior struggle and conflict of the person of communicator, God speaks to the nations. The whole person of Jeremiah carries the message.

There are songs which are called Servant Songs in Isaiah (42:1-4; 49:1-6; 50:4-11; 52:13—53:12). The writer of the Servant Songs portrays the image of the Servant who goes through the destiny of humiliation and exaltation. Scholars hold differing views on the identity of the Servant. He may be the nation of Israel, or an individual, or both. The point I wish to make is that the Servant (either Israel as a nation or an individual) is the communicator of God's purpose to history: "I gave my back to the smiters, and my cheeks to those who pulled out the beard; I hid not my face from shame and spitting" (Jer. 50:6).

The Servant accepts unbearable humiliation (see Jeremiah 11:19-21; 15:17; 18:18; 20:10). To be a communicator of God is not all an "armchair affair." It is a "calamitous" assignment! It is not a "part-time job." It requires all of man's life itself. In the conviction that "the Lord God helps me" (Jer. 50:7) he must accept rejection and humiliation. He becomes the rejected, the humiliated and the misunderstood (Jer. 53:4). This rejected, humiliated and misunderstood person is the communicator of the saving acts of God in history! He gives his "cheeks to those who pull out the beard." What an image of the communicator!

Paul's apostolic preaching is preached with his "body": "I bear on my body the marks of Jesus" (Gal. 6:17).

The marks may signify the scars from beating. Paul speaks about himself in the tradition of the other great communicators of God:

> For I think that God has exhibited us apostles as last of all, like men sentenced to death, because we have become a spectacle to the world, to angels and to men. We are fools for Christ's sake, but you are wise in Christ. We are weak, but you are strong. You are held in honor, but we in disrepute. To the present hour we hunger and thirst, we are ill-clad and buffeted and homeless, and we labor, working with our own hands. When reviled, we bless; when persecuted, we endure; when slandered, we try to conciliate; we have become, and are now, as refuse of the world, the offscouring of all things (1 Cor. 4:9-13).

Called to be a communicator of God's saving event, Paul's whole manner of life changes. The scars symbolize Paul's historical and human participation in God's concrete drama of the dead-alive-lost-found. His whole existence and theology demonstrate his personal experience of the power of God that stages the saving event of dead-alive-lost-found. Does not "reviled-bless-persecuted-endure-slandered-conciliate" have an amazingly similar note to that dead-alive-lost-found? He identifies himself "as refuse of the world, the offscouring of all things." Does this not, again, sound similar to the self-denial of the Servant who let others pull his beard out?

Seven letters attributed to Paul were written in prison. A great deal of Paul's message of the emancipating Christ comes from the wall of imprisonment. He is in prison, so he writes to the Philippians. Outside some are preaching Christ in envy and rivalry and others from good will. He cannot walk out of prison and speak to the people involved in this tragic division. He, the communicator of the Gospel, seems to be rendered helpless. But even remaining in prison, he senses the advance of the Gospel of Christ. In his imprisonment—in the situation of, as it were, others pulling his beard out—he witnesses the advance of the reality of Christ's emancipation among people. "If I must boast, I will boast of the things that show my weakness" (2 Cor. 11:30).

In inviting you to review—even though very briefly—the communicators of the saving act of God in history, I have tried to point out how deeply biblical communication is communicator-communication. God uses man in all his complexity. God lets him participate in his purpose in history. He does this in the midst of historical and human complexity. His love (*agape*) expresses itself not as a general philosophical principle of the world, but concretely and historically in the confusion of complexity.

IV

What a lengthy introduction to the question: "What makes a missionary?" I needed this introduction. It is in the context of the living man today and in the context of dead-alive-lost-found and reviled-bless-persecuted-endure-slandered-conciliate—the specific context of God's saving act in history—that I felt I could tackle this question of what makes a missionary. Simply it is not "what," but God, the Lord of history, who makes a missionary. Professional missionary? Non-professional missionary? We may make this distinction. Whether God will make this distinction or not, I do not know. God calls man and lets him participate in his purpose. God calls man *freely*. He calls man without the degree of bachelor of theology. He called a man who happened to be a Buddhist—one of the 30 millions in Thailand—for his purpose. Theology one can tame, but the living God no one can domesticate. No one can tell God what he *should* do. In the broad sense a missionary is anyone who increases by participation the concretization of the love of God in history. Some years ago, I visited a remote village in North Thailand. A group of government health officers were spraying DDT at that time. Eradication of the malaria mosquito is one concretization of the love of God. In this sense, those officers are missionaries. Is "missionary" an inclusive or exclusive concept? Is it a broad or narrow concept? It is a *theological* concept. "Theological" here means that the definition of being a missionary comes ultimately from God who missions man. He who missions knows the missionary. God makes the missionary because he missions man. It looks as though this is all one can say. But there is, as it were, the other side of the coin. The man missioned is the man who is placed in the continuous process of "making missionary" and "becoming missionary." "Missionary" is not a finished-product concept. It is a continuous-participation concept. A missionary lives with the consciousness of participating in the saving drama of dead-alive-lost-found. He grows. His missionary quality is enhanced as he lives a life of participation in the Pauline sense.

Then the question of what makes a missionary brings us to the question of the "nurture" or "growth" of the missionary. As he grows, he remains a missionary. Only in becoming is he a missionary. Only in hearing the call of God repeatedly "this day" does one become a missionary. Now, how about "missionary nurture"?

First, the missionary must live in the complexity of living man and living history. This call comes from God who loves man. Love approaches man carefully, feeling and knowing him to be someone who cannot be tamed and controlled. Love is the mind that appreciates complexity. The appreciation of complexity of man and history nurtures the missionary's life.

Second, the missionary's missionary quality will be nurtured in his life-participation in the apostolic existence of reviled-bless-persecuted-endure-slandered-conciliate. God calls man. In his call is included the call to go through the experience of "letting someone pull your beard out." Let me say a few words about the institutional implication this second point entails. Mission boards in the West must go through the 1971 experience of "letting someone pull your beard out." There are some historical connections and projects which form a portion of the proud heart of the mission boards. But the implication is that they may have to come out. It will hurt. However, if that is the way to enable our richer participation in that apostolic life, then it has to happen. Some of us are suggesting with sincerity and perceptivity that the time has come to dismantle the whole system of the mission boards.

The present mission system is a dead system. Bury it! Death of the mission system must not alarm us. On the other hand the death of the missionary mode of life participating in the dead-alive-lost-found process—if that happens—should alarm us. My attention is focused in the living man who is breathing air through his nostrils and whose life is a living participation in God's saving act in history. He, not system, is so important to me. When he comes to me I hesitate to raise questions as to the distinction between professional missionary, Western missionary, Asian missionary, part-time missionary, full-time missionary, etc. All these are reduced to the level of inconsequence. But if the present mission system does obscure and hinder man's participation in God's saving act in history, then that system must be buried. One cannot make a general statement as to whether the wholesale burial of the present mission system is desirable or not. Historical and human complexities must be fully appreciated. In the depth of involvement in the complexities of the historical situation, one must however make the decision that in this particular place, and at this particular time, overseas missionaries must be withdrawn. This decision must be based on observation as to whether the present mission system hinders God's living call in letting man participate in his dead-alive-lost-found history. The experience of "letting someone pull your beard out" will nurture the missionary's life.

Third, the missionary's missionary quality will be nurtured as he travels in the direction of the "unity of message and messenger." No missionaries will ever reach this unity. But that does not mean that one should not walk toward that goal. True, in man's disobedience as well as in obedience, the call of God makes one a communicator of God's history of salvation. But a missionary as a man must have "spiritual exercise." What direction should he go in his spiritual growth? The direction of the unity of message and messenger!

This article's subtitle includes the words "crucified mind, not crusading mind." I must close by explaining why it is called so. When I meet missionaries from the West in the variety of localities in Southeast Asia, what I call the Johannine principle —"He must increase, but I must decrease" (Jn. 3:30)—comes to my mind. John the Baptist introduced Jesus in these moving terms. He must increase! Missionaries must decrease *if* their decrease points to the increase of Jesus Christ. Increase of Jesus Christ? Yes! Increase of Jesus Christ in the given Southeast

Asian locality. How is Jesus Christ to be increased in Hong Kong? He is increased when the local people are increased in the knowledge of Jesus Christ in whom the dead-alive-lost-found history came to its final substance and expression. Missionaries must decrease then in order to make the local people increase. However, as soon as the given local people are increased, they must decrease for the sake of the increase of other local people. The chain reaction of increase and decrease must continue. This continuity of increase and decrease is the wave of salvation history, the beginning and the end of which is Jesus Christ. The Johannine principle of "he must increase and I must decrease" goes through a tremendous upheaval when the "he" decreases in order to make "us" increase: "For you know the grace of our Lord Jesus Christ, that though he was rich, yet for your sake he became poor, so that by his poverty you might become rich" (2 Cor. 8:9).

He is the author of reconciliation. In decreasing himself to the unfathomable depth, he becomes the foundation of reconciliation (Phil. 2:1-11). At this point, the Johannine principle is, as it were, swallowed up by the Christ principle. If missionaries decrease themselves, they are doing so not only in the light of the Johannine principle, but also in the revolutionary principle of Christ. Here lies the secret of the dynamic identity of the Christian missionary.

What does this "decrease" mean? Decrease in number? Decrease in influence? Decrease in prestige? I understand it in the framework of the history of "reviled (decrease)—bless (increase) —persecuted (decrease)—endure (increase)—slandered (decrease)—conciliate (increase)." It is the mind open to give. It is the mind that does not seek profit for itself. It is the mind which is happy in becoming refuse (decrease) of humanity since it will bring increase to others. It is a crucified mind, the mind of Jesus Christ: "Have this mind among yourselves, which you have in Christ Jesus" (Phil. 2:5-11).

It is a mind of self-denial based on Christ's self-denial. "Love does not insist on its way" (1 Cor. 13:5). The crucified mind is not a pathological or neurotic mind. It is *love* seeking the benefit of others. This mind sees man "as he is seen" (i Jn. 4:20). This mind creates the communicator's mind. This mind appreciates the complexity of man and history. This mind participates in the dead-alive-lost-found history in the way Christ participated. This mind does not bulldoze man and history without appreciation of their complexities. The crusading mind is not the mind of the biblical communicators. This must not be the mind of the missionary. The nurture of the crucified mind—is not this then a mark of all Christians, including missionaries? Is not the mind of the Crucified One the mind that creates the crucified mind within us and nurtures it? Isn't it true that only the crucified mind can respond joyously to the call of "dance, music and feast" in the event of dead-alive-lost-found?

A Moratorium
on Missionaries?

Gerald H. Anderson

One way of enabling the churches in Asia, Africa and Latin America to develop their strength and selfhood would be to withdraw all missionaries and foreign funding for a period of years—to give these churches a chance "to breathe," so to speak, without assistance. Such a proposal—for a moratorium on missionaries—has come from several respected churchmen in various parts of the world and will be a topic of debate wherever the future of the missionary enterprise is being discussed. While recognizing that there are situations in which the withdrawal of missionaries would be in the best interests of the Christian mission, Gerald H. Anderson suggests that as a general policy for *all* situations, the proposal is neither biblically sound nor in the best interests of the churches—either in the Third World or in the "First World." He urges instead the development of mutuality in mission, a relationship of interdependence between churches that would release the maximum resources for joint action in mission on an international basis. Dr. Anderson's article is reprinted with permission of *The Christian Century* (Chicago), where it first appeared in the issue for January 16, 1974.

An African church leader recently laid before the World and U.S. National Councils of Churches a proposal that there be a moratorium on sending and receiving money and missionary personnel. John Gatu, general secretary of the Presbyterian Church in East Africa, said that their continuing sense of dependence on and domination by foreign church groups inhibits many churches in Asia, Africa and Latin America from development in response to God's mission. "[Our] present problems," he explained, "can only be solved if all missionaries can be withdrawn in order to allow a period of not less than five years for each side to rethink and formulate what is going to be their future relationship. . . . The churches of the Third World must be allowed to find their own identity, and the continuation of the present missionary movement is a hindrance to this selfhood of the Church."

However shocking this proposal may seem, it is imperative that Christians in Europe and North America face the issue squarely—for one reason, because it will probably be a major item for discussion on the agenda of virtually every Protestant mission board and society that is related to the ecumenical movement; for another, because the feelings voiced by Mr. Gatu are shared by a number of Church leaders in Asia, Africa and Latin America, as well as in Europe and the United States.

Thus Emerito P. Nacpil, president of Union Theological Seminary near Manila, Philippines, told an assembly of Church leaders and missionaries gathered in Asia in 1971 that under present conditions a partnership between Asian and Western churches "can only be a partnership between the weak and the strong. And that means the continued dependence of the weak upon the strong and the continued dominance of the strong over the weak." The missionary today, he said, is

> a symbol of the universality of Western imperialism among the rising generations of the Third World. [Therefore] I believe that the present structure of modern missions is dead. And . . . we ought . . . to eulogize it and then bury it. . . . In other words, the most *missionary* service a missionary under the present system can do today in Asia is to go home.

Again, Father Paul Verghese, a former associate general secretary of the World Council of Churches and now principal of an Orthodox theological seminary in India, writes from that country:

Today it is economic imperialism or neo-colonialism that is the pattern of missions. Relief agencies and mission boards control the younger churches through purse strings. Foreign finances, ideas and personnel still dominate the younger churches and stifle their spontaneous growth. . . . So now I say, "The mission of the Church is the greatest enemy of the Gospel."

A third voice in harmony with Mr. Gatu's is that of José Míguez-Bonino, dean of Union Theological Seminary in Buenos Aires, Argentina. Recently addressing a group in the United States, Dr. Míguez said:

We in the younger churches have to learn the discipline of freedom to accept and to refuse, to place resources at the service of mission rather than to have mission patterned by resources. . . . We cannot for the love of our brethren or for the love of God let anybody or anything stand in the way of our taking on our own shoulders our responsibility. If, in order to do that, we must say to you, our friends, "Stay home," we will do so because before God we have this grave responsibility of our integrity.

I

The first thing to be said about this growing sentiment in Third World churches is that it should be seen as a sign of the world Church's vitality. It is an indication that the "younger churches" have come of age. And the leaders of those churches are ready and able to articulate what this new sense of strength and self-confidence implies with regard to the traditional structures of relationship to the churches of the West. The challenge they pose is the fruit of our labors in world mission over the past 180 years.

Second, the basic issue in the moratorium proposal is *integrity*—for both sides. On the part of the Third World churches it is a question of authority and control as they seek to establish and express their own identity. On the part of the churches in Europe and North America it is a question of accountability and faithfulness to the mandate for world mission inherent in the Gospel. Therefore the relation between selfhood and universality, while crucial, should not imply contrast or opposition, for a church ought to be both local and universal.

A recent study of this problem, carried out by George A. Hood for the Conference of British Missionary Societies and titled *In Whole and in Part*, suggests that a better formulation of the issue would be: How may the interdependence of the Church in mission be expressed throughout the world and in every place? Hood reaches the conclusion that "the clearest expression of interdependence across the whole spectrum of the Church's life is found in giving and receiving." Indeed, he says, "the greatest threat to interdependence is self-sufficiency. . . . Some parts of the Church are clearly being impoverished by feeling unable to give and others by their inability to receive." The most important implication of these facts for mission boards is that they need "to make the ideas of wholeness, interdependence, mutuality, more central."

Similarly, the WCC's 1973 Bangkok Conference on "Salvation Today" said (report of Section III) that "the whole debate on the moratorium springs from our failure to relate to one another in a way which does not dehumanize," and that "in some situations the moratorium proposal, painful though it may be for both sides, may be the best means of resolving a present dilemma and advancing the mission of Christ."

II

There are indeed situations in which withdrawal of missionaries may be in the best interests of the Christian mission—for instance, where the socio-political setup of a particular country or area is utterly contrary to the Gospel and where the established Church is identified with the status quo. It was a situation of that kind that, in 1971, led the White Fathers (a Roman Catholic mission society founded in 1868 and known officially as the Missionaries of Africa) to withdraw all their personnel from

Mozambique. The Vatican-Portuguese Missionary Accord has aligned the Roman Catholic Church and its local hierarchy with the colonial regime in that country, and when all positive efforts of the White Fathers failed to end the flagrant injustices visited on blacks in Mozambique, they decided, according to one report, that "they had to withdraw so as not to allow themselves to be considered partners of the Church-state collusion." While other mission societies operating in Mozambique have chosen to continue their witness there by a silent presence, the controversial decision of the White Fathers has been widely heralded as "an act of authentic Christian witness in the face of difficult options."

It was a different motive that, in 1969, prompted the unilateral decision of Methodist missionaries in Uruguay to withdraw for at least one year. They viewed their action as "a vote of confidence for the national church in its effort to work out a new life"—that is, as a way of supporting the indigenous church. Their voluntary withdrawal, they believed, would free the church of Uruguay to establish its own structures and to lay down the conditions under which whatever missionaries it invited to come back would be obliged to serve. (Thus far the Uruguayan church has invited only one missionary couple to return.) This move of the Methodists, like that of the White Fathers, has proved controversial. Some call it a bold act of witness, others see it as a new form of paternalism, this time telling the national church what it does not need.

These, however, were limited moves. The moratorium proposed by Gatu and Nacpil is much more far-reaching. They are talking about *all* missionaries under the present structures of sending and receiving. Surely their approach is too short-sighted and simplistic for an exceedingly complex set of historical circumstances. We cannot responsibly solve the accumulated problems of nearly two hundred years of missionary relationships by suddenly going into isolation, nor will the New Testament allow us to do so.

III

In the first place, so sweeping a moratorium would promote the domestication of the churches in their respective cultures, and this in turn would promote the further encroachment on them of tribal religion. Already cultural paganism infests the churches in most areas of the world—nowhere more so than around the North Atlantic basin. To insulate them further, as the moratorium would do, could only encourage this pagan trend. The fact is that the "foreign" missionary presence in the life of any church should serve as a particular reminder of the "alien" nature of the Gospel to every nation and culture. Unquestionably we in Europe and North America need this reminder especially. But churches in other parts of the world are not immune to some of the same temptations we face in the West.

In the second place, if we truly believe that Jesus Christ is Lord and Savior of all humankind, we must consider the effect of the proposed moratorium on the evangelization of the vast multitudes of non-Christians throughout the world, particularly in countries where the national churches represent but a tiny fraction of the population. One thinks immediately, for instance, of India's 575 million people, with Christians numbering only 2.6 percent; of Pakistan's 65 million, with 1.6 percent Christians; and of Bangladesh's 77 million, with 0.3 percent Christians. In these and many other countries, the population *increases each year* by more than their total Christian community. Yet the moratorium would serve to immobilize the churches of the West in relation to mission in these areas. It would limit us to mission where we are—an altogether unbiblical concept—and negate the concept of mission as the whole Church bringing the whole Gospel to the whole world.

In view of the enormous need and opportunity for missionary witness and service in all six continents, it is appalling that we of the West presently make so small a part of our resources available for this purpose. The mainline ecumenical denominations are particularly remiss in this respect. Thus the 11-million-member United Methodist Church—the largest denomination in the National Council of Churches—has seen a decline

of missionaries serving overseas from 1,450 in 1968 to 824 sche-
duled for 1974; and of every dollar given to that church, only 1.1
cents actually goes for work outside the U.S. Again, the Missionary Orientation Center once operated at Stony Point, New
York, by five of the major Protestant mission boards has now
closed because not enough missionaries are being sent overseas
to maintain it. And the number of U.S. Catholic missionaries
serving abroad is the lowest in ten years, down from a high of
9,655 in 1969 to 7,649 in 1972.

By contrast, many conservative evangelical Protestant
groups are increasing their overseas mission work. The Christian
and Missionary Alliance, for instance, with only 92,000 members
in the U.S., now has 893 missionaries overseas, and of every
dollar given to it for work beyond the local church, 85 cents goes
toward overseas missions.

IV

I cannot subscribe to the so-called "mystical doctrine of salt
water"—the idea that being transported over salt water, the
more of it the better, is what constitutes missionary service. Neither do I think that "more missionaries mean more mission." I
maintain, however, that men and women sent to proclaim the
Gospel of Jesus Christ in cross-cultural situations are integral to
the mission established in the incarnation. I agree whole-
heartedly with the policy summed up by one mission agency in a
recent working paper:

> We wish to affirm the validity of the missionary presence as
> an essential part of the Gospel. The good news of Jesus
> Christ is communicated through persons and becomes evi-
> dent through the interaction between persons. We believe
> the place of persons at the heart of mission to be an abiding
> reality. We also wish to affirm the validity of the missionary
> presence as essential to our understanding of the universal-
> ity of the Church.

If the participation of persons in world mission is lacking or
is limited by arbitrary rules, all areas of the Church's life will

suffer. In point here is R. Pierce Beaver's recent warning:

> One front of mission cannot be neglected or denied without adverse effect on other fronts; and already the domestic agencies of the churches are being afflicted with blight and malnutrition. The mission is one, and it is worldwide. . . . The sending mission of discipling the nations to the ends of the earth is always the spiritual thermometer which measures the faith of the Christian community.

This is not to suggest that the styles and structures of missionary involvement should be static. The WCC's Bangkok Conference cited above rightly urged missionary agencies to "examine critically their involvement as part of patterns of political and economic domination, and to re-evaluate the role of personnel and finance at their disposal in the light of that examination."

Yet the need to review and re-evaluate present structures and strategies does not *suspend* the Christian mandate for world mission—not if we see "the missionary presence as an essential part of the Gospel." Else we would be guilty of *sub*-mission. As the Bangkok Conference said (Section III):

> What we must seek is . . . a mature relationship between churches. Basic to such a relationship is mutual commitment to participate in Christ's mission in the world. A precondition for this is that each church involved in the relationship should have a clear realization of its own identity. This cannot be found in isolation, however, for it is only in relationship with others that we discover ourselves.

Actually, the overwhelming weight of opinion in the Third World, and in the "First World" too, is very much on the side of continued missionary presence. Even Mr. Gatu admits that "not many" African church leaders agree with his moratorium proposal. Nor do leaders of "younger churches" elsewhere. Recently, for instance, the United Church Board for World Ministries indicated to the Kyodan (the United Church of Christ in Japan) that, owing to budgetary stringencies, it might have to withdraw some missionaries. The response of the Japanese was that they would undertake to raise enough money to keep the missionaries, because—as they said—they felt that in their situation the foreign missionary presence was essential to the integrity of the Gospel and of the Church. This past year, in fact, the Kyodan raised about $100,000 for this purpose.

V

Finally, we must assess the moratorium proposal in the light of the increasingly vital internationalization of the missionary enterprise. Today, the Third World is not only sending missionaries to the Third World; it is also thinking in terms of mission to America and mission to Europe—thrusts that mission boards and the World Council of Churches are working hard to effectuate. A recently published research report, *Missions from the Third World* (available from William Carey Library, 533 Hermosa Street, South Pasadena, Calif. 91030), reveals that currently at least 209 Protestant agencies in the Third World are sending out 3,411 missionaries. This global interinvolvement in mission, going beyond traditional relationships and patterns for decision-making and exchange of personnel, holds enormous promise for the future.

The new era in world mission challenges all churches to manifest the universality of the *Ecclesia* by sharing resources in the common task of expressing the redemptive action of God in Christ. But, as the United Methodist Board of Global Ministries says, meeting that challenge will "require of us more total commitment and wholeness of vision, greater intentionality and receptivity, and more serious and joyous international sharing and interdependence than we have yet known."

The Development of Peoples and the Meaning of Service

Julius Nyerere

What is the Church's role and responsibility toward the under-developed—or developing—nations and peoples of the world as they struggle against poverty and oppression in search of justice and power? What does "service" mean in a situation calling for revolutionary change? What do the poor, the oppressed and the powerless peoples of the world look for in missionaries who come to serve them? In an address to the general assembly of Maryknoll Sisters in October 1970, an African statesman speaks candidly about these concerns. Julius Nyerere is the president of Tanzania. A Roman Catholic, a graduate of Edinburgh University, and a champion of African nationalism, he is known for his efforts to forge a Tanzanian consciousness through a policy of socialism and self-reliance. Here he issues "a call to the Church to recognize the need for social revolution, and to play a leading role in it." The Church and those who serve it, he says, must be "consistently and actively on the side of the poor and underprivileged"; otherwise "the Church will become irrelevant to man and the Christian religion will degenerate into a set of superstitions accepted by the fearful." His speech first appeared in *The Tablet* (London) for January 23, 1971, and is reprinted by permission.

Poverty is not the real problem of the modern world, for we have the knowledge and resources that could enable us to overcome poverty. The real problem—the thing which creates misery, wars and hatred among men—is the division of mankind into rich and poor.

The significance about this division between the rich and the poor is not simply that one man has more food than he can eat, more clothes than he can wear and more houses than he can live in, while others are hungry, unclad and homeless. The significant thing about the division between rich and poor nations is not simply that one has the resources to provide comfort for all its citizens, and the other cannot provide basic services. The reality and depth of the problem arises because the man who is rich has power over the lives of those who are poor, and the rich nation has power over the policies of those which are not rich. And even more important, our social and economic system, nationally and internationally, supports these divisions and constantly increases them, so that the rich get even richer and more powerful, while the poor get relatively poorer and less able to control their own future.

This continues despite all the talk of human equality, the fight against poverty, and development. Still, the rich individuals within nations, and the rich nations within the world, go on getting richer very much faster than the poor overcome their poverty. Sometimes this happens through the deliberate decision of the rich, who use their wealth and their power to that end. But often—perhaps more often—it happens "naturally" as a result of the normal workings of the social and economic systems men have constructed for themselves.

Both nationally and internationally this division of mankind into the tiny minority of rich and the great majority of poor is rapidly becoming intolerable to the majority—as it should be. The poor nations and the poor peoples of the world are already in rebellion against it; if they do not succeed in securing change which leads toward greater justice, then that rebellion will become an explosion. Injustice and peace are in the long run incompatible; stability in a changing world must mean ordered change toward justice, not mechanical respect for the status quo.

It is in this context that development has been called another name for peace. It is this context which gives urgency to your deliberations on participation in the development of peoples.

The purpose of development is man. It is the creation of conditions, both material and spiritual, which enables man the individual, and man the species, to become his best. That is easy for Christians to understand because Christianity demands that every man should aspire toward union with God through Christ. But although the Church, as a consequence of its concentration upon man, avoids the error of identifying development with new factories, increased output, or greater national income statistics, experience shows that it all too often makes the opposite error. For the representatives of the Church, and the Church's organizations, frequently act as if man's development is a personal and "internal" matter, which can be divorced from the society and the economy in which he lives and earns his daily bread. They preach resignation; very often they appear to accept as immutable the social, economic, and political framework of the present-day world. They seek to ameliorate intolerable conditions through acts of love and kindness where the beneficiary of this love and kindness remains an object. But when the victims of poverty and oppression begin to behave like men and try to change those conditions, the representatives of the Church stand aside.

Rebellion as Development

My purpose is to suggest to you that the Church should accept that the development of peoples means rebellion. At a given and decisive point in history men decide to act against those conditions which restrict their freedom as men. I am suggesting that unless we participate actively in the rebellion against those social structures and economic organizations which condemn men to poverty, humiliation and degradation, then the Church will become irrelevant to man and the Christian religion will degenerate into a set of superstitions accepted by the fearful. Unless the Church, its members and its organizations express God's love for man by involvement and leadership in constructive protest against the present conditions of man, then it will become identified with injustice and persecution. If this happens, it will die— and, humanly speaking, deserve to die—because it will then serve no purpose comprehensible to modern man.

For man lives in society. He becomes meaningful to himself and his fellows only as a member of that society. Therefore, to talk of the development of man, and to work for the development of man, must mean the development also of that kind of society which serves man, enhances his well-being, and preserves his dignity. Thus, the development of peoples involves economic development, social development, and political development. And at this time in man's history, it must imply a divine discontent and determination for change. For the present condition of men must be unacceptable to all who think of an individual person as a unique creation of a living God. We say that man was created in the image of God. I refuse to imagine a God who is poor, ignorant, superstitious, fearful, oppressed, wretched—which is the lot of the majority of those he created in his own image. Men are creators of themselves and their conditions, but under present conditions we are creatures, not of God, but of our fellow men.

Surely there can be no dispute among Christians about that. For mankind has never been so united or so disunited, has never had such power for good nor suffered under such evident injustices. Man's capacity has never been so clear, nor so obviously and deliberately denied.

The world is one in technological terms. Men have looked down on the earth from the moon and seen its unity. In jet planes I can travel from Tanzania to New York in a matter of hours. Radio waves enable us to talk to each other—either in love or abuse—without more than a few seconds elapsing between our speech and the hearing of it. Goods are made which include materials and skills from all over the world—and are then put up for sale thousands of miles from their place of manufacture.

Yet at the same time as the interdependence of man is increased through the advance of technology, the divisions between men also expand at an ever-increasing rate. The national income per head in the United States is said to be more than 1,000 pounds a year; in Tanzania it is approximately 26 pounds. In other words, it would take a Tanzanian forty years to earn what an American earns in one year, and we are not the poorest na-

tion on earth. Further, it has been estimated that while the rich
countries are adding approximately twenty pounds a year to the
per capita income of their citizens, the average increase per capita in the poor countries is less than one pound per year. It has
been estimated that up to five hundred million people on the
earth today are suffering from hunger—from never having
enough to eat. Further, one out of every two of the world's people is suffering from malnutrition—from deficiencies of protein
or other essential health-giving foods. And finally, let me remind
you that even within the wealthiest countries of the world, the
misery and oppression of poverty is experienced by thousands, or
even millions, of individuals, families and groups.

So the world is not one. Its peoples are more divided now,
and also more conscious of their divisions, than they have ever
been. They are divided between those who are satiated and those
who are hungry. They are divided between those with power and
those without power. They are divided between those who dominate and those who are dominated, between those who exploit
and those who are exploited. And it is the minority which is well
fed, and the minority which has secured control over the world's
wealth and over their fellow men. Further, in general that minority is distinguished by the color of their skins and by their race.
And the nations in which most of that minority of the world's
people live have a further distinguishing characteristic—their
adoption of the Christian religion.

These things cannot continue, and Christians above all
others must refuse to accept them. For the development of men
and the development of peoples demands that the world shall
become one and that social justice shall replace the present op-
pressions and inequalities.

The Development of Peoples

In order to achieve this, there must be economic development and equitable distribution of wealth. The poor nations, the
poor areas and the poor peoples must be enabled to increase
their output; through fair distribution they must be enabled to
expand their consumption of the goods which are necessary for
decency and for freedom.

For what is required is not simply an increase in the national income figures of the poor countries, nor a listing of huge increases in the production of this crop or that industry. New factories, roads, farms and so on are essential, but they are not enough in themselves. The economic growth must be of such a kind, and so organized, that it benefits the peoples, which means that social and political development must go alongside economic development—or even precede it. For unless society is so organized that the people control their own economies and their own economic activity, then economic growth will result in increased injustices because it will lead to increased inequality, both nationally and internationally.

In other words, the development of peoples follows from economic development only if this latter is achieved on the basis of the equality and human dignity of all those involved. And human dignity cannot be given to a man by the kindness of others. Indeed, it can be destroyed by kindness which emanates from an action of charity. For human dignity involves equality and freedom and relations of mutual respect among men. Further, it depends on responsibility and on a conscious participation in the life of the society in which a man moves and works.

The whole structure of national societies and of international society is therefore relevant to the development of peoples. And there are few societies which can now be said to serve this purpose; for there are few—if any—which both accept and are organized to serve social justice in what has been called the revolution of rising expectations.

Let us be quite clear about this. If the Church is interested in man as an individual, it must express this by its interest in the society of which those individuals are members. For men are shaped by the circumstances in which they live. If they are treated like animals, they will act like animals. If they are denied dignity, they will act without dignity. If they are treated solely as a dispensable means of production, they will become soul-less "hands" to whom life is a matter of doing as little work as possible and then escaping into the illusion of happiness and pride through vice.

Therefore, in order to fulfill its own purpose of bringing men to God, the Church must seek to ensure that men can have dignity in their lives and in their work. It must itself become a force of social justice and it must work with other forces of social justice wherever they are, and whatever they are called. Further, the Church must recognize that men can only progress and grow in dignity by working for themselves and working together for their common good. The Church cannot uplift a man; it can only help to provide the conditions and the opportunity for him to cooperate with his fellows in order to uplift himself.

The Meaning of Service Today

What does this mean for those who give their lives to the service of the Church?

First, it means that kindness is not enough, piety is not enough, and charity is not enough. The men who are now suffering from poverty, whether they are in the Third World or in the developed world, need to be helped to stretch themselves, they need to be given confidence in their own ability to take control of their own lives, and they need to be helped to take this control and use it themselves for their own purposes. This is important to the Church as well as to mankind. For until men are in a position to make effective choices, few of them will become Christians in anything but name. Their membership in the Church will be simply another method by which they seek to escape from a consciousness of their misery; if you like, religion becomes a kind of opium of the people.

Everything which prevents a man from living in dignity and decency must therefore be under attack from the Church and its workers. For there is, in fact, nothing saintly in imposed poverty, and although saints may be found in slums, we cannot preserve slums in order to make them breeding grounds for saints. A man who has been demoralized by the conditions under which he is forced to live is no use to himself, to his family, or to his nation. Whether he can be of much use to God is not for me to judge.

The Church has to help men to rebel against their slums; it has to help them do this in the most effective way it can be done. But most of all the Church must be obviously and openly fighting all those institutions and power groups which contribute to the existence and maintenance of the physical and spiritual slums —regardless of the consequences to itself or its members. And, wherever and however circumstances make it possible, the Church must work with the people in the positive tasks of building a future based on social justice. It must participate actively in initiating, securing, and creating the changes which are necessary and which will inevitably take place.

Only by doing these things can the Church hope to reduce hatred and promote its doctrine of love to all men. Its love must be expressed in action against evil, and for good. For if the Church acquiesces in established evils, it is identifying itself and the Christian religion with injustice by its continuing presence.

Secondly, the members of the Church must work with the people. It is important that we should stress the working with, not the working for. What is necessary is sharing on the basis of equality and common humanity. Only by sharing work, hardships, knowledge, persecution, and progress can the Church contribute to our growth—and this means sharing in every sense as "members one of another." For if the Church is not part of our poverty and part of our struggle against poverty and injustice, then it is not part of us.

In many areas of the world—and particularly in Africa—the Catholic Church has built its own schools and its own hospitals. These have been invaluable; they have provided education and medical care when there would otherwise have been none. But I believe that such provision should be an interim measure, and that, wherever possible, the Church members should be working with, and through, the organizations owned and controlled by the people themselves.

Members of religious organizations must encourage and help the people to cooperate together in whatever action is necessary for their development. What this will mean in practice will vary from one country to another, and from one part of a country to another part. Sometimes it will mean helping the people to form and to run their own cooperative villages. Sometimes it will mean helping the people to form their own trade unions—and not Catholic trade unions, but trade unions of workers regardless of religion. Sometimes it will mean the Church leaders involving themselves in nationalist freedom movements and

being part of those movements. Sometimes it will mean cooperating with local governments or other authorities; sometimes
it will mean working in opposition to established authorities and
power. Always it means the Church being on the side of social
justice and helping men to live together and work together for
their common good.

Let us admit that, up to now, the record of the Church in
these matters has not been a good one. The countries which we
immediately think of as Catholic countries are not those in
which the people enjoy human dignity and in which social justice
prevails. Nor are they countries in which there has been great
economic progress. The Church is not without influence in Latin
America, and I am told that one-third of all the Catholics of the
world live in that sub-continent. Yet we do not associate that
part of the world with progress and social justice. On the contrary, the conditions of poverty, exploitation, and misery in
Latin American countries are too well known to require com-
ment from me.

I am not asking that the Church should surrender its functions or allow itself to be identified with particular political parties or political doctrines. On the contrary, what I am saying
amounts to a demand that it should stop allowing itself to be
identified with unjust political and economic power groups. The
Church should want to be identified with the pursuit of social
justice, and that is what I am asking you to promote. The poor
and the oppressed should come to you not for alms, but for support against injustice.

It is necessary to recognize, however, that others—non-
Catholics and non-Christians—will also be working to promote
social justice; we have no monopoly of virtue. We must not be
afraid of this. On the contrary, we should welcome other workers
for justice. It is not necessary to agree with everything a man
believes or says in order to work with him on particular projects
or in particular areas of activity. The Church must stand up for
what it believes to be right; that is its justification and purpose.
But it should welcome all who stand on the same side, and continue regardless of which individuals or groups it is then opposing.

We know that we are fallible men and that our task is to

serve, not to judge. Yet we accept into the Church (provided only that they come to Mass every Sunday and pay their dues or contribute to missionary activities) those who create and maintain the present political and economic system. But it is this system which has led to millions being hungry, thirsty and naked; it is this system which makes men strangers in their own countries because they are poor, powerless and oppressed; it is this system which condemns millions to preventable sickness, and which makes prisoners of men who have the courage to protest. What right, then, do we have to reject those who serve mankind, simply because they refuse to accept the leadership of the Church or to acknowledge the divinity of Jesus or the existence of God? What right have we to presume that God Almighty takes no notice of those who give dedicated service to those millions of his children who hunger and thirst after justice, just because they do not do it in his name? If God were to ask the wretched of the earth who their friends are, are we so sure that we know their answer? And is that answer irrelevant to those who seek to serve God?

The Role of the Church

What all this amounts to is a call to the Church to recognize the need for social revolution and to play a leading role in it. For it is a fact of history that almost all the successful social revolutions which have taken place in the world have been led by people who were themselves beneficiaries under the system they sought to replace. Time and again members of the privileged classes have joined, and often led, the poor or oppressed in their revolts against injustice. The same thing must happen now.

Within the rich countries of the world the beneficiaries of educational opportunity, of good health, and of security must be prepared to stand up and demand justice for those who have up to now been denied these things. Where the poor have already begun to demand a just society, at least some members of the privileged classes must help them and encourage them. Where they have not begun to do so, it is the responsibility of those who have had greater opportunities for development to arouse the poor out of their poverty-induced apathy. And I am saying that Christians should be prominent among those who do this, and that the Church should seek to increase the numbers and the power of those who refuse to acquiesce in established injustices.

The same is true also as regards the international scene. The poor and backward countries are beginning to speak up and to protest against their condition. But they gain strength and effectiveness because of countries like the Scandinavian nations and Canada which are beginning to recognize the insecurity and the injustice of their wealth in a world of poverty and to take a leading part in urging change.

I am saying that the Church should join with these nations and, if possible, help to increase their number. I am saying that it should be one of the group of nations and institutions which reject domination by the rich for the benefit of the rich. And it should be the function of Church members in wealthy countries to enlarge the group opposed to international exploitation of the poor and oppression of the weak.

Only by its activities in these fields can the Church justify its relevance in the modern world. For the purpose of the Church is man—his human dignity and his right to develop himself in freedom. To the service of man's development, any or all of the institutions of any particular society must be sacrificed if this should be necessary. For all human institutions, including the Church, are established in order to serve man. And it is the institution of the Church, through its members, which should be leading the attack on any organization or any economic, social, or political structure which oppresses men and denies to them the right and power to live as the sons of a loving God.

In the poor countries the Church has this same role to play. It has to be consistently and actively on the side of the poor and underprivileged. It has to lead men toward godliness by joining with them in the attack against the injustices and deprivation from which they suffer. It must cooperate with all those who are involved in this work; it must reject alliances with those who represent Mammon and cooperate with all those who are working for man.

IV: Churches in Mission

Structures
for Mission

Emilio Castro

"A new way must be found" to do mission in "the new situation
of Church and society today." That means finding "more adequate working structures" that will "express mature relationships" between churches in mission, according to Emilio
Castro, director of the World Council of Churches' Commission
on World Mission and Evangelism. Four convictions that are
fundamental in any search for new missionary structures are discussed by the author in this article which appeared in the October 1973 *International Review of Mission*, published by the
Commission on World Mission and Evangelism of the WCC.
Previously, Mr. Castro was president of the Evangelical Methodist Church of Uruguay and coordinator of UNELAM (Provi-
sional Commission for Latin American Evangelical Unity). His
article was translated from the Spanish by Helen Franco.

Those concerned with Christian mission today live in the
growing conviction that a new way must be found to relate the
abiding concern for mission to the new situation of Church and
society today. There is scarcely a book or an article on mission
which does not raise this issue. Even among those missionary
groups which continue to grow in the amount of money and personnel sent overseas, there is a desire to find more adequate
working structures.

Times are changing. The Church today is present in all
parts of the world; indeed it is difficult to find a place without
Christian witness. The missionary expansion of the Church has

resulted in the assumption of responsibility by Christian communities throughout the world for mission in their own societies. The missionary task, then, becomes either support for the local witness of Christian communities, or competition with them. It can be, therefore, either a mutually enriching experience or a source of endless frustration.

But we cannot forget that the Church lives amid today's human tensions. The growing disparity between the so-called developed and underdeveloped countries, and the factors of prestige and power which accompany the relationships between nations, unfortunately have their echoes in the relationships between churches. Called to obedience to a Lord who transcends political and economic frontiers, how can we express this situation in our relationships? Pious phrases and good intentions abound, but we do not know how to implement them, submitting ourselves to the discipline of the Christian community—the brotherhood of the faith—which demands of us a common responsibility. But if we do not find adequate structures, we shall destroy relationships. (This has happened not infrequently in the history of mission.) We must find the means to express mature relationships appropriate to the present time, seeking new possibilities for mission boldly and fearlessly.

Perhaps this raises the problem in a negative way when it ought to be stated from within the joyful perspective of the Gospel. After all, it is precisely because missionary work has been so successful that we find ourselves faced by a situation which demands radical revision. But the success of Christian mission has, of course, also borne the marks of human sin. Consequently, any revision of former patterns must be marked by repentance and openness to new obedience. We face this task, not with a feeling of frustration or desire to break with the missionary experience, but out of a discovery of new and greater possibilities for mission. Karl Barth has pointed out that while human sin is pride, the special sin of Christians is laziness. In the missionary task this sin takes the form of inertia, a tendency to repeat, a clinging to the past and the fear of taking up the challenge of the new situation in which we find ourselves.

We undertake this work with some basic and prior convictions. The first is that mission belongs to God. Christians are called by the Spirit to follow the example of Jesus Christ in the missionary action of the Father. "As the Father sent me, so I send you." But this is not the end of our quest. What we must find are the means of expressing intelligently the fulfillment of this mission in today's situation. This conviction is fundamental because it gives us a value by which we can judge what already exists and plan for the future. Obviously it can easily become an excuse for fanaticism, and instead of following the invitation of the Holy Spirit we can follow the inclinations of our own hearts as if they were the sole possessors of the truth. Unfortunately, faith and fanaticism have always been very close companions in human history. We must guard against any such tendencies through our mutual recognition of the gifts which the Spirit has given to the Christian community in all parts of the world. Under the common discipline of the faith, we can collaborate, submitting ourselves to each other through love. A decision in obedience to break the fellowship at the international or local level will always be the exception and never the rule.

The second conviction fundamental to our search for new missionary structures is that we are a servant people, a pilgrim people, never settled in one place. We cannot accept the past as the norm because we are seekers of him who makes all things new. This does not mean that we reject out of hand the experience of the past, nor do we engage in a restless search for novelties or the latest fashions. Rather we have the freedom to recognize in the past the obedient and the sinful ways in which our elders tried to interpret and obey the mission of God, so that we can use both the inspiration and the warning of their example to guide our own choices of obedience in the new circumstances and opportunities which face us. This quality of an obedient people, a holy people, available for God to use in the world, must be continually refreshed and renewed in Christian conversation.

A third basic consideration is the priority which must be given to the local church for the fulfillment of mission in its area of influence. It is interesting to note how the apostle Paul first sought contact with the synagogue, recognizing the existence in a given city of a people who bore the revelation of God as it was known up to that moment. From this starting point, he planned the formation of Christian communities. Once they were established, it was to those communities that he respectfully addressed himself when talking of his missionary plans. To Rome he wrote announcing his desire to visit them, expressing the hope that together they could bring spiritual benefits to that area, and asking for their support for the extension of his missionary campaign in the Spanish peninsula. While we are called by God to serve him throughout our planet, we live in local communities in which we receive inspiration and vision, and we plan our task in collaboration with other local communities who also receive inspiration and vision and who therefore have the prime responsibility in their local setting.

Yet precisely as we understand the importance of the local church we also recognize the importance of the presence of the foreigner in the midst of a Christian community. The Letter to the Churches written from the Salvation Today Conference in Bangkok says: "It is at the local level that the reality of the Church universal must be lived. In today's world, with an ever-growing migration which challenges our communities, all of our churches are called to receive the strangers in their midst as brothers and sisters who manifest the catholicity of the Church and share in its local mission. God has set before us riches that we must learn to receive." The missionary, insofar as he reminds us of the dimension of sending, puts himself at the frontiers of the Church and the world, thus contributing to the understanding of sending in the local church. Our obedient missionary participation must contribute to the unity of the Church and never destroy it through ecclesiastical imperialism or national chauvinism. But whether it be the traditional figure of the missionary, the visitor or the migrant worker, the foreigner is necessary to the mission of the local church throughout the world. We must find the structures which will both acknowledge local responsibility and reflect the relationship of the local to the universal community.

Our fourth conviction is that we live in the age of ecumenism. The concept of mission as the transplanting of our own particular version of Christianity from one country to another simply cannot stand up before the demands of our times. What matters is that the world must have the opportunity to receive the Christian witness. The support of whoever can best bring that witness is more important than sustaining our denominational loyalties.

The need to respond structurally to a vision of mission that includes all areas of the world has led many missionary societies to build a two-way traffic scheme into their relationships with local churches, but today we must move toward an even wider relationship. A multiple traffic system, under the name of Ecumenical Sharing of Personnel, is being constructed which will separate funding from personnel and channel the support of Christians in all parts of the world for the exchange of missionary forces in all possible directions. Three thousand missionaries from the Third World are already at work outside their home countries, and this missionary potential in rapidly growing churches will no doubt continue to grow in the near future. The necessary financial resources must be found to permit them to travel and to work. What is needed from the financially strong churches is the imagination and generosity and spirit of sacrifice to support this new movement of the Holy Spirit, forsaking the patterns of missionary support dependent upon the sentimentality or paternalism inherent in all human beings.

It is the context of this experimental search for new forms of mission that the Bangkok discussion on moratorium, which has already attracted much attention, must be understood. A moratorium on the sending of funds and personnel may be necessary in a particular situation if it is the best way of rediscovering mission in that place and carrying it out. Moratorium should never be the expression of a desire to break off relationships or to reject the call to mission. Moratorium must be *for* better mission; this is its only justification.

Violent or obligatory moratoria have taken place at various times in the history of the Church, with varying results. During the war the German churches were not able to send personnel and funds to their traditional mission fields in Africa and Asia. The churches of Japan went through a period of moratorium during the Second World War. There was a period of moratorium in the Pentecostal Church of Chile when it broke away from the Methodist Church and began an independent pentecostal movement which has been very fruitful. But today we have to examine the idea of moratorium as a means of providing a possibility for the recovery of the freedom of missionary planning for a church in a given situation. The reason for the disengagement of a moratorium is to produce new commitment.

For the sending church, moratorium may mean calling a halt to the routine repetition of its work and the beginning of a consideration of the fullness of mission, starting with that church's own country and moving out toward others. It is, perhaps, because we rarely question our models of relationship that missionary work goes ahead with no consideration of the new and creative possibilities that lie before us. For the church which requests a moratorium, this can be an opportunity to re-examine its priorities, to rediscover its identity and to develop better communication with its own people. How many churches arising out of missionary work are weighed down by the heritage of missionary institutions, such as hospitals and universities, and thus are prevented from establishing their own priorities? Moratorium is a new weapon in the Christian missionary arsenal.

We must also create structures for dialogue on mission as well as those for sharing resources in mission. We call your attention to the experiment of the Evangelical Community for Apostolic Action (CEVAA) which is an attempt to bring to the same table for discussion the financial and personnel resources and the theological vision of a group of churches joined together to work in various parts of the world. Whether it be through this type of organized forum, with its own continuous life, or through a process of consultation and reflection carried out every few years, it is clear that we must undertake together an examination of our missionary priorities and structures in order to increase the efficiency of our action. The present bilateral relationships between the badly named "mother" and "daughter" churches need to be assessed not in the light of loyalties inherited from the past, but rather in the light of the prime loyalty we all have to the common mission of Jesus Christ.

Bilateral relationships can also be enriched by being submitted to analysis, criticism and challenge from a wide ecumenical group. We need to look at the creation of missionary relationships between churches having no exchange of funds or personnel. The churches of Eastern Europe, for example, are prevented from participating in the world missionary task through such exchange. Does this mean that they cannot take part in the missionary task? Have they not an important contribution to make through prayer to the missionary work of the whole Church? Can their witness and their experience be made available through visits? Has the witness and experience of Christians in other parts of the world, for example in the Third World, something to say to the mission of the Church in socialist countries? Mission cannot simply be seen in terms of sharing funds and personnel; mission is a sharing of all the gifts of the Spirit.

The Life and Growth
of Churches in Mission

James A. Scherer

How is Church growth to be measured? The answer to that question tells a great deal about one's entire theology of mission —motive, message, method, strategy, aim—and is a matter of vigorous debate among missiologists. Two books representing divergent schools of thought about Church growth are reviewed here by James A. Scherer, professor of world mission at the Lutheran School of Theology, Chicago. *Understanding Church Growth* by Donald A. McGavran is—Dr. Scherer points out— "a passionate defense of *numerical* growth as the only ultimately valid criterion of Church growth." While acknowledging that McGavran's "penetrating analysis of the underlying sociological factors . . . is a great contribution," Scherer considers the author's "vision of fantastically multiplying churches . . . a kind of 'last hurrah' for the spirit of Edinburgh 1910." McGavran rightly dispels "romantic notions and false theological rationalizations of non-growth . . . but in general his treatment of the relationship between rapid numerical increase and other aspects of Church life remains simplistic." The other book, *Can Churches Be Compared?* edited by Steven G. Mackie, contains the reflections of an international panel that reviews the findings from a series of situation studies of fifteen churches in five continents undertaken by the World Council of Churches' Department of Missionary Studies. Rather than the single criterion of numerical increase, this study suggests that Church growth should be measured in terms of "organic wholeness"—the ability of a Church to "respond positively to the factors that impinge upon the whole human society." If this appears too indefinite, it is intentional. Scherer concurs with the panel that there is "no

universal model or pattern for Church life and growth." The
study concludes that "the only criterion of vitality and obedience
is the readiness to respond at the point when response is demanded." McGavran's evangelical enthusiasm and the WCC's "humble agnosticism," seen together, provide a confident call to mission. Dr. Scherer's review first appeared in the January 1971
International Review of Mission (Geneva).

At a time when the popularity of Church-centric missionary
thinking has sunk to a low ebb, and when advocates of Church
planting appear to have lost the initiative to various proponents
of secularization, it is salutary to note the appearance of two
books dealing almost wholly with the life and growth of churches
in mission. Each of the two volumes gathers up and summarizes
assumptions and findings of an entire related genre of mission
study literature. *Understanding Church Growth* [1] represents
Donald McGavran's mature and complete statement of Church
growth philosophy and methodology. It draws upon the numerous reports, both published and unpublished, prepared under
the supervision of Dr. McGavran at the Church Growth Institute
in Pasadena, California. *Can Churches Be Compared?* [2] is edited
by Steven G. Mackie and consists of the "reflections" of a com-
petent international panel of experts upon the now completed
thirteen volumes in the "World Studies of Churches in Mission"
series. Initiated by the Research Department of the International
Missionary Council after Willingen (1952), this ambitious project has now been carried to completion by the WCC Department
of Missionary Studies under the leadership of Victor Hayward
and Steven Mackie.

Concentration of both books upon the area of Church life
and growth helps to illuminate still another area in the continuing conversation between conservative evangelical and WCC-
related mission groups. It is apparent that the two schools of
thought, despite their growing convergence on many points and
in some specific aspects of the present study—most notably the
marked sociological and cultural orientation of the two present
volumes—do not view *growth* in the same way. Dr. McGavran's
book is a passionate defense of *numerical* growth as the only ul-

timately valid criterion of Church growth. He makes the *a priori* claim that all other areas of Church life—evangelism, ministry, cultural adaptation, stewardship, social witness, etc.—are tied in an absolute way to the one overriding factor of numerical increase. Rapid increase in numbers thus becomes the article by which a Church in mission stands or falls. *Understanding Church Growth* is an apologia for systematic Church planting and development aimed at numerical increase, and for research into factors which help or hinder such increase. It is currently the most eloquent statement on behalf of Church-centrism and, with its vision of fantastically multiplying churches in what Dr. Mc-Gavran calls "Africasia," a kind of "last hurrah" for the spirit of Edinburgh 1910. Its challenge to ecumenical missions is its claim to set forth a theologically irreproachable and scientifically tested norm for mission policy in a time of general crisis and confusion.

The WCC study is, by contrast, a modest, low-keyed, probing analysis of churches in the missionary situation around the world. Proceeding inductively, it reflects on the findings of situation studies of fifteen churches in five continents which have been described in terms of their organic wholeness and relatedness to the local environment. Eschewing any *a priori* definitions of growth, the panel poses the question of what promotes "a continual living response to God" (p. 16). It defines vitality and aliveness as the ability to "respond positively to the factors that impinge upon the whole human society" (p. 17) as well as to adjust to environmental conditions. Church growth thus includes growth in numbers but also in "new ways and dimensions in which living faith is expressed" (p. 21). The WCC study prefers to describe Church life and growth in terms of "organic wholeness" (p. 14) rather than the single criterion of numerical increase. *Can Churches Be Compared?* limits its task to detailing and classifying what it regards as an astonishing variety and diversity of growth patterns, but it modestly prescribes no solutions and draws no lessons. It extends our understanding of the process by which churches seek to fulfill their missionary calling, but it issues no ringing challenge to action because it discerns no all-embracing solutions.

Dr. McGavran is at his best when bringing the wealth of his

own personal experience and observation and the fruits of
Church growth research to bear upon actual situational analysis.
His method displays growing exactitude and refinement in the
gathering and use of information, in the drawing up of illustrative graphs and charts, and in the pinpointing of critical factors.
Under his leadership Church growth analysis has advanced in
sophistication to the point where it has become an indispensable
tool for the study of local churches. His ability to illuminate
otherwise meaningless or colorless facts through penetrating
analysis of the underlying sociological factors and the cultural
dynamics involved in the response of what he calls "homogeneous units" is a great contribution. Dr. McGavran's goal is to
"lift the fog" which, as he believes, obscures the real causes hin-
dering Church growth. So rigorous is he in dispelling romantic
notions and false theological rationalizations of non-growth that
he may be said to have demythologized this subject. His own interpretation stresses measurable environmental factors and in-
sists that situations be weighed in terms of their social and cultural complexity. The rigor and honesty brought to the task will
put students of Church growth in Dr. McGavran's debt. Much to
his credit, the author is even-handed in his criticism of conservative evangelical and ecumenical groups for the rationalizations
(theological and promotional) which both employ in justifying or
covering up non-growing situations.

On the other hand, Dr. McGavran indulges in some roman-
ticizing on his own, and not a little polemicizing, and these have
a tendency to detract from the valuable scientific contribution of
his work. A tone of censoriousness characterizes his description
of critics of Church growth philosophy. He would have us believe
that numerical increase is rejected by the majority of persons
concerned with mission work—a view that many readers are not
likely to accept—and that he alone remains faithful to the commission to disciple the nations, while others have gone whoring
after the *Baalim* of social relevance, ecumenical relations, institutional witness, and so on. Because he remains persuaded that
others will continue hostile or indifferent to Church growth
unless convinced by him, he feels a mandate not merely to en-
lighten his readers but also on occasion to chastise them for
apostasy. He stands forth from the pages of *Understanding*

Church Growth as a fervent apostle and crusader for a particular ideology, but it is questionable whether this advances the scientific nature of his objectives. A second dogmatic notion which the author holds to in the absence of *prima facie* evidence is the belief that numerical growth is the master key which unlocks every other problem area in the life of the Church. This view may certainly be argued as a plausible hypothesis, but it lacks conclusive proof. Dr. McGavran himself recognizes that great people movements demand effective follow-up and shepherding lest they become stagnant, but in general his treatment of the relationship between rapid numerical increase and other aspects of Church life remains simplistic.

Dr. McGavran is at pains to lay a biblical and theological foundation for his philosophy of Church growth, yet his appeal to the Scriptures should not go unexamined. Unquestionably he is right in claiming the New Testament as the authority for his theology of a "God who *finds*" and does not merely *search* for the lost. Mission, he says, is "an enterprise devoted to proclaiming the good news of Jesus Christ, and to persuading men to become his disciples and dependable members of his Church" (p. 34). Therefore conversion is necessary, and Church growth is an indispensable goal of mission work. There is no biblical justification, McGavran finds, for "detached witness"; mission is always "purposeful finding." Salvation is the supreme need, and from this all other necessary goods can be expected to flow. McGavran stands for Church growth and conversion over against anonymous presence, humble service, or witness that does not seek conversions. He is undoubtedly right that the triune God is a "God who finds," but what does it mean in the context of the world for God to find? The bland equation between God's finding of men and the process of churchification begs too many questions and ignores the issues related to the current discussion of evangelism and conversion, the spiritual alienation of the Christianized masses in the West, and the necessity for a meaningful witness to God's action outside the ecclesiastical sphere. It may be that McGavran's two-stage counsel of baptize now, teach the implications of discipleship later, has pragmatic relevance for the approach to primitive peoples undergoing "people movements" into the Church. It can hardly be regarded as infallible guidance for mission in six continents, least of all in urban industrial areas and among intellectuals. It also ignores the plain fact that past people movements among the European tribes are at least partly responsible for the spiritual condition of the West today. There are deeper theological questions to be probed in connection with the assertion that God is a God who finds.

In his concern to accelerate efforts toward conversion Dr. McGavran appears to have conceded too much to his own pragmatic spirit and his buoyant evangelical optimism. Like the world missionary movement on the eve of Edinburgh, he sees "Africasia" (Asia, Africa and Latin America) ready and waiting for the Gospel, and the task as essentially that of finding the correct methodology for capitalizing upon the opportunity. The chief variation from Edinburgh is that for McGavran the resources are ready to hand, only they are being directed toward wrong goals and employed in the service of wrong strategies. The pedagogical requirement is to redirect missionary effort toward proper goals and to reorder priorities in favor of Church growth. Ignorance and blindness of churchmen and mission administrators are the chief causes of failure, but these obstacles can be overcome by a fundamental change in methodology and objectives. It would appear that ultimate theological questions cause little more than a passing ripple, e.g., the nature of evil, the reality of the cross, demonic forces opposing the Gospel, unbelief, indifference, etc. All hesitation is overcome in a supreme act of confidence in the transcendent will of God who desires that his lost sheep be found. Church growth thinking is handicapped by Dr. McGavran's failure at this point to provide larger and more satisfying answers regarding the nature of the Gospel, the Church, and the kingdom. What kind of eschatological framework is presupposed? Shall we assume that "Africasia" is capable of undergoing an irresistible Christianizing movement at precisely the moment that "Eurica" (Europe and North America) are sliding in the direction of progressive de-Christianization? Ironically, there is some evidence (see *IRM*, January 1970, pp. 39ff.) that this may be happening in Africa. If and when it does occur, it ought to give rise to some deep theological soul-searching and not simply to increased efforts to accelerate growth rates.

From a purely methodological point of view one must also ask whether analysis after the fact and prognosis are the same thing. Dr. McGavran has done much to illuminate the causes of non-growing churches by combining statistical analysis with insights from the social sciences. Can such analysis also be used programmatically to forecast when and where a given Church will grow? The unspoken assumption of *Understanding Church Growth* is that Church growth analysis can be used not only predictively but also catalytically to influence growth where it might not otherwise have occurred. One should not dismiss many excellent examples of numerical growth through "homogeneous units" (tribe, caste, etc.) or "web movements." Yet it is never made clear whether these movements occurred spontaneously or through the application of correct methodology. Fine examples of successful people movements are cited, but unfortunately there is no clinically controlled evidence for successful movements in virgin situations where good rather than bad methods were applied. If field "x" is ostensibly ripe for harvest and Church growth methods are employed but no results follow, who or what is to blame? The question is how far Church growth can be processed through computer-like methods. One senses an element of determinism in calculating the relation of cause and effect which only remotely fits the actual empirical situation where results are frequently unpredictable and an open-ended approach must be taken. At the same time, however, we must agree with Dr. McGavran that practical failure need not be attributed to inscrutable causes or to theological mystery, but that it is a valid subject for investigation and criticism.

One basic assumption in Church growth philosophy should be lifted out for further discussion because of the manner in which it contradicts much recent ecumenical missionary thinking. Dr. McGavran asserts that "men like to become Christians without crossing racial, linguistic or class barriers" (p. 198), and from this he argues that successful evangelism should not challenge the reality of race, language and class. Generations ago Bruno Gutmann, Gustav Warneck and others argued that mission work must be adjusted to given social and cultural realities, and their work led to the formation of impressive folk churches. McGavran believes that the ability to transcend racial and ethnic barriers is a fruit of the Spirit reserved for those who have already made considerable progress in the Christian way. It is not a virtue that can be expected of neophytes. The question is whether the stress at the last CWME Assembly (Mexico City, 1963) on the Church as a community with a special calling to transcend and cross the frontiers of race, religion, class, etc., is sound in the light of Dr. McGavran's position. He believes that the mission approach should be to a single homogenous unit and that the "correct policy of Christian mission is to disciple each unit out to its fringes" (p. 212). According to this view, world mission becomes home mission infinitely extended and operating chiefly through local groups reaching out among their own kind. This may or may not signal the end of the traditional "foreign missionary" enterprise. Of greater moment is the question whether the missionary approach is allowed, even required, to preserve and confirm existing folkways and social structures. Does the Gospel take the line of least resistance, or should it challenge ethnocentric prejudices and practices? Does it merely confirm the givenness of local beliefs and customs, or does it include a note of judgment and issue a call for repentance and change? In McGavran the prophetic task is definitely subordinated to that of social conservation.

A further question for discussion is the place which motivation plays (or should play) in people movements. Dr. McGavran follows Bishop Pickett (*Christian Mass Movements in India*, 1933) in arguing that impure or dubious motives which bring people into the Church are not necessarily a bad thing, for these motives can be Christianized and purified after conversion. Here it would seem that the end justifies the means and that God's mercy is sufficient to cover man's weakness. It is for this reason that Dr. McGavran is so insistent that people movements must be viewed as more than numerical accessions; they demand wise and continuing pastoral care, instruction and upbuilding in the Christian life. The authors of *Can Churches Be Compared?* tend also to support this view, for they see groups turning to the Christian Church in search for humanity, meaning of life, community, messianic support, or simply recognition of human significance (p. 31). This raises interesting questions about the nature of the "faith," whether of individuals or of groups, that leads to conversions. Faith can be relativized and declared to be little more than a sociological symbol of group adherence to Christ or to the Christian community. It can also be psychologized and viewed chiefly as an emotional attitude or inclination without clear dogmatic content. Justification by faith would then include the reality of forgiveness for error, subjectivism and incompleteness. It is then not the dogmatic correctness of faith which justifies but the human movement toward God in Christ as the source of blessing and salvation. The latter interpretation is more descriptive of the faith of the Canaanite woman or of the Roman centurion than are many propositional statements about faith from the Reformation period. Here is an area where missionary practice corrects and overrules confessional theologies from the West. The nature and function of faith in the missionary encounter, as depicted in these two studies, should be the subject for further study.

Even when he hyperbolizes and dogmatizes, Dr. McGavran remains a valuable friend and critic and an indispensable gadfly to the missionary movement. His evangelical sincerity and utter commitment to the cause of world mission go far to overcome occasional defects in his presentation, while his perceptive insights and sound criticisms more than compensate for certain extravagant claims and off-target judgments. There is much sound evangelical wisdom embodied in *Understanding Church Growth*, and it should be read as a healthy counterweight to much sensational journalism which dismisses the historical missionary task as a thing of the past, or condemns Church planting and conversion to irrelevancy. Dr. McGavran issues a clear call to mission and a challenge to go forward with the help of new insights and tools. Those who ponder the lessons of this lengthy book will do so to their profit.

Can Churches Be Compared? can be dealt with more summarily because of its brevity and the greater modesty of its claims. As noted, it is a preliminary evaluation of the volumes in the "World Studies of Churches in Mission" series, a project that has been hailed as marking the birth of a new style of "missionary historiography." The thirteen volumes in the series, published between 1958 and 1970, cover fifteen separate local or regional churches in five of the six continents. The writers do not continue the pattern of recounting the traditional historical and institutional development of churches based on their Western antecedents. Instead, they break new ground by attempting to describe the churches as they are in their social, cultural and environmental *Sitz im Leben*, an approach heretofore characteristic of anthropological studies but largely missing from missionary writing. In these volumes one acquires some feeling for what Christians are like in their everyday lives, how they relate to their fellow countrymen, what convictions they hold, what penalties they pay for their faith, and how they try (or fail) to express their discipleship in relation to their own time and place. Gone for the most part as the center of attention are the pioneer missionary hero, the mission society, and the preoccupation with Western patterns and precedents. In their place emerges a series of contemporary pictures of fifteen struggling earthly communities seeking in their own way to express the divine calling, but all mindful that the treasure is mediated in earthen vessels. Not the least interesting feature is the fact that churches in the West (England, Germany and the USA) are also represented. Africa is represented by four studies (Uganda, Zambia, Togo and Congo-Brazzaville), India by four, and Japan, East Java, the Solomon Islands and Chile by one each.

The instructions of the editorial committee were to describe a particular Church at some depth in terms of its organic relation to its total environment, giving attention to both positive and negative responses (aliveness vs. retrogression), in such a way that the resulting picture would satisfy both an outside observer and a member of the local church. The extent to which the results match these criteria must be judged by the individual reader of the thirteen volumes. The present report does not evaluate the individual studies but merely reflects on the task as a whole and on what was learned in the process of completing it. The picture that emerges is one of growing frankness and maturity in recognizing what churches are and (equally important) what they are not, and an increasing readiness to strip missionary reporting of the "mythology" which Stephen Neill referred to when he noted (*The Unfinished Task*, p. 111) that "for forty years it has been difficult . . . to tell the truth and nothing but the truth about the younger churches." Now the time has come when the truth can be told about churches in both East and West, and the honesty of the telling is refreshing. One may even hazard the guess that unvarnished facts, plainly told, contain more encouragement than the pleasant mythologies of yesteryear. We are moving beyond the period in which defensiveness —on the part of Western missionary or national—made the plain truth unacceptable and well nigh undiscoverable. If it had done nothing else, the present series would have made a valuable contribution to healthy, open-minded, six-continent missionary thinking. The report describes its findings in terms of "humble agnosticism" (p. 101). The main conclusion reached seems to be that we are only beginning to understand what *life* and *growth* mean when applied to living churches. One cannot dogmatize too much about the criteria for a healthy Church, for a growing Church is like a sensitive plant reacting to its local soil and ecological conditions. It must be understood *organically* and not institutionally or administratively. Nor can numerical increase be taken as the sole or principal criterion of aliveness, for a Church grows in a variety of ways. It is highly significant that the panel has set aside the time-honored (since Venn and Anderson) "three-self" criteria of Church development (self-government, self-support, self-propagation) in favor of other criteria which are primarily sociological and cultural, and which have always figured prominently in continental missionary thinking. The demise of the older pattern of thinking should not be lamented, for it was rooted too exclusively in structural and political concerns and could at best contribute to the solution of the authority problem. Its ecclesiological insights were shallowest precisely in the area where the new series of studies makes its greatest contribution, namely, in the understanding of the organic relatedness of the Church to its local environment. It is in this sense that *Can Churches Be Compared?* heralds a new style of missionary historiography.

The report draws extensively upon the local situation studies to illustrate its major findings. There is a variety of patterns of Church genesis, it says, all related to the felt needs of the surrounding society. These patterns are related to a variety of motives, none of which is judged to have more validity than any other. *Congruence* and *detachment* describe two dynamic modes

of relationship between Church and community. Environmental
factors influence local teaching, Church discipline, and forms of
nurture and ministry. Churches are never static but appear to
move either in the direction of greater *distinctiveness* from society or greater *identity* with society. Churches express their responsibility for others through evangelism, living example, service, and social or political involvement. They present an
astonishing diversity of forms, there being no universal model or
pattern for Church life and growth. A Church's self-consciousness—necessary to the fulfillment of its mission—grows out
of its relationship to its surrounding culture and determines the
shape of its obedience. "The dynamic of a Church's growth and
development is an internal dynamic. It is inadequately explained
in terms of external agencies, but arises from the interplay of environmental factors and the work of the Spirit" (p. 94). Here the
report allows scope for intangible factors, and parts company
with the deterministic assumptions of the Church growth philosophy. "The only criterion of vitality and obedience is the readiness to respond at the point when response is demanded" (p. 98).
Even these tentative conclusions, the report intimates, should not
be pressed too far, for the panel modestly feels that it has only
touched the fringes of God's ways of dealing with the Church.
For the Church has an inward being which is known only to God
and which cannot be penetrated by researchers.

Can Churches Be Compared? contains little that is startling-
ly new but it does serve as a useful introduction to the entire
series of studies on churches in mission. Readers should turn directly to the primary volumes for the rich insights they afford.
Hopefully others will now begin to study and describe still other
churches, making use of the excellent guidelines laid down by the
editorial committee and using earlier studies as models. A similar word of encouragement should be extended to students of
Church growth working under the supervision of Dr. McGavran.
The growing number of situation studies in the "Church
Growth" series may also be read with immense profit. The two
approaches would seem to complement and correct one another.
The Church growth emphasis on numbers as primary needs am-
plification in terms of the organic criteria of the WCC study.
The ecumenical report with its "humble agnosticism" can per-

haps gain something from the evangelical enthusiasm of Dr. Mc-Gavran and the confident call to mission embodied in his Church growth philosophy.

NOTES

1. *Understanding Church Growth*, by Donald A. McGavran (Grand Rapids, Michigan: William B. Eerdmans Publishing Company, 1970).

2. *Can Churches Be Compared?* Edited by Steven G. Mackie, WCC-CWME Research Pamphlet No. 17 (Geneva: World Council of Churches, and New York: Friendship Press, 1970).

Black Consciousness and the Black Church in America

C. Eric Lincoln

The black church is "the mother of the black experience in America," the key to understanding the experience of thirty million black Americans. Yet to most non-blacks the black church remains an interesting but enigmatic phenomenon on the American religious scene. One of the foremost interpreters of the black experience in America is C. Eric Lincoln, a sociologist of religion, formerly on the faculty of Union Theological Seminary, New York, and now chairman of the philosophy and religion department at Fisk University in Nashville, Tennessee. Dr. Lincoln describes here the development of the black church, as distinct from American Christianity, and discusses the vital role it has played in forging a black consciousness and a new "ethnic profile," the Afro-American. He maintains that while the black church is the black American's most focal institution, the one that has given unity and cultus to their struggle from slavery to freedom and—currently—for liberation, the black church is now confronted with the necessity of redefining its role and mission if it is "to retain its viability and its credibility as a factor important to the black experience." This is crucial not only for black Americans, but ultimately for all those to whom they relate in the quest for a more human existence. Dr. Lincoln is the author of *Black Muslims in America, My Face Is Black, The Black Church Since Frazier, Is Anybody Listening to Black America?* and *Sounds of the Struggle.* This essay, which was the 1973 Fondren Lecture at Scarritt College for Christian Workers in Nashville, is reprinted from the April 1973 issue of *Missiology: An International Review* (Pasadena, California), the quarterly journal of the American Society of Missiology.

If there had been no racism in America, there would be no racial churches. As it is, we have white churches and black churches, white denominations and black denominations, American Christianity and black religion. From the very beginning, American Christianity was in a quandary about what to do with black Christians once their numbers began to grow. It seems that they were a problem inside the white church, and out of it.

The Presbyterian Synod of South Carolina and Georgia addressed the subject in 1834 in this way:

> The Gospel, as things are now, can never be preached to the two classes successfully in conjunction. The galleries or the back seats on the lower floors of white churches are generally appropriated to the Negroes, when it can be done without inconvenience to the whites. When it cannot be done conveniently, the Negroes must catch the Gospel as it escapes through the doors and windows (A.U.P., 1968:27).

Professor Kelly Miller (1968:193), whose forebears knew from first-hand experience the inner torture of trying to worship God in a gallery, explains that "when the Negro worshiper gained conscious self-respect he grew tired of the back pews and upper galleries of the white churches, and sought places of worship more compatible with his sense of freedom and dignity." The problem was that finding more compatible places of worship was not always a simple matter. The only place a black Christian was likely to find where he could worship in an atmosphere compatible with his sense of freedom and dignity was, in the nature of circumstances, in a black church. But black churches were considered dangerous, and in every southern state they were forbidden, suppressed or regulated by law until the Civil War settled the black Christian's right to independent worship as one of the incidentals to the termination of slavery. As early as 1715 a North Carolina law provided a heavy fine:

> If any master or owner of Negroes, or slaves . . . shall permit or suffer any Negro or Negroes to build . . . on their lands . . . any house under pretense of meeting-house upon

account of worship . . . and shall not suppress or hinder them (A.U.P., 1968:11).

In 1800, a law in South Carolina made it unlawful for: Any number of slaves, free Negroes, mulattoes or mestizoes, even in the company with white persons to . . . assemble for the purpose of . . . religious worship, either before the rising of the sun, or after the going down of the same (*ibid:* 22).

In North Carolina no slave or free black could legally preach or exhort "in any prayer meeting or other association for worship where slaves of different families were collected together" (*ibid*: 25). Other laws required the presence of whites— from five or six to "a majority" at any meeting or worship service blacks could attend. Some of the harsher laws were in response to the slave insurrections of L'Ouverture in Haiti, and Nat Turner and Denmark Vesey in Virginia. But a far-reaching deliberate intention to control the black man's religion seems discernible even underneath the cover of a practical response to the always present danger of insurrection.

Because of the disparity of their respective interests, and because of their differences in the ordering of priorities, some spiritual and some profane, the black-church-within-the-white-church arrangement was never a completely satisfying experience for either blacks or whites. As a matter of fact, the peculiar arrangements for black worshipers to attend white churches was nothing less than the calculated subversion of the sacred to the crassest interests of the profane. The blacks recognized and resented so obvious an abuse of the faith. They were never reconciled to their status in the white church, and when the occasion presented itself they made their own arrangements. The benevolent arms of white Christendom were found to be quite cold. Black Christians had their own thoughts about their bodies and their souls and their destinies, but it was polite to humor the white man's Christian judgment because the white man represented the sum total of temporal power within the universe of the black experience. So in the white man's church they sat wherever his pleasure indicated they should. They stifled the urge to scream and to shout and to raise their arms to heaven, and they strangled the sobs and the moans that welled up inside and made their bodies shake and tremble like leaves in a storm. Only their tears could not be stayed—tears of sorrow and distress—so often mistaken for tears of joy for having the privilege of confronting God in the presence of the slavemaster.

But it was when the white man's worship service was over that the black man's might begin. For neither his heart nor his private membership was in the white man's church—a church that scorned him and demeaned him.

There was that *other* church, that invisible institution of black religion which met in the swamps and the bayous, and which joined all black believers in a common experience at one level of human recognition. Deep in the woods where nature's own artifices could hold and disperse the sound, away from the critical disapproving eyes of the master and the overseer, the shouts rolled up—and out. The agony so long suppressed burdened the air with sobs and screams and rhythmic moans. God's praises were sung, his mercy enjoined, his justice invoked. This was the invisible church, where the black man met God on his own time and in his own way without the white intermediary.

One of the most critical interests of the contemporary black American is the search for the definition of the black heritage—a search which begins inevitably with the black church, for the black church is the mother of the black experience in America. When I say "black church," obviously I do not refer to the blacks gathered in white churches, nor to those black gatherings monitored by white overseers, for the inherent limitations such instances imposed upon the black psyche made for the negation rather than for the flowering of an authentic religious experience. Today's black Americans are very earnestly involved in the struggle to determine who they *were* in order that they may better know who they *are* and who they may become. The process of rediscovery is complex and difficult. The official version of the history of this nation and its people is laid down with intended finality in our official literature of instruction. But much of that literature is often consciously, and sometimes inadvertently, committed to perpetuating the Great American Myth of white supremacy and black debasement. The myth is protected by an intricate system of taboo, and it is buttressed with a clever folk-lore which functions to lend credence to what is patently incredible. Fortunately, the "finality" of American history is of course not final at all. This is an age of skeptics, an age in which "men want dug up again." A new breed of scholars more interested in recovering the truth than in merely covering up the past are at work re-examining the evidence of the American experience, for the prevailing interpretation of that experience as it is laid down in the textbooks, romanticized in the supportive literature, and sanctified by racial fervor was designed for a society which is past. Most black Americans and an increasing number of white Americans have grown weary of the myth. They want to know the facts behind the myth. And this is as true of our true religious heritage as for any other.

Any understanding of the significance of the black experience in America, and any successful attempt to put that experience in perspective, must begin with the black church, for this is the key institution which spans most of the history of the black experience and offers the most readily accessible doorway to understanding the complexity and the genius of the sub-culture that is black America. The part that the Christian religion played in shaping the identity of the black American has been interpreted variously, depending upon the perspectives brought to the situation. But while the consequences of the Christianization of the slave have been the subject of debate, no one has ever denied that there *are* consequences, and that they are of the highest order of significance.

Perhaps for more than any other people since the Israelites were enslaved in Egypt, the black American's religion has been characterized by the absolutely unique place it occupied in his personal life and in his understanding of his existence. For much of black history, religion was all he had to give meaning to that existence. There were no other institutions upon which to fall back for strength to confront the exigencies of his uniquely distressed condition. It was he and his God, God and his people in the intimate intercommunion shaped by that very "peculiar institution" called human slavery. The Christianity that the black man received at the hands of the slavemasters was not calculated to make him, the black man, free in either his mind, his body or his spirit. Freedom was not a possibility for which he was considered worthy this side of the grave. That version of the faith given to the slaves was administered as a spiritual narcotic intended to protect the economic interests of the slavemaster by so confusing the mind of the slave as to make his dehumanization seem to him reasonable, right and consistent with the will of God. Was he not the accursed son of Ham? (Albeit he was not a Hebrew!) Was not his blackness a sign of his degradation? And did not Paul admonish the slave who wanted to join his fellowship of Christians that he must return to his master? "Double, double, toil and trouble" was the proper lot of the black slave, and this by divine decree. He must labor in the fields for his earthly master "from can-to-can't," from "can see to can't see"—i.e., from daylight until dark, the traditional work day for slaves. And he must not complain. It was God's will. He must not run away, because to do so would be to steal his master's property, viz., himself. Above all, he must not commit suicide, because to do so would be to destroy property not his own, to the extreme and final disadvantage of those God had set over him and given stewardship of his body. A slave who committed suicide could receive no rites of the Church and must burn in hell forever for his crime against his master. But if he bore his lot with love and patience, being at all times loyal and obedient to the masters set over him in this world, would not God see him properly rewarded in the world to come? Such were the teachings of the Christian Church as they were offered to the African who, because of the white Christians' alleged concern for the purification of his black and heathen soul, found himself involuntarily resident in America.

But that was not black religion and that was not the black church.

Those who laid claim to the black man's body, his labor, his children, born and unborn, were Christians, and the strange claims these white Christians made upon their fellow black Christians were validated by a system of law anxious to accommodate the claims of property, but peculiarly insensitive to the claims of persons—black persons in particular. In the context of the American priority of interests it could have been reasonably expected, and it did in fact develop, that when the question arose as to whether the saving of the black man's soul ought to make his retention in slavery no longer defensible, the accepted answer was that the black man had no soul and could therefore not be a proper subject of salvation in heaven or freedom on earth, or that God only required that he be free from sin, not free from men. The point is that, with his body already in eternal bondage, the religion given to the black man was calculated to put his soul in perpetual escrow. And there it undoubtedly would have remained save for the development of the invisible institution, the black church.

If the matter had ended with the fulfillment of the white man's intentions, the development of black religion would have been quite different from what did in fact occur. Unquestionably, three centuries or so of the American Protestant ethic—well augmented by and indistinguishable from a counterpart American Catholic ethic—have left their mark. The black Christian, who still yearns to have his blackness washed away at that magic fountain believed to flow beyond the veil of mysteries deep in the inner sanctum of the American church, has not fully recovered from the spiritual narcolepsy engendered by his uncritical acceptance of that version of the faith he received as a slave in his spiritual infancy. In contrast, the liberated, self-confident black Christian is fully aware of himself as a Christian among Christians, possibly for the first time since the declamations on the status of his soul were the popular sport of the learned divines who perceived it to be their duty to account for his blackness as an act of God, and his bondage as an act of man.

Whenever the black man accepted uncritically the American version of the Christian faith, he was stifled by it, for from the beginning the American version was designed to reduce the inherent hazards of slave-keeping to manageable proportions by interposing God's will between master and slave. Christianity was the critical link in a malevolent strategy by means of which the involuntary diaspora of West Africa were to be the uncompensated human instruments by means of which white Christians intended to enrich themselves, and Christianity came to be a prime agency of control in an interlocking system of physical intimidation, legal manipulation and religious divarication. Contemporary history does not rule out the possibility that such a strategy so combining the law, religion and force, in whatever guise, may still function with sinister effectiveness in controlling or augmenting the control of the aspirations and the possibilities of black people in America. Certainly, the dehumanization of Christians by Christians is not unheard of in our day. Yet so bald a strategy, even in the days of slavery, was seen for what it was, and rejected. The remarks of Lunsford Lane, an ex-slave, are illustrative:

> I was permitted to attend church, and this I esteem a great blessing. It was there that I received much instruction, which I trust was a great benefit. . . . [But] there was one hard doctrine to which we . . . were compelled to listen, which I found difficult to receive. We were often told by the ministers how much we owed to God for bringing us over from the benighted shores of Africa and permitting us to listen to the sound of the Gospel. In ignorance of any special revelation that God had made to [the white man] or to his ancestors, that my ancestors should be stolen and enslaved on the soil of America to accomplish their salvation, I was slow to believe all my teachers enjoined on this subject. Many of us left [the church], considering like the doubting disciple of old: this is a hard saying; who can hear it? (A.U.P., 1968:29-30).

Despite this aspect of the Christianization of the black contingent of the faith, the *black* church as an institution soon took on important ramifications for the unfolding of the black experience in America. Religion implies a cultus, a church, and the church became the organizing principle for the social development of the black American. The story of the black slaves' disjunction from their African heritage and the ancient cultures to which they had belonged previously is well noted and frequently employed as a kind of "missing link" explanation for all that is not known or understood about the black experience in the West. Whether the disjunction was as summary or as conclusive as some scholars assume it to be remains, I think, a question not satisfactorily resolved. Some vestiges of social and cultural traditions which could not possibly be "American" do persist in the black sub-culture. Nevertheless, the fact is that the most important structural and unitizing institutions through which the individual African in America might have hoped to retain some sense of social identity—the tribe, the council, the tribal societies, etc.—could not be replicated under the circumstances of American slavery. The oral literature recounting the ancient cultures could, and did, survive for a time, but, generally speaking, the African's cultural institutions could not hope to survive for long under the all-encompassing suppression that was the American slavocracy. The dispersal of slaves owning a common language or tribal tradition was a routine precaution against revolt. The suppression of the African languages was accomplished through threat and ridicule. The fine art of oral history of the Africans was reduced to the harmless tales told by the plantation's Uncle Remus, and the African religions were relegated to the realm of paganistic superstition. In the void left by the fragmentation and the distortion of the African heritage, the Christian religion eventually caught fire and flourished, and the church became the inevitable central institution around which the social development of the black American could take place. The black church became the chief organizing principle around which and through which the slave and his successors would find meaning and identity in the land of the Western pharaohs.

The genius of the Christian religion is that it has always managed to survive its distortions. For two thousand years the faith has been compromised by countless schisms and "isms" without succumbing completely to any of them. Popes, priests, preachers, parishioners, governments and private interests have sought to convert the authority and prestige of the faith to private ends. None has enjoyed lasting success. Hence, the strategy of the slavocracy to use religion as the clinch pin for the perpetuation of slavery and caste in America was ultimately doomed to failure, although the failure of that strategy is hardly due to its renouncement, early or late. To be sure, there have always been prophetic voices in the American church, but they have never been of sufficient power or amplitude to effectively dampen the racism which still structures that church and determines the behavior of its constituency. The strategy of white Christianity failed in its intent to make black Christians its spiritual subordinates because, in accepting Christianity in America, the blacks were not accepting American Christianity. Rather, when it was offered to them, they availed themselves of the opportunity to reidentify with a God and a faith which transcended the parochial interests of the American Christians.

Probably the first church intended specifically for blacks was established between 1773 and 1775 "on the South Carolina side of the Savannah River . . . twelve miles from Augusta, Georgia," at Silver Bluff, South Carolina, and later moved to Savannah (Brawley, 1970:66). In 1791, a group of blacks in Philadelphia, having first formed a benevolent society, erected a building and voted to become an Episcopal church, subject to certain conditions named in their petition to the bishop. The conditions stipulated that they be received as a body, that they retain local autonomy, and that their lay reader be ordained as minister. These conditions were acceptable to the bishop, and in 1794 St. Thomas Church became the first black Episcopal church in America. Absolom Jones was ordained a deacon and, shortly afterward, the first black Episcopal priest (Wesley, 1969:72-73). There were to be thirteen others by the end of the war in 1865.

The first black denomination grew out of the humiliation of black Christians attending St. George Methodist Episcopal Church in Philadelphia in the late eighteenth century. Richard Allen, a lay minister who had preached frequently at St. George since 1786, Absolom Jones and other black worshipers were on an occasion removed bodily from the gallery of the church as they knelt in prayer. Stung by the behavior of the white brethren, Allen subsequently organized Bethel African Methodist Episcopal Church (1794) (*ibid:* 78),[1] and was ordained by Bishop Asbury in 1799. Blacks in other middle Atlantic communities soon began withdrawing from white churches and organizing their own "African Methodist Episcopal" churches. In 1816 these independent churches met in Philadelphia to establish the African Methodist Episcopal Church as a denomination, and Allen was elected first bishop. Thus was the black church formally established as a separate entity of the Protestant Church in America.

Today the AME denomination has over a million members. The African Methodist Episcopal Church Zion, which was organized in 1796 when black members withdrew from the white John Street Methodist Episcopal Church in New York (Brawley, 1970:69-70), has a membership close to a million. There are more than eight million black Baptists in three "conventions," and a half-million black Methodists in the Christian (previously "Colored") Methodist Episcopal Church (*ibid:* 78).[2] Perhaps two million other blacks are scattered among various sects and cults including "store front" communions and Black Muslims. What is left belong to the "white" denominations, principally Roman Catholics, United Methodists, and Presbyterians, with smaller numbers of Episcopalians and Congregationalists.

One of the peculiar attractions Christianity could offer blacks was that it provided a ready-made culture and a ready-made tradition for a people who had been brutally separated from their own. The Christian God was active in history. He involved himself in human affairs. He delivered Israel from bondage. Were the black slaves themselves not in the hands of Pharaoh, and would not God deliver them? If God was just and if God was merciful, if God was on the side of the oppressed, then must not they be the chosen people of God? Who else could better qualify? But the blacks were not looking for a tradition to adopt; they had their own. While the bondage of Israel was a useful illustration of the power and justice of God, except for an occasional sect with severely limited membership, the blacks in America never confused themselves with Israel. They knew themselves to be God's *black* people—an affirmation of the illimitability of divine love and concern. If God could choose once, God could choose again. He could choose *black* people. Although they have been wasted in the drainage of the white man's culture, to the surprise and consternation of well-meaning social scientists, theologians and government planners, black Americans have resisted all efforts to deny them a sub-culture of their own. Out of the body of their unique experiences in America, there gradually emerged a new ethnic profile that is neither African nor American, but distinctly *Afro-American*. The black experience looks back to its long pilgrimage from slavery to freedom and remembers all the techniques of survival, and it looks forward and addresses itself to a strategy of complete liberation. The black experience is inevitably modified and constricted by the white overculture which surrounds it, but it has deep roots in the black church and black religion, and these have always been beyond the effective reach of white America.

The black Christians identified themselves as the people of God, but they did not attempt to substitute the history and the traditions of the Jews for their own. Like the Jews, they chose God and conceived themselves as chosen by God because of their understanding of the nature of the love of God and the character of his justice. While there have been some minor cults which found the appropriation of a synthetic Jewish culture less anxiety-producing than the search for and the development of their own cultural identity, black Christians have generally avoided the fantasies of such cults without submission to the even more demeaning presumptions of American Christianity. Black religion is assuredly not the religion the blacks received from the American practitioners, for that religion was compromised by racism and human slavery. By contrast, black religion sees itself as the religion of liberation, bringing good news to the poor in spirit and freedom to the oppressed. It is a faith born of the black experience, a unique encounter with God in the concept of a developing American civilization.

The black church, the cultus of black religion, was affected with a crucial social interest from its inception. It was for much of its history an invisible system of relationships, a nexus of ungathered power. It was not a place, and often it *had* no place except the bayous and the swamps where, in the search for a more suitable truth than a segregated church provided, the black faithful gathered in furtive, clandestine assemblage. It was the black church that organized the energies and systematized the beliefs and practices of the slaves and their descendants in such a way as to transcend the cultural deficit caused by their estrangement from Africa. But more than that, the black church was the unitizing agent which, more than any other factor, made of a scattered confusion of African peoples *one* people, a self-conscious ethnicity with a common religious reference.

The black church has always been more than a religious society. It has been the black man's government, his social club, his secret order, his espionage system, his political party and his vanguard to revolution. It became the counterpart of the important social institutions he had known and participated in under the African culture from which he was separated so precipitously. Under its aegis were the rites of passage from puberty to adulthood, from singleness to marriage, from life to death. The church sponsored the communal meal, the ritual of community togetherness. When freedom came and the invisible church could be made manifest in wood and glass and stone, wherever black people gathered, and by whatever exigencies of fortune, there they built a church, a symbol of their faith in God's continuing deliverance and of their common bond in the black experience. The church house was funded and raised as a community effort. The church building was the community forum, the public school, the conservatory of music, the place where the elocutionary arts, the graphic arts, the literary arts and the domestic arts were put on prideful display. It was *lyceum* and *gymnasium* as well as *sanctum sanctorum*. It was the prime developer of black leadership, a fact that is still critical to the black struggle for full participation in the American spectrum of values. The black church produced Nat Turner and it produced Martin Luther King, and, ranging between their respective conceptualizations of the most effective means to accomplish black liberation, the black church has been womb and mother to an extraordinary phalanx of black leaders for every generation of its existence.

The black church has been the one institution the black man could call his own. During the slave era it was monitored by the white overseers or by white clergymen, but there was little proclivity on the part of the white man to take it over or to identify with it except to neutralize it as a potential focus of rebellion. So long as he could be satisfied that the black church was not a threat to his economic and political interests, the white man was willing to let it alone. There were exceptions, but for the most part white people were careful to ignore what went on in black religion except insofar as they were amused by its style or made patrons to its indigence. In consequence, the way in which the black church has contributed to the shaping of the developing cultural ethos is essentially a reflection of the character of black

involvement. The black church has been the definition and determination of the black experience which in turn produced the
black church.

The black church is the black American's most focal institution, but times change and institutions change. Institutions do
not change precipitously, and not always perceptibly, but they do
change. It is the nature of an institution to resist impulsive
change, lest the appearance of stability be compromised or destroyed, for an institution is a social device by means of which
the salient values of a community are preserved from generation
to generation with a high degree of integrity. Yet if the institution is to remain viable and relevant, it must not confuse integrity with intactness. Integrity demands the responsible transmis-
sion of the spirit or the essence of the values institutionalized.
Intactness demands that the institutionalized values be transmit-
ted as received, without change or modification. The black
church is now confronted with the necessity of redefining its role
in the contemporary scheme of things. How it shall finally conceive itself will determine whether it shall continue to be a key
factor in the liberation and dignification of black people, or
whether it will yield its place to some of the rapidly proliferating
secular institutions which are bidding for its traditional position
of pre-eminence, or whether it will opt to lose itself in the larger
communion of American Christianity. Religion is a basal, vital
aspect of the black man's identity and of his concept of who he is
in a world where his humanity is still questioned by many he
must confront at various levels of human intercourse. At the
same time, the contemporary world is a kaleidoscope of changing patterns in social relations. The religious presuppositions
upon which we used to rely for interpreting the world and its
meaning are no longer a sufficient index to that end. What is the
future of black religion and of the black church in times like
these?

First of all, if it is to be true to its institutional heritage,
black religion (or any religion) must not limit its perspective to
the short-term interests and to the problems of immediacy which
demand instantaneous solution or response. That may be the role
of magic, or of politics, or of social welfare. It is not and cannot
be the responsibility of religion. On the other hand, religion can-

not remain totally static in a world of change and still command the world's interest or respect. The relevance of religion derives from its ability to relate change and the consequences of change to itself, and to interpret the world at any given moment in terms of the internal truths which are not the subject of change. If the black church is to retain its viability and its credibility as a factor important to the black experience, it must withstand transition while at once anticipating and evaluating new patterns of human existence and interpreting them in terms of the values of black religion and what transcends black religion. In short, a viable religion must change, but it must persist through changes, always remaining what it was, always becoming what it must be as it unfolds itself to meet the needs of its people wherever they are in the flux of human history. And since the black church is the cultus of black religion, its credibility and its viability cannot be separated from the aspirations and the hopes of the black people it represents. A church which does not lead where the people should be going is a dead church, and a church that goes where the people are leading is superfluous. The black church will remain alive and necessary so long as it has credibility, and it will retain its credibility only so long as its fundamental values, i.e., its basic appeals, transcend the parochialism which called it into being.

Revolution is the characteristic phenomenon of these times. The black revolution is the corporate expression of thirty million people of African descent against the ancient regime which has used religion as an instrument of dehumanization and exploitation. The critical, evaluative faculties which inform human behavior in ordinary times are often muted or short-circuited in the fervor of social change. The validity of all religion in general and certainly the relevance of black religion in particular is, and will be, called into question again and again.

If the black revolution intends to transform this society into the democratic entity it has so long claimed itself to be, if in the process of democratizing America the revolution intends to legitimize and dignify the black experience for all time to come, and if it expects to be relevant tomorrow, the black church may not rest on the accomplishments of yesterday. The revolution I am talking about is a revolution of ideas and of attitudes. It is a revolution of perspective and of response to perspective. It is designed to insure the emergence of the black American as a full man with full responsibility and full power to make responsibility real. It intends to help America move back from the edge of the abyss. It is redemptive rather than retaliatory, but it must not close its mind to the realities which scandalized the traditional faith, aborted the noble intentions of the founding fathers, and brought us to our present predicament in religion and social relations. To do so would be to deny the relevance of history, and history is the experience by which we learn.

NOTES

1. Separated from the (white) Methodist Episcopal Church, South, and formally incorporated at Jackson, Tennessee, in 1870. See H. Shelton Smith, 1972, p. 231.

2. Historian Charles Wesley points out that only twelve days separated the dedication of St. Thomas Protestant Episcopal Church and Bethel African Methodist Episcopal Church, founded by Absolom Jones and Richard Allen respectively, who had shared racial humiliations at St. George Methodist.

REFERENCES CITED

A.U.P.: *Atlantic University Publications* (New York: Arno Press, 1968).

Brawley, Benjamin: *A Social History of the American Negro* (New York: Collier Books, 1970).

Miller, Kelly: *Radicals and Conservatives and Other Essays on the Negro for America* (New York: Shocken Books, 1968).

Smith, H. Shelton: *In His Image, But . . .* (Durham: Duke University Press, 1972).

Wesley, Charles: *Richard Allen: Apostle of Freedom* (Washington, 1969).

Change
in the Church

Manas Buthelezi

The socio-political dynamics in South Africa provide a critical testing ground for the Church as it seeks to engage in mission to the nation. Unfortunately, the voices of black Christians in that situation are not often heard. Dr. Manas Buthelezi, a leading black Lutheran clergyman, is the Natal regional director of the interdenominational Christian Institute, an organization that is openly critical of apartheid (separation of the races) in a Christian society. In this article, Dr. Buthelezi—the only black South African with a doctorate in theology—examines the urgent need for change in the church in South Africa, if the church is going to be faithful and effective in mission. Speaking of "the systematic apostasy of the white man," he says: "What has happened in this country is that the white man in his stewardship has violated the integrity of God's love and justice." This "spiritual vandalism on the part of the white man" leads the author to question "whether Christian love is safe at all in the hands of the white man." The same would apply, he says, to social justice. A few weeks after this article had been published in the August 1973 issue of the *South African Outlook* (Mowbray, Cape), the South African Minister of Justice issued a "banning order" against Dr. Buthelezi, prohibiting him from attending social, political or educational gatherings and from teaching students, although he may still conduct church services. Under the "banning," however, no newspaper may publish what he says—or anything he has ever said in his life.

To some people "change" and "Church" seem to be two irreconcilable concepts. The Church as an institution stands in sharp contrast to the transitoriness of the things of this world.

While permanence and continuity describe the character of the Church to them, it is to worldly things that "change" relates.

In the Middle Ages "seculum" of which secularization and secularism are modern English variations, pointed to a category of time: it meant "age" or "century" as opposed to "eternity." It also came to designate those members of the clergy who ministered to people in their daily life in contrast to the members of the monastic orders. In "seculum" there was a notion of that which is passing away or temporal in contrast to that which is eternal.

Thus the secular was a realm of temporal political power, of labor and trade and natural law. This was in contrast to the Church which was a dispensary of grace that related man to the eternal. Timelessness and permanence was to the Church what change and transitoriness was to the world.

Heresies

Since the earliest times of Church history the category of antiquity was used to demonstrate the permanence and continuity of the Church vis-à-vis sects and heretical groups. The novelty of the sects and heretical groups stood in sharp contrast to the antiquity of the Church which dates back to the times of the apostles. Thus in his *Prescription Against Heretics*, Irenaeus challenges the heretics thus:

> If there are many heresies which are bold enough to plant themselves in the midst of the apostolic age, that they may thereby seem to have been handed down by the apostles, because they existed in the time of the apostles, we can say: Let them produce the original records of their churches; let them unfold the roll of their bishops, running down in due succession from the beginning in such a manner that that first bishop of theirs shall be able to show for his ordainer and predecessor someone of the apostles or of apostolic men —a man, moreover, who continued steadfast with the apostles.

It is the wrong notion of what the Church stands for that causes many people here in South Africa to find it difficult to see the Church as an instrument of social change and social process. To them that is social gospel. This poses the problem of the solidarity of the Church with the mass of people among whom it ministers. The issue at stake is whether the bridge between the Church and the secular world is just the mission of the Church to the world or whether this mission presupposes an already existing solidarity between the two.

Gustaf Wingren has made the observation that the salvation event which is the content of the message of the Church took place outside the religious center of Jerusalem. It took place in the world, in the sphere of the "secular." Not an apostle but a stranger, Simon of Cyrene, under compulsion, carried the cross of Christ. A criminal at Jesus' side and not a disciple received the promise of the kingdom. Both the death and resurrection were enacted before pagans, Roman soldiers, and not before a crowd of disciples who, as a matter of fact, had run away and were in hiding. Thus, this event in Jerusalem, which is to be proclaimed to all people "beginning from Jerusalem" is, as much as any could be, an event in the world.

From the beginning the Church is part of God's transforming social process in the world. Is there anything more transforming than the power of the Gospel to the lives and destinies of the peoples of the world? When Christ sent his disciples to make disciples of all nations, he was in effect prescribing that the Church should be an instrument of change in the historical destinies of those nations.

Structural Change

Therefore when we speak of change in the Church, it is not just a question of change in Church structures—even though that is also included—but also change in the role of the Church in the South African society. The Church does not exist for itself but for ministering to South Africa. Therefore what is of primary importance is not just structural change within the Church but how the Church projects itself as a catalyst in changing the thinking and behavior of South Africa's politicians, economists and citizens.

Let us take the question of social justice. There are Christians who believe that the active promotion of social justice is outside the purview and competence of the Church. They believe that this is something that should safely be left in the hands of politicians. They forget that justice belongs to God and not to the discretion of politicians. There are people who believe that the social and political structures in South Africa radiate justice and fair play to all and that it is only political agitators and Communist-inspired churchmen who see the situation as problematic at all.

Talking about change, one of the things that should change is this type of thinking. Therefore there should be change within and through the Church.

Why There Is Need for Change

Rightly or wrongly the white man has been regarded as the standard-bearer of the mission of Christ in South Africa. He was the protector and watchdog of all the values that the Christian Gospel is designed to uphold.

We have, however, witnessed one of the greatest spectacles in the history of the Church in South Africa, namely, the systematic apostasy of the white man. Let me give a theological setting to this charge.

Justice and love are two concepts that are theological in the strict sense of the word. As far as the imperfect human language can go, "holy" and "love" are words which almost define the nature of God. We say that "God is holy" and "God is love."

The idea that God cares for his creation in general and for his people in particular is central in both the Old and New Testaments. In contrast to the gods of the Greek and Roman religious world, who were sometimes represented as jealous of and competing with man, the biblical God is characterized by his active interest in the welfare of his people: he loves and is just to them.

In one of the stories of Greek mythology it is told how sex came about among men. Man was originally a very beautiful being with four legs, four arms and two heads. The gods became so jealous of his beauty that they clove him in half. Since then the two halves have been trying to come together in the form of man and woman.

Shepherd

When we encounter the "shepherd" of the psalms or that of St. John's Gospel, we not only get a glimpse of how a rural culture conceptualized its God, but, more important, we find an instance of what I shall call biblical oeconomia—that is, God not only produces the means of sustenance but he also distributes it equitably like a shepherd who tends his flock. The communism of the New Testament Church was a social extension of this biblical concept of "God's economics." The author of the Book of Acts portrays this social extension as a communal life of sharing, that is, a pooling together of God's gifts for common consumption.

The social extension of "God's economics" contains a moral element of stewardship. The story of Ananias and Sapphira dramatizes the moral accountability of the stewards of God's stewards. The point of reference is always how man's stewardship reflects God's justice and love.

What has happened in this country is that the white man in his stewardship has violated the integrity of God's love and justice.

It is common knowledge that in this country the active promotion of love between black and white is looked at with suspicion. Any fraternization between races, which should naturally develop from faith in Christ, instead of being a cause for praise, brings with it serious consequences, such as being visited by the security police or simple exposure to one form of censure or the other.

As a black Christian I have come in anguish to the conclusion that the white man, through his political and social governmental institutions, no longer services the promotion of God's love between black and white but is really doing his best to kill and frustrate it. This spiritual vandalism on the part of the white man has brought with it consequences so serious that it is no longer a theoretical possibility that Christians suffer just for the sake of promoting love and good will between black and white.

After the end of it all, South Africa will have a unique distinction of producing martyrs who suffered simply because they were trying to promote good will between the races.

Intriguing Question

The current and intriguing question is whether Christian love is safe at all in the hands of the white man. The same applies to social justice. As far as the question of the violation of social justice is concerned, there is a sense in which one can say that the black man has become a "Christ" to the white man: he has been "crucified" so as to bring security and social salvation to the white man. What counts for his insecurity means security to the white man; his poverty is the yardstick of the white man's affluence. In other words the white man would not be as affluent if the black man were less poor than he is.

The irony of all this is that Christianity in South Africa has a white image. This is in spite of the fact that almost all the major multi-racial churches are overwhelmingly black. "What the churches in South Africa are thinking" is very often identical to "what white people in South Africa are thinking." The voice of the black man has not yet been heard in the Church in any significant manner. Added to this is the fact that the white man has discredited himself as the protector of Christian values. The situation becomes very desperate indeed.

There must, therefore, be change in the Church in order to reflect a changed situation, namely, the white man's turning against that which promotes Christian love and justice. The Church must release its potential by promoting the reflection of its black constituency in both its structure and proclamation. The Church must cease to be sectarian in order to reflect the whole of the people of God. It must cease to be a satellite of white power politics in order to become a forum of communion for the whole people of God.

The Black Man Has Changed

The last three years have been characterized by the evolution of black consciousness in South Africa. This in turn called for the need to relate the Christian faith to the experience of the black man.

"But God, Why Did You Create Us?" was the title of an article published in a church periodical some years ago. The article as a whole reflects the mood of a black man who cries from the abyss of the shackles occasioned by the fact that he is black. He is seeking for meaning for and destiny in a life in which blackness is not a favorable intellectual point of orientation.

The theological meaning of this question cannot be appreciated in isolation from the whole gamut of social, political and economic problems. This is not the place to discuss the content of the question as such since here we are discussing change in the Church in broad terms. I only wish to point to the reality of its existence as a primary pre-theological question. In other words there are certain questions which are suggested by the reality and mode of human existence. Any healthy theological reflection uses these questions as points of orientation.

In his critique against "kerygmatic theology," Paul Tillich cautions us against the danger of "throwing" the Christian message at those "in the situation." One need not follow all the turns and twists in his method of correlation in order to appreciate the validity of his caution. He defines the "situation" as follows: "Situation: one pole of all theological work does not refer to the psychological or sociological state in which individuals live. It refers to the scientific and artistic, the economic, political and ethical forms in which they express their interpretation of existence. . . . The situation to which theology must respond in a special period."

Christian Message

Paul Tillich asserts that the Christian message supplies answers correlated to the existential questions which arise from the human situation. The task of systematic theology, according to him, is to analyze the human situation from which the existential questions arise, and to demonstrate that "the symbols used in the Christian message are the answers to these questions."

When man—even an unbeliever—raises moral and existential questions about his life and environment, he is impelled by his condition of creatureliness. Gustaf Wingren argues that "men ask themselves questions like these because of the very fact that they are alive. They can ask them, even though they have no belief in God at all, but what they are really questioning is their relationship to God. For this relationship is given with life itself, and even when men have ceased to be related to him."

We can even go further and say that the preaching of the Word of God by missionaries in Africa did not serve to pull down God to the African situation, because he was already there protecting and sustaining life as Creator. All the preaching did was to bring the message of a God who was already there. The important soteriological motif out of which arises the question as to how man can be reconciled to God should not make us oblivious to the creation motif out of which arises the question of how God commands the situation in the fallen world. Neither should epistemological considerations, namely as to when man "graduates" from a lack of certain knowledge to ascertained knowledge of things divine, determine our conception of the temporal order of the events of God's active presence among sinful men.

From the above it follows that the existential questions which arise from the soul of the black man are the legitimate frame of reference for the Gospel which sums up God's design for the situation of man. If the Gospel is to save the black man, it must relate to such basic questions as: "Why did God create me black? What is the ultimate destiny of the black man in a world governed by the values of the white man?" It is the task of theology in Africa to use these questions as the frame of reference while it defines the content of the Gospel which is designed also to save the black man. The classical themes of theology and their formulation should only serve as starting points and not mark the final and ultimate points of the task of theologizing.

The so-called black theology is the intellectual arm of the spiritual awakening of the black man toward the message of the Gospel. The black man, for the first time, is beginning to hear the message directly from God's mount. For the first time he hears God from the depths of his existence as a black man.

The Church can no longer pretend that nothing has happened. It cannot close its ears forever toward the witness of faith —liberation by the majority of the South African believers. The Church must change so that the black man's witness to the Christian faith may also be heard. In a eucharistic tone the black man is singing: "Out of the depths I cry unto thee, O Lord!" Who has the authority to silence the black man?

God Demands Change Now

This is the time of crises—the crises of Christian discipleship. South Africa urgently needs the Gospel of liberation, a Gospel that will liberate the whites from the bondage inherent in the South African way of life—a way of life that chokes brotherhood and fellowship between black and white. This is the Gospel which will liberate the white man into the realization of the fact that he is nothing but a fellow human being in relation to the black man, and a Gospel which will liberate the black man into the realization of the fact that he is nothing less than a human being.

South Africa urgently needs security—a security that results from fellowship between black and white, not a security created by distance between black and white, since the consciousness of distance does not lead to a feeling of security, but leads to fear and suspicion.

God demands that the white man repent of the political, economic and social sins he has committed over the last three centuries. If the white man will be saved at all, the English and the Afrikaners of this country must say in unison: "Mea culpa, mea culpa, mea maxima culpa."

God is greater than the power which the white man wields today. The white man is nothing but the creature of God for whom Christ also died on the cross. The white man is guilty before God because he has manipulated his political and social institutions against the promotion of love between brothers and against justice toward brothers.

The Church must change because God demands it now. Both the white man and the black man must be liberated from the present bondage. That will be meaningful change because the whole Church, black and white, will have been instrumental in it.

The "Third World" and the Twentieth-Century Church

John Schumacher, S.J.

To what extent has the experience of the Church in the Third World affected the writing of Church history? Not much, according to John Schumacher, S.J. He describes significant elements in the new self-understanding of the Church which are clearly contributions of the Third World, but Church historiography continues to neglect the experience of Third World Christians—much to the disappointment of Church historians and theologians working in the Third World. "A radical shift of perspective" is required, he says, to make the Church conscious of "the new center of gravity of the people of God." Father Schumacher, an American Jesuit who teaches history at Ateneo de Manila University in the Philippines, is widely known for his published writings on Philippine history. This essay first appeared in the September 1971 issue of the international journal *Concilium* (London).

The first obstacle for the historian who attempts an analysis of the twentieth-century perspective of the Church's self-understanding resulting from its impressive extension in the Third World is one of complexity—the complexity of the term "Third World" and the complexity of its impact on the Church. If we are to define the Third World as those countries "still seeking the means to escape from the domination of the great powers and to develop freely,"[1] we find very different types of national churches, distinct in their development.

There are, first, the churches which largely grew out of the century of worldwide missionary expansion preceding World War II, an expansion paralleling, and all too often uncomfortably implicated in, the imperialist expansion of the major Western powers in Asia and Africa. They are young churches, and generally minority groups suspect of being alien to the majority culture of their peoples, of which a non-Christian religion seems to form an integral part. In the second place we find the churches which grew out of the Iberian expansion of the sixteenth century. They are churches with well-established traditions, endowed with a hierarchy since the sixteenth century, but also usually stunted in their development through the failure of the *Patronato-Padroado* system to develop an adequate indigenous clergy. Though majority churches, intimately bound up with the culture of their peoples (at times even to an extent which makes their more vital elements seek to disentangle the Church from a suffocating embrace), they too find themselves threatened with the loss of their identity by their excessive dependence on missionaries from abroad. Finally, there are many of the Eastern churches, no less venerable for the antiquity of their tradition than the churches of the West, but, by the minority status they occupy in predominantly Muslim countries, likewise struggling to maintain their identity and develop freely.

Though the coming to maturity of the churches of Asia and Africa created by the nineteenth-century world-mission is the most obvious element of the extension of the Church in the Third World, the churches founded in the sixteenth century as well as the Eastern churches of antiquity may be truly said to have entered into the mainstream of Church life only in the twentieth century, and only then to have been accepted—even imperfectly as yet—as equals among the churches making up the people of God. As we have come to recognize, there are many kinds of imperialism and dependency—not only political, but economic, cultural and religious. The political emancipation which has been so rapid since 1945 has only served to heighten the consciousness of other forms of dependency and to intensify the search for means to eliminate them. Not least is this true in the life of the national churches as they seek, not independence from the universal Church, but a realization by themselves, and a recognition by others, of their own unique character within the universal

Church, as well as full integration within their own national cultures.

The entrance into the full life of the Church of these peoples of the Third World, acutely conscious of their aspirations to national development and self-realization, has had a manifold effect on the whole Church's self-understanding. The principal elements in this new self-understanding due primarily to them would seem to be the following: (1) a realization of the essential pluralism amid unity which belongs to the universal Church; (2) a new attitude toward the values of non-Christian religions and consequently a new concept of the relation of the Church to them; (3) a broader understanding of the role of the Church as a witness to the Word of God and its demands on men; (4) a fuller concept of the mission of the Church as embracing not only the ministry of word and sacrament, but active involvement in economic and all human development.

Other elements in the contemporary Church's self-understanding might be mentioned, which, though they had their principal origin in a European or North American milieu, have also to some extent been the fruit of Third World experience: for example, the new understanding of religious freedom, and the altered concept of ecumenical relations among the Christian churches. The lived experience of Protestants and Catholics working in the Third World has made its own contribution here, too. But the four elements named above would seem to deserve more extended consideration, as being more clearly specific contributions of the Third World.

At a time when the vast majority of Catholics lived within the geographical boundaries of Europe, even the presence of sizable minorities in "the missions" did not significantly affect the European character of the Church as a whole, for the mission churches were governed by a European hierarchy, and largely, if not exclusively, staffed with a European-born clergy. In spite of the efforts at accommodation on the part of a few missionaries of vision, the Catholicism implanted and lived among the peoples of the mission lands bore the characteristics of its European origin, and the local churches remained essentially appendages of the Church in Europe, itself increasingly centralized and brought into uniformity in liturgy, law and theology.

It would perhaps be an exaggeration to say that the contemporary recognition of the Church as essentially embracing a legitimate pluralism, not only in the forms of its liturgy and law, but even in its theology and the expression of its faith, has been solely due to the striving of the peoples of the Third World to express more fully their own identity and the uniqueness of their own cultures. But the theologian reflecting on the incarnational nature of the Church could not fail to take account of the variety of peoples which had entered into the Church, bearing cultures and civilizations often just as venerable and of greater antiquity than those of the West. The point had not totally escaped the followers of Matteo Ricci in seventeenth-century China, but the European church had been unable or unwilling to recognize it at the time.[2] In the twentieth century the conclusion could not be so easily evaded, particularly as the Western political hegemony began to fade and the rising nationalisms of the new nations looked back to their own cultural heritage as the source of national spirit to unify their peoples. Once the step of recognizing that Catholicism might express itself differently in Asia than in Europe had been taken, it became clear that even in those peoples who had shared a common experience of a European culture accompanying the implantation of the Church in their midst (as in the countries formerly subject to the Spanish *Patronato*), the cultural heritage, for example, of the Philippine church was not that of the churches of Hispanic America,[3] nor even was the national character of the Peruvian church the same as that of Argentina.

The conscious recognition by the Church of a legitimate and even necessary pluralism in its life has manifested itself most obviously and most readily in the adaptation of the liturgy since Vatican II. The substitution of the vernacular for Latin in the Roman rite, a development aided by the existence of Eastern vernacular liturgies, was a first tangible step. More recently, and as yet somewhat tentatively, the recognition of diverse expressions of worship proper to a plurality of cultures has been accepted. The impulse behind the creation of national episcopal conferences and the widespread desire for greater room for initiative on their part likewise correspond to the realization of the pluralistic nature of the Church. But the area in which the need for pluralism has been most felt has been that of theology itself. Not only those cultures with ancient and well-developed philosophical and religious traditions of their own demand this pluralism, but other peoples whose ways of thought are less obviously distinct to the superficial Western observer feel strongly the need for an indigenization of theology among themselves. Though the task has scarcely begun in most cases, the reality of its need (if the Gospel is to be truly made relevant to all men) has become ever more evident.

Intimately related to the encounter of a Western Church with the great non-Christian cultures of the non-Western world has been the Church's changing attitude toward other religions and its relation to them. The encounter did not, of course, occur for the first time in the twentieth century. Christianity had met Islam in the Middle Ages, but the result had been the Crusades; the missionary expansion of the sixteenth century in turn had seen only the hideous work of the devil in the religions it met. It is true that Ricci and his successors had learned to value the ethical system of Confucianism in the Jesuit mission to seventeenth-century China, and Roberto de Nobili had even perceived some of the religious values of Hinduism. But even apart from the rejection of their views by the European church, their fundamental attitude was rather one of openness to what might be found compatible with Christianity than a seeking of positive values in the religion of the peoples they were striving to convert. Their understanding of the Church itself was scarcely altered.

The twentieth-century Church, however, has not merely made an effort to understand the religion-inspired cultures with which it lives in contact so as to be able to present its message in their culture-forms. Rather it also looks at them to find true religious values which perhaps have been obscured in the Western Christian presentation or formulation of God's Word to man. It even finds in them in some fashion authentic vehicles of God's saving grace in which men truly find him.[4]

This in turn implies an altered concept of the Church itself and its mission to the nations, an understanding which has as yet perhaps not been fully clarified. But whatever the full understanding of the mission of the Church today may be, few would disagree that an essential part of it is its role as witness to, and servant of, God's Word to men—however that may be expressed. To be sure, the Church has always conceived itself as a witness to God's Word, and one can certainly not deny all understanding of humble service to Christians of earlier ages. Yet one must confess that the Church's understanding of its witness to God's revelation has usually been that of the crusader, the inquisitor, or —in modern times—the beleaguered and persecuted defender of the truth against modern atheism.

The most striking manifestation of this self-understanding of the Church as witness to and servant of God's Word, wherever found, is the one which has been forced on it most clearly by the Third World in its midst. It is the role of the Church as bearing a responsibility for all human development, even for temporal and economic development. For it is precisely the deprivation of economic development and, as a consequence, of access to other forms of national and human development which constitutes the Third World as such. Again, to be sure, the Spanish church which produced Francisco de Vitoria and Bartolomé de las Casas was not totally deaf to the cries for justice in the preaching of the Gospel to developing peoples.[5] But the justice of which the Church recognizes itself as prophet today has another content. It is no longer a question primarily of individual rights but of the rights of nations. Moreover, the presumption in favor of legitimately acquired wealth no longer exists for nations. In the face of the growing gap between the nations which possess and those which do not, and which cannot acquire the means of doing so, the Church sees itself as committed to demand the liberation of the Third World from the forces inherent in an international situation tending to maintain that imbalance of justice.[6].

Yet the prophetic role of the Church in its demand for justice for the Third World does not fully express its conception of itself today. It must also play an active role in the achievement of economic development and, through it, of all human development. The Church must actively involve itself in temporal realities, not to dominate or to control, but to promote effectively and assist in its servant role the attainment of a human society in which human culture and development are available to all men. Again it can be noted that this is not the first time that the

Church has played an active role in the human and even economic development of nations, as both the history of medieval
Europe and the history of "the missions" bear witness. The difference perhaps lies in the view of the work of development not
merely as a means to attract men to the Gospel, nor even as a
kind of pre-evangelization to establish the necessary human conditions in which the Word can be preached. Rather this contribution to human development is increasingly recognized as an integral part of the mission of the Church, so that even if there is no
possibility of actually preaching the Word or administering the
sacraments, the Church, by its contribution to human development, is fulfilling its mission of working for the realization of
God's kingdom.[7]

If the history of the Church is a progress in its understanding of itself, to what extent has the evolution sketched here affected Catholic ecclesiastical historiography? For the most part,
the judgment must be quite negative. The writing of Church history has increasingly detached itself from the older models in
which popes and emperors, councils and heresies, and the vicissi-
tudes of ecclesiastical politics and diplomacy occupied the center
of the stage. The shift in emphasis in secular historiography from
political and diplomatic history to social, cultural and economic
history has been paralleled in Church historiography by a shift of
interest to the life of the people of God, their faith and their spirituality, their forms of piety and even their superstitions. It is
these which the ecclesiastical historian seeks to understand and
depict.

Yet when one looks to the standard manuals of Church history, and even to some multi-volume extended treatments,[8] the
result is disappointing to the Church historian or theologian
working in the Third World.[9] At worst, they are narrowly national histories focusing events upon the preoccupations of the
national church of the author. At best they are conceived on the
broader scale of Europe, with increasing attention being given to
the experience and piety of the Eastern churches. But the rest of
the Third World (Latin America, South and East Asia, and
Africa—if they appear at all) is treated in a few pages. What is
worse, these appendixes, besides being limited for the most part

to the barest facts of the foundations of these "missions," commonly include numerous errors of fact in the meager information they supply.

The "mission histories," though filling the gap to a certain extent and somewhat less inaccurate in their factual presentation, likewise fail to solve the problem. For all churches have been mission churches in their origins. Yet even though no Church historian could conceive ending the history of the German church, for example, with the work of St. Boniface, whole Christian peoples numerically larger by far than the German church disappear from the consideration of the Church historian with the substantial completion of evangelization in the seventeenth century, when their life as churches had scarcely begun. The underlying, though unspoken, theological assumption vitiating such mission histories is that these missions are considered more as manifestations of the Christian life of the church which evangelized them than as new incarnations of the Church in cultures having their own contribution to make to the fullness of the people of God.

If the churches of the Third World, precisely because they are developing churches, have themselves as yet produced little in the way of scientific theological syntheses, each in its own unique fashion has lived and is living the Christian life. A theology which finds a *locus theologicus* in the life of the people of God must consider itself as at best half-true if in practice it leaves out of account the Christian experience of the majority of national or ethnic manifestations of Christian experience—even within the Catholic tradition. But the Christian experience of the Third World churches can only become that *locus theologicus* once it has been brought from the margin into the mainstream of Church history. If the Church historian is to be truly such and not merely an ecclesiastical antiquarian, it is surely far more important to know the progress of Christian life during a single century among one entire people of the Third World than to investigate the *minutiae* of the history of any number of medieval European monasteries, long since extinct.

This much being said, the practical difficulties of such a reorientation of the historiography of the Church to correspond to its contemporary self-understanding must be confessed. Not only does it require a radical shift of perspective on the part of the Western Church historian to make himself conscious of what we may call the new center of gravity of the people of God, it also requires an intensive work of research and of self-reflection on the part of the historians of the Third World. For just as the churches of the Third World for the most part have scarcely begun the indigenization of their theology instead of accepting the problematics and formulations of the West, so too they have for the most part done relatively little to write the history of the unfolding of God's grace among themselves. In the urgent preoccupation with what seemed to be "more necessary" and "more practical" matters, they have failed to lay the foundations for their own particular self-understanding, which alone can be the basis for their perception of their own unique insertion into the history of salvation.

To many today, the task of the Church is to recognize the designs of the Spirit to the extent that they manifest themselves in the aspirations of peoples. These aspirations, purified, clarified and energized with the "salt" of the Gospel, help to manifest to the Church its role in each people, its mission to them. The historian of the Church in the Third World must help Christian people to read the signs of the times in their midst, not only in unfolding the history of the people of God in this nation, but in placing it in the context of the whole history of the people of God. Much indeed of what is recounted in the standard histories of the Church has little relevance to the younger churches. But much is very relevant, for it forms an integral part of the continuation of the history of salvation into which the younger churches have been inserted in God's due time. As the Gospel came from Jerusalem through Greece and Rome to Europe, so it has been passed on to most of the Third World through Europe. The task of the Church historian is to delineate what in this past is the particular current into which the history of God's manifestation among this particular Christian people has been inserted. This will be his contribution to the urgent theological enterprise of understanding the Church's mission in this particular people. This in turn will make possible a fuller understanding of itself by the universal Church as the people of God, with all that this implies.

NOTES

1. "Message de quelques évêques du Tiers-monde," *La Documentation Catholique* 64 (1967), p. 1899.

2. G. Dunne, *Generation of Giants* (London, 1962).

3. J. L. Phelan, *The Hispanization of the Philippines* (Madison, Wisconsin, 1959), pp. 72ff. However, Phelan judges the "Philippinization of Catholicism" by a rather narrow theological criterion of orthodoxy.

4. Cf. the decree *Nostra Aetate* of Vatican II, and, more explicitly, "Conclusions du Symposium sur la théologie de la mission," sponsored by SEDOS, 27-31 March 1969, in *La Documentation Catholique* 66 (1969), pp. 887-889.

5. Cf. L. Hanke, *The Spanish Struggle for Justice in the Conquest of America* (Philadelphia, 1949); J. Hoffner, *La ética colonial española del Siglo de Oro* (Madrid, 1957) (*Christentum und Menschenwürde*, Trier, 1947).

6. *Gaudium et Spes*, n. 86; *Populorum Progressio*, nn. 47-49, etc.

7. Cf. P. Land, "*Populorum Progressio*, Mission, and Development," *International Review of Mission* 58 (1969), pp. 400-409.

8. The two major multi-volume series currently in progress, *Handbuch der Kirchengeschichte*, edited by H. Jedin, and *The Christian Centuries: A New History of the Catholic Church*, edited by L. Rogier, R. Aubert, M. D. Knowles and A. G. Weiler, have not yet reached a point in publication chronologically advanced enough to make possible a judgment on them with regard to this point.

9. E. Dussel, "Cultura latinoamericana e Historia de la Iglesia," *Anuario de Sociología de los Pueblos Ibéricos* 5 (1969), pp. 113-118.

V: Humanization,
Dialogue and Liberation

Salvation and Humanization:
A Discussion

*M. M. Thomas
and Lesslie Newbigin*

Salvation and Humanization by M. M. Thomas was published in 1971 by the Christian Literature Society in Madras. Bishop Newbigin reviewed the book in the March 1971 issue of *Religion and Society* (Bangalore). It was an appreciative review, but the bishop sought clarification from the author on two important points and challenged the author's conclusions on a few crucial issues. What did Mr. Thomas mean by expressions such as "a Christ-centered secular fellowship outside the Church" and "a Christ-centered fellowship of faith and ethics in the Hindu religious community"? Can we equate, or identify, humanization with evangelization? What indeed is the nature of evangelism? This discussion, consisting of letters exchanged between Mr. Thomas and Bishop Newbigin, first appeared in *Religion and Society* for March 1972. These excerpts from the letters were published originally in *Asia Focus* (Bangkok), Volume VII, Number 4, 1972. Mr. Thomas, a lay member of the Mar Thoma Syrian Church, is director of the Christian Institute for the Study of Religion and Society in Bangalore and chairman of the World Council of Churches' Central Committee. Lesslie Newbigin is the bishop in Madras of the Church of South India.

M. M. Thomas

My starting point is that the new humanity in Christ, that is, the humanity which responds in faith and receives the liberation of Jesus Christ as Lord and Savior, transcends the Church.

217

This is a point which you seem to have no difficulty in accepting, for you say: "Clearly we must agree that the Church—meaning by that word the visible and recognizable groups of people whose names are on our various membership roles—is not to be identified with the new humanity. God's saving purpose is not limited to the Church. We may believe that the Church is the nucleus, the first-fruit, the sign and the instrument of God's purpose to unite all things in Christ, but the Church is not itself the new humanity."

Let me explain where I see the realities of faith and grace outside the Church to which the Church must open itself if it is to be the Church, the nucleus of the new humanity. I mention two areas where this sign of the wider new humanity must be looked for:

1. First, in the area of the struggles of societies for a secular human fellowship. Many of those struggles by themselves may be only within the structures of law and idealism, and therefore only self-defeating like the Tower of Babel. But not all. There are some struggles in which the men involved have come to realize the frustration of the path of self-righteousness, of principle, law and ideology, and are looking for a new path beyond it, and open themselves up to the reality of transcendent forgiveness in the secular experience of mutual forgiveness which makes love and community real at the I-Thou plane. This may not have in it the full acknowledgment of Christ as person; however, there is a partial but real acknowledgment of him. And the Church cannot be the sign of the new humanity unless it is present at this point, discerning the reality of the new humanity which is there. This is possible only if the Church itself is concerned with active participation in the struggle for secular fellowship on a Christ-centered basis. It is this plea that I made in my lecture. Indeed, the point I am making is related to what you have said in the review— namely that in the area of humanization the Church must be able to meet, outside the Church, not only "fighters" for freedom but also "bearers" of it and the grace behind it. I made the point that the fellowship within the Indian Christian community often became sour and selfish and ceased to be Christ-centered precisely because it was indifferent to its task of creating fellowship in the wider community. It was indifferent because the

Church became a closed introverted community among other such religious communities.

2. Second, among the adherents of other religions (especially of Hinduism) who have gone beyond the recognition of Christ as the ideal to the faith-response, however partial, to him as person and as "decisive for their existence," but who, however, consider that conversion to Christ does not necessarily imply conversion to the Christian community isolated from the communities in which they live but rather that it implies the building up of a Christ-centered fellowship of faith within the society, culture and religion in which they live, transforming their structures and values from within. Keshub Chander Sen's Church of the New Dispensation in the nineteenth century and the Subba Rao movement today are clear examples of this approach. There have been many individuals like Kandaswamy Chetty who sought to live as members of the Hindu community but as committed to Christ. They have been opposed to baptism because it had become—as they saw it—a sign not primarily of incorporation into Christ but of proselytism into socio-political-religious communities. Here again, how does the Church discern and open itself to and become a sign of the reality of the new humanity in Christ present outside? It can be done only by the Church extending the hand of fellowship to those across the "communal" barrier, and recognizing a form of the Church (partial, no doubt) in the Christ-centered fellowship of faith emerging outside the Church. This the Church in India has been unable to do because of its character as a closed religious community, over against other religious communities. Thereby these new emerging forms of Church life get more perverted.

BISHOP NEWBIGIN

What I really want to do is to take separately the two "areas" where signs of the wider new humanity must be looked for. I would like to take them in the reverse order, starting with the form of the new humanity within the Hindu religious community. You have developed this idea most fully, I believe on page 40 of *Salvation and Humanization*. You speak there of a

Chirst-centered fellowship of faith and ethics within the Hindu religious community in which Christ is allowed to judge and fulfill not only the cultural and social but also the religious life of the Hindu, and you add that this depends upon the assumption that faith is different from religion and that religions—like culture—can be redeemed of idolatry and self-justification and—in the process—secularized through bringing them into relation with Christ. This is a very challenging idea. I think it raises very difficult questions. For instance:

1. In what sense is it meaningful to speak of religions being secularized? In the normal meaning of these words, that which has been secularized has ceased to be religious. Do you mean that the process of secularization gradually eliminates the religious elements in the Hindu socio-religious complex, leaving only the social and cultural forms? Or do you mean that *religion* continues in a form which is both secular and Hindu? If the latter, can you say what that would mean? What does "religion" mean in this picture?

2. Can acceptance of Jesus Christ, as we know him through the Bible as the absolute Lord of all things, be combined with Hinduism as a religion? Is it not the case that such people as Chander Sen and Subba Rao have absolutely rejected many of the specifically religious elements in Hinduism?

3. I think there is (perhaps) a meaningful sense in which one can speak of Christ "judging and redeeming religions and cultures" (though I am not quite sure). But if there is, how does he do it? Has it not always been the case that an essential part of the process has been the breaking of existing socio-religious solidarities? Has the Church ever taken form in a new culture by a mere process of painless infiltration which did not involve such breaks? The ancient world was full of movements which sought to combine allegiance to Christ with maintenance of the general framework of Graeco-Roman religious thought and life. (See, e.g., Glover: *Conflict of Religions in the Early Roman Empire*, or Cochrane: *Christianity and Classical Culture*.) But it was not through any of these that the Gospel won its way in the classical world. These movements are now of historical interest only as a reminder of the struggle which was involved if allegiance to

Christ as absolute Lord was to replace the ancient socio-religious forms of life and thought.

4. Christians in the past have generally distinguished between the specifically religious elements in the total socio-cultural-religious complex and the rest, and have said that while the Church can take form within the cultural and religious milieu, whatever it may be, any religious dogma or practice which is incompatible with absolute allegiance to Christ has to be rejected at the outset. Thus the early apologists rejoiced to accept and use the ideas of the great pagan philosophers, but absolutely rejected the ancient pagan religions. Thus also De Nobili in his long arguments with the Franciscans sharply distinguished between practices which were religiously neutral and those which implied a religious belief incompatible with the Christian faith. You insist on keeping the total religious-cultural-social complex intact, and you do so by maintaining that faith is distinct from and transcends religion, though it must have a religious expression. (Logically it seems to me that you should look for a total religious-cultural-social expression of Christianity, which would be the old Christendom heresy which we both reject.) Of course everything depends upon what we mean by "religion," which is a slippery word, but if it connotes those beliefs and practices which are concerned with what we believe to be ultimate and decisive, then those religious elements in the total complex which imply another ultimate than Jesus Christ must be eliminated from anything which can be called a Christ-centered fellowship of faith.

5. You may say: "Yes, perhaps eliminated eventually, but not necessarily at the outset." If so, I would agree. This is the point—I think—which is at issue in what you say about the Church "extending the hand of fellowship" to such bodies as Subba Rao's movement. I am at one with you in believing that wherever Christ is accepted as Lord, there the Church is present in some sense. I am very happy with the radical Christo-centricity of your writing—for example, your report to the Central Committee at Addis. But would we not agree on the following?

(a) While we agree that wherever Christ is accepted as Lord, there the Church is present in some sense, nevertheless we would not be willing to relativize all our conceptions of the Church. We are bound to believe that some forms, structures, practices, and beliefs are more congruous with the Lordship of Jesus Christ than others.

(b) None of our existing churches embodies the plenitude of what the Church is intended to be.

(c) There is a mutual obligation among those who accept Jesus as Lord to carry on a continuous process of mutual criticism and correction concerning our various imperfect and partial embodiments of "what-it-is-to-be-the-Church."

(d) This mutual obligation has to find some visible form. This is what I understand the WCC, NCC, etc. to be all about.

From this I would conclude that if—for example—Subba Rao said that he wanted to bring his movement into the NCC or the WCC, we should welcome it. The question is—Would he? To judge from Baago's pamphlet it would seem that the main drive of his movement is polemic against the churches. You have rightly quoted (if I take your reference rightly) the recent admission of the Kimbaguist Church into the WCC. I am very happy about this. It is surely an illustration of the fact (which can be documented from the studies of Sundkler and Barrett) that these African independent churches are likely to move in one of two possible directions—either into the broad fellowship of churches in the ecumenical movement, or into a more and more explicit paganism.

6. This brings me to my final point. In speaking about the possibility that forms of the Church might appear within the Hindu (and presumably other) socio-religious-cultural communities, you seem to speak of separate entities unrelated to each other or to the entities which already exist and which are called churches. Jesus did not come to create a variety of unrelated groups, each expressing some particular cultural ethos. He came—as you often stress—to sum up all things. The sign, therefore, of the new humanity must include a capacity to embrace people of varying cultural backgrounds in one fellowship. It is this that seems to be vehemently rejected by the movements which you are commending to our attention. You seem to imply (e.g., the last page of *Salvation and Humanization*) that we simply have to turn our backs on the Church as it is in India and

seek a wholly new form. I don't think we differ about the need for radical reformation in the Church. But surely history teaches us that these attempts to achieve reformation by disowning the existing churches and starting something wholly new only end in new sectarianism. It would be very easy to envisage—around the year 2100 A.D.—a litter of small Indian sects embodying in a fossilized form the particular ideas about secularization, dialogue, etc., which happen to be fashionable just at the moment, comparable to the litter of American sects which are the fossilized reminders of the living religious ideas of the mid-nineteenth century. Surely we do not want that.

Here we are dealing with a quite different set of issues from those I have just discussed. We are not thinking about bodies which acknowledge Jesus and have therefore some of the character of the Church; we are dealing with men who, in the struggle for secular human fellowship, are sharing in something which we must recognize as having some of the character of the new humanity. I do not think that such groups of men and women can be described as "Christ-centered." In the sense that everything which exists has its origin and goal in Christ the Logos, they are indeed related to Christ. And we believe that they manifest the signs of his saving power to re-create man. But they are not characterized by an explicit faith in Jesus as Liberator, Lord and Savior. We might say that they are part of the new humanity, but not that they are forms of the Church. I want to discuss later the sense in which they are part of the new humanity, but meanwhile I want to take up your very important discussion on the last two pages of *Salvation and Humanization* regarding the form of the Church in a secular society.

You very rightly speak of the danger that in a secularized society, where the Church no longer has—institutionally—political responsibility, Christianity may become simply an affair of inward piety. This is the same danger which A. K. Saran foresees for Hinduism. You speak of the alternative that the Church could be—corporately, I suppose—related to society as suffering servant and witness, without coercive power, but nevertheless involved. I am sure we are agreed about this. But:

(a) What does it mean to speak of the Church (as distinct from individual Christians) suffering and witnessing? Suffering requires a body to feel pain. The text of Hebrews is relevant: "Sacrifice and offerings hast thou not desired, but a body thou hast prepared for me." There is no meaning in speaking about the sufferings of the Church unless the Church is a corporate entity—which means a sociologically recognizable reality, distinct from other realities of a similar kind, distinct from the corporate bodies of Islam or Hinduism—a body of which one can say either "I am a member" or "I am not a member." I suppose you would agree with this, though some of your phrases would seem to make it doubtful.

(b) I do not believe that the role of the Church in a secular society is primarily exercised in the corporate actions of the churches as organized bodies in the political or cultural fields— even when these actions are cleansed of ontocratic pretensions and bear the genuine marks of suffering and witness. On the contrary, I believe that it is exercised through the action of Christians as lay people, playing their roles as citizens, workers, managers, legislators, etc., not wearing the label "Christian" but deeply involved in the secular world, in the faith that God is at work there in a way which is not that of the "Christendom" pattern. We agree about this. But this means that it is the specifically religious component in the life of the Church which has to be strengthened. It is precisely in this way that the Church manifests its character as a community which transcends other sociological categories. The obedience-in-freedom of the believing Christian will be expressed in a great variety of ways—even at times in mutually contending forms of political action. The "Christian cause" will not be interpreted as one among the various political or cultural movements. But Christians will be deeply involved in them. I am sure that there is no difference of opinion between us on this. But it will mean that the character of the Church as a religious community is strengthened—for everything depends upon the constant renewal through worship, and prayer, through word and sacrament, of the living relation with Jesus himself. This means a profoundly inward and personal dimension to the Christian life which does not lead to an escape from involvement in secular affairs.

I want to say that I am completely with you in believing that the saving work of Christ is going on in those secular relationships of real community and forgiveness of which you speak. I have said that I do not think we can use the phrase "the new humanity" to describe these situations if we accept your definition of the new humanity as "the humanity which responds in faith and receives the liberation of Jesus Christ," etc. But if we define the new humanity differently, then I would agree that the phrase is correctly used to denote such situations. I think I would want to say this: that Christ's work of making men truly human after the pattern of Jesus Christ is going on in such situations and that therefore we can speak of the new humanity being manifested there even though there is not the response of explicit faith in Jesus.

What, then, of the relation of this to the Church? I would state it dialectically: on the one hand the Church cannot grow into the plenitude of its proper character unless it is completely open to such movements; on the other hand such movements will become trapped in legalism and self-justification if they are not being opened up to encounter with Jesus Christ himself as a living person.

Perhaps our differences arise because we are stressing the opposite sides of these mutually necessary propositions. You are stressing the necessity for the Church to be fully opened up to these secular movements. I am stressing the fact that if there is to be a Church at all, there must be an active effort to bring people into full commitment to Jesus through baptism and incorporation into the sacramental-congregational-liturgical life of the Church. I feel the force of your contention, and I hope I am as open to it as an aging ecclesiastic can be. I hope and believe that you share my concern that evangelism—in the sense of the open and explicit proclamation of Jesus as Savior and the invitation to men to be committed to him in the fellowship of the Church—is in danger of being left to people who do not at all understand your concern for openness. This seems to me to be one of the really dangerous things in our situation.

M. M. Thomas

It is in this context that I have raised the question of the

form of the Church in India and criticized the present form of
the Church as religious community.

1. The "religious community" of Christians in India is a
communal group, "with the religion, social structure and even
politics of the group integrated into one totality," so that if a
Hindu becomes a Christian he moves from the jurisdiction of
Hindu law to Indian Christian law and separates himself from
the Hindu community in the social, legal and religious sense.
And conversion in this context largely becomes proselytism, and
baptism is like circumcision, which is the mark of transference of
communal affiliation. I am glad that you agree that this is a
travesty of the idea of the Church.

The Church must become the bearer of Christ in all Indian
communities, and Christians should not become a separate judi-
cial-political community.

2. I note that you approve of the De Nobili experiment of
forming the Church within the Hindu community as "a fellowship which through word and sacraments was linked explicitly
and decisively with Jesus but remained sociologically part of the
surrounding Hindu community, continuing to observe caste, to
wear the thread and to carry on many traditional practices." Of
course I have some difficulties here because De Nobili separated
sociological realities entirely from renewal in Christ. It was all
right in his day, but today the nation is moving in the direction
of a casteless society. And I would emphasize the need for accepting the total milieu of Hindu religious community with the
secular impact made on it as the contemporary context for the
formation of fellowships of word and sacraments "linked explicitly and decisively with Jesus" but remaining religiously, culturally and socially part of the Hindu community.

3. The Church should have "certain given elements"—e.g.,
Scripture, creeds, sacraments and ministry—which "belong to
the proper character of the Church" in its *plenitude*. But which
Church in history has had this plenitude and all these given elements? Plenitude cannot be present in the Church in all times
and in all places, though it is proper to it. And I raised the question at Nasrapur whether it was not better to recognize a fellowship with the basic minimum of the given elements as belonging
to the historic continuity of the Church. What is that minimum

except faith-acknowledgment of the centrality of the person of Jesus Christ for the individual and social life of mankind? The growth of these fellowships to plentitude should take place within the ecumenical fellowship of churches. There are independent churches in Africa which have faith in Christ but no sacraments and which have now been accepted into the fellowship of the World Council of Churches, hoping of course that they would grow into fuller plenitude along with other churches. The Church in India can extend into the religious and secular communities of India only if we are prepared to recognize partial formation of Christ-centered fellowships as valid beginnings of the form of Church life itself in these communities. It is the only way in which the form of Church life in India could be renewed. Otherwise the rigidity in the name of plenitude in a situation which is far from having plenitude will continue to pervert the Church into a closed religious community.

BISHOP NEWBIGIN

In speaking of the Church-as-it-is you use a number of phrases such as "a socio-political-religious community," "a closed religious community over against other religious communities" and "a separate judicial community." You seem to accept the fact that there should be a Hindu religious community, and to advocate the formation of Christ-centered groups *within* this community, "remaining religiously, culturally and socially part of it." But there should *not* be a Christian community in this sense.

But in your polemic against the Church-as-it-is there are two elements which need to be distinguished. At several points you speak of the Church as a closed-in, self-regarding body. We agree, of course, in condemning this. But do we not also agree that this is the temptation of all organized bodies? I see absolutely no evidence that the alternative forms of the Church which you propose would be free from this. But—and this is my main point—you seem to tie this criticism up with another quite distinct one—namely that the Church is concerned with other things than religion, that membership involves socio-political and cultural commitments, and that this has made it impossible for the Church in India to be the sign of the new humanity for all men. You often seem to imply that these two things (self-centeredness and socio-political-cultural involvement) are necessarily tied together. I do not think they are. It is this second which is the real point for debate.

Presumably the acceptance of Jesus Christ as central and decisive creates *some* kind of solidarity among those who have this acceptance in common. If it did not do so, it would mean nothing. The question is: What is the nature of this solidarity? It has always been understood to include the practice of meeting together to celebrate with words, songs and formal actions the common faith in Jesus. How far beyond this should it extend? This question has been answered in different ways at different times and places. The earliest Church thought that the *koinonia* (common sharing) in the Spirit called for a *koinonia* in material goods such as to exclude all private property. This view did not prevail, but there has always been a sense that mutual helpfulness among believers was required by the common confession of Jesus. It is almost inevitable that some common cultural forms and some common social bonds will develop among those who are united by a strong faith in Jesus. This will be accentuated if—as in India—the society in which Christians find themselves is already an extremely closely knit unity of religious, cultural and social bonds. In other words, the "communal" character of the Indian church has been—to some extent—forced upon it by the communal character of Indian society as a whole. This is confirmed by observing that the churches formed by the same Western missions in—for example—Japan do not have this communal character.

I do not think that your statements about the Church are sociologically realistic. You seem to want a kind of Church in which membership does not break any of the other solidarities which men have. You express the desire for forms of fellowship which are explicitly linked to Jesus Christ but remain "religiously, culturally and socially part of the Hindu community." I think that this is quite unrealistic. A man who is religiously, culturally and socially part of the Hindu community is a Hindu. If, at the same time, his allegiance to Christ is accepted, that allegiance must take visible—that is social—forms. He must have *some* way of expressing the fact that he shares this ultimate allegiance with others—religious, social and cultural elements. This is why I still feel that you are really docetic in your thinking about the Church. You seem to envisage a form of Christian corporate entity which never has existed and which never could exist.

Mission
and Humanization

Peter Beyerhaus

What are the opportunities given by God in our time "to testify
to the non-Christian world about his whole purpose of love"?
Peter Beyerhaus, professor of missions at the University of Tübingen, Germany, sees "two conflicting answers to this task,
each one represented by a respectable missionary force throughout the world." The *evangelical* answer looks "for such new historical opportunities where the Gospel finds responsive populations" and then moves in with missionary resources to take
advantage of the opportunities for evangelization and Church
planting. A different answer, he believes, is represented by those
related to the Commission on World Mission and Evangelization
of the World Council of Churches who see *humanization* and
systemic change as the missionary answer today. Dr. Beyerhaus
discusses why these two concepts of missionary strategy "have so
far failed to meet each other in a complementary synthesis." In
particular, he voices "the fear on the part of the evangelicals that
the present attempts to redefine the goal of mission in terms of
humanizing the social structure reveal a decisive theological
deviation at the very heart of the Christian faith." Dr. Beyerhaus
was one of the chief architects of the 1970 "Frankfurt Declaration on the Fundamental Crisis in Christian Mission" and is the
author of *Missions: Which Way?* and *Shaken Foundations: Theological Foundations for Missions*, both published by Zonder-
van. This piece is reprinted by permission from the January 1971
International Review of Mission (Geneva).

World mission, world history and social change are inseparably interrelated in a dialectical tension. For the motive and goal of world mission is the kingdom of God, which in spite of growing resistance is also the goal of world history, and which even now is seeking to permeate human society. This destination, the kingdom in power and glory, has always been in the consciousness of Christian missions. And missions were always reminded that their obedience to the great commission was tested by their responsiveness to the opportunities of world history. For if God is the ruler of both world history and mission history, then it is clear that he directs world history in such a way that the world is continually confronted in ever new situations with the offer of salvation in Christ. Thus in each historic moment the Church in mission has the task of asking what opportunities God may give us to testify to the non-Christian world about his whole purpose of love. In thus asking it will firmly keep in mind that this purpose looks beyond the preservation of the world to its final salvation.

I

Today there are two conflicting answers to this task, each one represented by a respectable missionary force throughout the world. The pity is that they seem to be unable to find each other in a constructive synthesis.

One of them is the *evangelical* answer. Consistent with the tradition of Protestant world missions as a whole, evangelicals— I am speaking of those with a statesman-like vision—would look for such new historical opportunities where the Gospel finds responsive populations. Here they would mobilize as strong missionary forces as possible both from the indigenous churches nearby and also by recruiting new missionaries from the larger churches in the West in order to secure a maximum of new disciples. In the past, evangelicals used to call such openings revivals and ascribed them solely to the work of the Holy Spirit. Today, while not diminishing the stress on prevenient grace which is at work in such group movements, many evangelicals would admit that sociological factors may also play an important part. This is, at least, the conviction underlying the worldwide studies of the Institute of Church Growth at Fuller Theological Seminary in Pasadena, California. Anthropological and historical questions are treated with no less scholarship than theology and biblical missionary methods. The whole purpose is to find out where at present within non-Christian populations conditions appear which could make them responsive to the missionary challenge. These situations would be the main concentration points of a wise strategy of mission. This concept has been officially adopted by American evangelical missions in general at the Wheaton Congress on Worldwide Missions in 1966. Regretting their former "complacency with small results long after a larger response could have been the norm" and their "failure to take full advantage of the response of receptive peoples," the Wheaton Declaration urged "that research be carried out by nationals and missionaries in all parts of the world to learn why churches are or are not growing . . . to evaluate Church growth opportunities now overlooked and to review the role, methods and expenditures of our agencies in the light of their significance to evangelism and Church growth."[1] This strategy combines the theologically valid conviction of the absolute priority of eternal salvation with a new understanding of history as a dynamic process which conditions the *kairoi toon ethnoon*, i.e., the opportunities when people at large beecome responsive to the proclamation of the Gospel.

It cannot be denied that this evangelical view not only shares the soteriological concern of the first apostles but is verified today by major ethnic movements which can and do contribute greatly to the multiplication of Church membership in several parts of the world. Contrary to the popular impression that the advance of the world missionary movement has been brought to a standstill by nationalism and renascent indigenous religions, the evangelicals can point out that the Church today faces missionary opportunities as seldom before in its entire history.

In Africa alone during the years 1950-70 the number of Christians has risen from 20 to 50 million. In Indonesia from 1966-68 alone 400,000 people applied for Church membership, and the movement is still going on. One might object that the Indonesia Mass Movement has more political than spiritual causes. But this is exactly our point. In mission history we cannot soberly divide the motives and factors which condition the process of Christianization. The decisive question for the Church is whether it is responsive to the occasions in which God as the ruler of history demands its special attention and obedience. The Gospel has the inherent power to transform even such an inquirer who first asked for baptism with very mixed and doubtful motives. Otherwise Europe would always have remained a heathen continent!

Now evangelical mission leaders are worried that within many churches and mission societies the awareness of such evangelistic opportunities has considerably declined. As a matter of fact, as far as Western churches are concerned, the old evangelistic incentive to preach the Gospel to those who have never heard it—"that they may turn from darkness to light and from the power of Satan to God, that they may receive forgiveness of sins and a place among those who are sanctified by faith" (Acts 26:18)—seems today to be a decisive motive for missionary recruitment only in evangelical mission societies. Organizations like the Worldwide Evangelization Crusade or the United Mission to Nepal are still moved by the concern for unevangelized areas in the world which have been newly opened up for mission work.

Within the other churches, and not least within those missions which are affiliated to the Commission on World Mission and Evangelism, the evangelistic drive seems to have been more or less replaced by social-ethical interest. Not Christianization and Church planting but *humanization* and radical change of the structures of society seem to be the new ecumenical missionary strategy, at least since the preparation for Uppsala 1968. In the Draft for Section II, "Renewal in Mission," the place formerly taken by the mission fields was dedicated to the "points of tension within contemporary human existence,"[2] which means to racial strife, social upheaval or student revolts in all parts of the world. Achieving more satisfactory horizontal relations seems to have gained the upper hand over against Paul's interpretation of his apostolic ministry: "We beseech you on behalf of Christ, be reconciled *to God*" (2 Cor. 5:20). The concern caused by such apparent "displacement of their primary tasks" in ecumenical missions, as the Frankfurt Declaration later called it, caused Dr. McGavran to put the searching question to all Assembly delegates: "Will Uppsala betray the two billion?"[3]

In terms of this provocative question, converting non-Christians or rendering social service seemed to be exclusive alternatives. Maybe it was the false impression that the alternatives were in fact exclusive, so that one or the other was vigorously attacked by some and defended by others, which led to the strong polarization between "evangelicals" and "ecumenicals," between "traditionalists" and "progressives," that marked the heated deliberations in Section II.

Now the two tasks of proclamation and service form no genuine alternative in view of the total commission of the Church. Neither need they be alternatives in the task of mission. It was a committed British evangelical, Rev. J. R. W. Stott, who after Uppsala in the same "Church Growth Bulletin" proposed the new formula: "Evangelicals should proclaim the equation that 'mission = witness + service.' "[4]

In fact there is a legitimate way today to view the relation between mission, history and society from an angle different from the evangelical one sketched above. Newly-opened up geographical and ethnic areas are one form in which even today missions meet the challenge of history. Here the Church Growth Institute and the Worldwide Evangelization Crusade are right and deserve our wholehearted support. There are even today wholly untouched tribes in the valleys of central New Guinea, on the heights of Himalaya, and in the primal forests of the Amazon where the touch of cultural contact calls for a new pioneering missionary enterprise.

But we also have to consider such situations which could not be called "pioneer mission," but where new forms of mission are called for to open up new areas by witness and service. I would mention only three examples to illustrate this point:

1. One of the catch-words in Asia and Africa today is the term "nation building." Here one of the main problems is what is called in India "communalism" and in Africa "tribalism." As N. Sithole[5] has shown, it was mission itself which helped to create the spiritual foundation of modern nationalism in Africa. But since nationalism in its initial stage has been a reactionary

movement against Western colonialism, it has largely lost its unifying force in the newly independent states. Thus from the past the old unresolved frictions of tribes and castes are again emerging. They frustrate the unifying efforts of national governments and can cause such horrible fratricidal wars as in Nigeria. Who is able to point out a spiritual force which could reconcile such dissensions? Here the national and regional Christian councils have demonstrated a significance which has been taken seriously by the national governments.

2. All young nations are forced to introduce industrialization in order to solve their economic problems. But industrialization produces estrangement from the familiar patterns of life and brings forth new social antagonisms. Who will help the factory laborer to find meaning in his job at the conveyor belt? Who will encourage the various groups to see each other not as opponents but as partners? Who will exhort management not to sacrifice human personality to the principle of productivity and efficiency? All these questions point to the growing significance of industrial mission in many parts of the world.

3. Industrialization necessarily means *urbanization*. In our age of automatic production methods the migration to the towns exceeds in speed the creation of new jobs. In the slums of Calcutta, Bangkok, Lagos and Rio de Janeiro the cities are surrounded by septic belts of an uprooted proletariat with all corresponding hygienic, social and moral evils. Who helps to ameliorate these emergency situations and to integrate these stranded persons into the new society as respected citizens? The answer of the National Christian Council of Kenya was the creation of a number of exemplary community centers in Nairobi, which were built in partnership with the cooperating missions.

These three examples may serve to show how the social and political problems of the nations today put a genuine question as to whether Christian missions might be able to mobilize spiritual forces to meet them. Giving aid to people in emergency or in developmental crisis out of the love of Christ, overcoming old or new enmities through the power of reconciliation, witnessing courageously on behalf of the dignity of all discriminated persons because Jesus died for them: all these are occasions where the oral proclamation of the Gospel can be verified by the serving fellowship of love and thus demonstrate its winning power.

I myself once saw in a Nairobi community center how the Christian help given there toward the social integration of stranded migrants from the tribal areas made them very receptive to the Christian message. Each Sunday three services in different vernaculars had to be held at this center. They were so crowded that loudspeakers had to be used for the people who could not find room in the church.

In the countries of the Third World the Christian mission still meets many people who are fully prepared to listen to a religious interpretation of their social need at its deepest level. These people are aware that a new culture needs an integrating religious center. The social challenges are at the same time opportunities for genuine evangelism.

Thus we find that the two ways of developing a missionary strategy which relates the saving message to an opening historic situation need not be exclusive alternatives. If mission means crossing new frontiers, there is no reason why these frontiers should be defined only in geographical and ethnic ways. To cross social and historic frontiers can be a very legitimate missionary challenge as well.

II

What then is the decisive reason why the two concepts of a missionary strategy relevant to the present historic situation have so far failed to meet each other in a complementary synthesis?

I do not think that the main reason lies in a controversy about suitable policies. It is rather the fear on the part of the evangelicals that the present ecumenical attempts to redefine the goal of mission in terms of humanizing the social structure reveal a decisive theological deviation at the very heart of the Christian faith. The shock of the deliberations in Uppsala Section II, where evangelicals had to struggle with all their strength for such elementary Christian convictions as the need for a new birth or a biblical nurture of the congregation in mission to be included in the report, will not easily be forgotten. Neither will it be forgotten that Canon Douglas Webster had to make three

abortive attempts to get in the reference to the two billion who
had never fully heard the Christian message, until it was finally
included in the form of a somewhat reduced number.[6] According
to Douglas Webster the weakness of the report "is less in what it
said, than in what it refused to say."[7] Why was there such a
resistance to including statements which only sought to affirm
the central concern of Christian missions ever since the days of
the apostles? Could it be that social compassion has swallowed
up soteriological compassion, because the dogmatic convictions
underlying such soteriological compassion have faded away at
least with some of the most vociferous protagonists of humanization?

We have to be aware that to be open to the historical situation faces the Christian mission with an acute danger of being
led astray. For in world history we do not encounter the *Deus
revelatus* but the *Deus absconditus*. And far too easily we forget
that in world history the rule of Christ is still contested by the
prince of this world.

In past epochs missions were tempted to pervert the sign of
the cross into a symbol of imperialistic robbery. Today our
temptation is that Christians yield to the voice of syncretistic tol-
erance and perform their service silently "with no ulterior motives," as it is said. But by doing so they are bound to be subject-
ed to other motives which their non-Christian partners most
tenaciously keep in mind.

The malady which most of our major missions have never
dared to examine closely is the insidious paralysis in the biblical
convictions of many theologians and ministers in our churches.
Critical methods of exegetical research have undermined the authority of Scripture. Demythologization and existential interpretation have dissolved the concept of Christ's expiatory sacrifice
as well as the reality of his future kingdom still to be established
in power by his second coming. Situationalist views of the Bible
deprive its texts of their normative significance for faith and
ethics and reduce them to the level of answers to the socio-political problems which men in their time had to face. What remain
are some vague principles like responsibility, solidarity, openness
for the future, etc., completely abstracted from the specific histo-

ry of revelation and salvation in which they occur.

Even Jesus becomes just the prototype of an ideal social attitude, the "man for others" whose resurrection and Lordship mean hardly more than that the community of his followers is still inspired by his example. Christological affirmations are thus abstracted from the living person of Christ and interpreted as reflections of the Church about its own mission. The conclusion drawn by the members of a missiological seminar under the guidance of a well-known ecumenical theologian sounds like this: "The traditional statements about the return of Christ, that God be all in all, etc., aim functionally at man's becoming man, a goal to which Christian mission is calling and paving the way, but which it is not given for man to reach on his own."[8]

By such theological methods biblical prophecies are deprived of their realistic content. They are not disputed in their form and their original content is not directly negated, but by a process of philosophical or sociological abstraction they are transformed into anthropocentric statements which in spirit and wording appear merely to be reflections of a current humanistic ideology.

It is obvious that in such a general theological situation the question of the primacy of oral witness in the total framework of Christian mission is answered more and more skeptically.

We encounter today the strange concept that the socially desirable consequences of the Gospel will still allow us to call our historical engagement "mission" if we deliberately abstain from calling upon people to believe in Christ and to be baptized in his name. To quote the minutes of the above-mentioned missiological seminar again: "It cannot be regarded as the goal of Christian mission to 'make' non-Christians Christian, to 'convert' them, to 'win' them, etc. To practice the function of the Christian faith—in a theoretically responsible way—is the only method of spreading it. Thus to communicate Christian ideas (e.g., 'God', 'sin') and practices (e.g., prayer, worship, baptism, Eucharist) without being asked, to non-Christians and children, is an obstacle to mission. (The Christian education of children is always authoritarian. To abandon it would be a sign of *shalom*.)"[9]

The argument for defending such a form of mission without proclamation is that any form of humanization would stress the authority of Christ. Even if this is not done expressly, such a humanizing process—e.g., breaking down the barriers of caste in Indian school classes—can only be made possible by the risen Christ, who is understood to be the anonymously directing power of world history. Thus it does not matter which group actually brings about the desirable social change; they may be Christians, Marxists, Humanists or neo-Hindus. For world history as such is understood as the result of God's mission, and in the transformation of the social structures we are told to realize the features of the coming kingdom of God. From here the conclusion is not far off that historical engagement as such is already mission, i.e., the participation in the *missio Dei* in world history.

What we observe here is a most dangerous short-cut in theological reasoning. The whole concept is no longer clearly focused on two indispensable biblical data, the crucifixion and the second coming of Christ. The dialectical tension between world history and salvation history, which is expressed by these two events and which is not removed within this present eon, is overlooked. Church and mission are leveled down to the dimension of the world. In such a concept the eschatological kingdom of Christ is swallowed up by the immanent achievements of historical evolution. Even if such evolution is ascribed to the work of the anonymous Christ, we are nearer to the monistic philosophy of history of Hegel and Karl Marx than to the prophecies of the Bible.

III

The question is whether we really sacrifice something indispensable if we agree to this program. Is it not true that the coming kingdom already becomes transparent when social structures are humanized according to the will of God? Should we not be glad to observe that a number of contemporary political ideologies and syncretistic movements have received their dynamic direction by being infected with the hope of the prophetic faith of Christianity? Should we not even admit that such liberation movements could be more genuine fruits of Christian mission than many sterile younger churches? Should we not even support the revolutionary movements as our partners or agents in the struggle for better justice in the world?

Some experts like W. Freytag and Lesslie Newbigin observed long ago that most revolutionary movements bear messianic features. Some of them have even produced their own political and/or religious messiahs who have been described in terms borrowed from the pattern of Jesus of Nazareth in his struggle, suffering, death and resurrection. Here Christian missions have achieved an exciting effect which they would never have anticipated.

What hinders us from recognizing such unexpected and indirect results as legitimate fruits of mission? Why can we not really rejoice at this transformation of history which may exceed by far the social results of missions? Our reason is that here the ultimate aim is a perfect society in which there is neither demand nor room for salvation. Humanization has become separated from evangelization of the world. Man is putting himself into the center. He declares himself to be the measuring rod of all things and creates for himself a paradise without God. He is not in need of any God because he is replacing God. This "theology of the snake" is, according to Ernst Bloch,[10] the secret atheistic theme of the Bible—the emancipation of man over against the concept of a sovereign God: "Ye shall be like God." Here Bloch echoes Karl Marx who in 1841 wrote in the introduction of his doctoral thesis: "The confession of Prometheus: 'With one single word, I hate all gods' is the confession of philosophy itself, its verdict against all celestial or terrestrial gods who do not acknowledge the human self-consciousness as the highest deity. There shall be nobody besides him."[11]

Being aware of this inherent atheistic trend within the whole history of humanism, we are shocked to see how naively current ecumenical missiology can take up the concept of humanization and put it one-sidedly into the center of its motivation and goal. True enough, the New Testament does describe Jesus as the new man and the beginner of a new humanity. But this is a complementary exposition to the other, more central concept that in Jesus Christ we are meeting the pre-existent Son of God who wrought our salvation and is risen to receive our adoration and obedience. Separating these two concepts and putting his human nature into the foreground will always create the risk of perverting the Christian faith into a humanistic syncretism which at the same time removes the ontological diastasis between biblical faith and non-Christian religions and ideologies. Rather we are told along with the adherents of other "living faiths" to discover the manhood of man.

There is one text in recent ecumenical documents which goes to an unsurpassable extreme in separating the concept of humanization from the doxological and soteriological context of biblical faith. It occurred first in the American contribution to *The Church for Others*[12] and was quoted in the commentary to the Draft for Section II in Uppsala 1968:

> We have lifted up humanization as the goal of mission because we believe that more than others it communicates in our period of history the meaning of the messianic goal. In another time the goal of God's redemptive work might best have been described in terms of man turning toward God rather than in terms of God turning toward man. . . . The fundamental question was that of the true God, and the Church responded to that question by pointing to him. It was assuming that the purpose of mission was Christianization, bringing man to God through Christ and his Church. Today the fundamental question is much more that of *true* man, and the dominant concern of the missionary congregation must therefore be to point to the humanity in Christ as the goal of mission.[13]

Here, it seems to me, we are encountering nothing less than the bankruptcy of responsible missionary theology. One forgets that being missionaries means to be the heralds of a sovereign Lord who has entrusted to them an unchangeable message, the true knowledge and acceptance of which decides about the eternal life and death of its destinees. Instead the destinees themselves with their concerns determine the scope and content of the message, even if this leads to a radical stripping down of that message. In former ages people were religious and asked for the true God, and Christian missions directed them to him. Today people do not care for gods any more, but for better human relations. Thus mission does not speak of God but directs them to the humanity in Christ as the goal of history.

True, all this is done in the concern of missionary accommodation. By confining ourselves to the concept of humanization we hope to find a field of common concern with Hindus, Moslems, Marxists and Humanists. For, according to the concept of the anonymous Christ *extra muros Ecclesiae* we are already sharing in Christ if we together with them work for the humanization of mankind. Perhaps by means of dialogue, if the others ask us for the motive of our actions, they might even become disposed to accept Christ and to integrate him into their present faiths.

IV

But when arguing like this one overlooks the fact that missionary proclamation calls for a wholehearted decision. It is not possible to say "yes" to the gift and remain indifferent to the giver. It is possible, however, to reach out for the gift and to say "no" to the giver. This is what all post-Christian religions and ideologies have done. They have borrowed principles and visions from the Christian message and have enriched or transformed their own previous systems. Thus, when engaging in dialogue with representatives of such syncretistic movements we will always discover a certain degree of unanimity with them as far as situational analyses, general principles and visions of hope are concerned. But all these conversations, including the Christian-Marxist dialogue, come to a sudden end when we speak of Christ and him crucified. Maybe one does like Ernst Bloch and places his cross within the row of the thousand crosses of the followers of Spartacus at the Via Appia. But one does not accept the cross as the altar at which our guilt was expiated and our peace with God was restored. There is no bridge which leads us over from a social concept of humanization to the biblical mystery that by Christ's sacrifice we were not only vested with our true humanity according to his image, but made children of God and thus partakers of his divine life.

But because of this syncretistic rejection of the unique offer and claim of Christ, all post-Christian movements betray either a mild but intransigent or an aggressive anti-Christian character. Thus their ultimate destination is to prepare the final, dramatic conflict with the community of Christ, where the dominating figure will be the antichrist. He will fulfill the legacy of a Christless humanization program by appearing to be Christ himself. He will untie the whole of humanity under his rule, a rule which will appear to be a paradise of social justice. But this paradise will end up in terror, blood and tears.

There is one basic and fatal error in a theology of mission which locates the missionary work of God one-dimensionally in world history: it overlooks or belittles the demonological crack which runs right through history from the fall to the end of the world. Therefore it is unable to put the cross of Christ with all that it stands for in the center. Its propitiatory purpose is as much overlooked as its prototypical significance, i.e., to make us endure our own cross and the growing antagonism of the world in view of its conquest by Christ's final triumph in history at his second coming.

There is no direct road which leads from the present state of injustice through the transformation of all social structures toward a united humanity which is equated with the messianic goal. The Bible clearly teaches us that world history finds its way toward salvation only where its encounter with the way of the messengers results in the obedience of faith in Christ. Where, however, the world rejects his offer of grace and his royal authority, it definitely falls under the wrath of God and proceeds to meet its final judgment. Mission, according to Lesslie Newbigin, is the cutting edge which God introduces into the stream of history.[14] By this edge people are forced to make their decision about Christ. Thus the saved new humanity and the doomed old eon are separated. It is the specific mandate of mission to erect the cross of Christ in ever new human spheres of life. This cross is a power of salvation for those who believe, but a fragrance from death among those who are perishing (2 Cor. 2:15f.).

Fully aware of these two exit-routes at the end of world history, Christian mission will still rejoice at all truly humanizing changes in society. We evaluate them as direct or indirect effects of the ministry of reconciliation and as anticipatory reflections of the coming kingdom.

But abiding salvation is to be found only where people who were alienated from God are rescued and incorporated into the body of Christ. This determines the priorities of our missionary functions and keeps alive our hope in the coming Christ. For he himself will resolve the dialectical tension between world history and mission history. He will remove their tragic dichotomy by his final victory in the anti-Christian cataclysm of world history. Then the common goal of world history and mission history, the kingdom in power, will definitely be established.

NOTES

1. "The Wheaton Declaration," *IRM*, LV, 220, Oct. 1966, pp. 467-468.

2. *Drafts for Sections* (Geneva: World Council of Churches), p. 30.

3. "Church Growth Bulletin," Institute of Church Growth, Fuller Theological Seminary, 135 N. Oakland, Pasadena, Calif. 91101, Vol. IV, No. 5, May 1968, p. 1.

4. *Ibid.*, Vol. V. No. 2, Nov. 1968, p. 39.

5. N. Sithole, *African Nationalism* (Capetown: OUP, 1959).

6. *The Uppsala Report 1968* (Geneva: World Council of Churches), p. 32.

7. *Bible and Mission* (British and Foreign Bible Society, 1970), p.3.

8. This quotation is taken from the mimeographed minutes, p. 4, of a university seminar on mission led by Prof. H. J. Margull in the summer of 1970. [See also the article by Prof. Margull in this volume, "Mission '70—More a Venture Than Ever."—Eds.]

9. *Ibid.*, pp. 3 and 4.

10. Cf. Ernst Bloch, *Atheismus in Christentum* (Suhrkamp Verlag, 1968).

11. Karl Marx, "Über die Differenz der demokritischen und epikureischen Naturphilosophie," in *Frühe Schriften I*, edited by H. J. Lieber and P. Furth (Darmstadt, 1962), p. 3.

12. WCC, Geneva, 1968.

13. *Drafts for Sections, op. cit.*, p. 34.

14. *The Relevance of Trinitarian Doctrine for Today's Mission* (London: Edinburgh House, 1963), p. 37.

Dialogue as a
Continuing Christian Concern

S. J. Samartha

In this survey of recent developments in dialogues between Christians and people of other faiths and ideologies, S. J. Samartha discusses the theological imperative behind dialogue. "It is Christology, not 'comparative religion,' that is the basis of our concern. Our primary interest," he says, "is to be with Christ in his continuing work among men of all faiths and ideologies." Christians have an obligation to listen and learn as well as to speak and teach. In dialogue, others may help us to understand our own Christian faith better, even as our listening can be a form of proclamation in the quest for truth. This text was an address to the Central Committee of the World Council of Churches, meeting at Addis Ababa in 1971, and is reprinted by permission from *The Ecumenical Review* for April 1971, published by the World Council of Churches, Geneva, Switzerland. Dr. Samartha, a minister of the Church of South India, was formerly professor of history of religions and principal of Serampore College, West Bengal. Since 1968 he has been on the staff of the World Council of Churches and is at present the director of its Program on Dialogue with People of Living Faiths and Ideologies. He is the editor of *Living Faiths and the Ecumenical Movement* (Geneva: WCC, 1971), in which the essay is reprinted.

Dialogue is part of the living relationship between people of different faiths and ideologies as they share in the life of the community. Christians in different countries of the world are already engaged in dialogue with their neighbors. Factors in contemporary historic situations in which Christians find themselves today, and the theological imperatives of the Christian faith itself, make it necessary that this concern for dialogue be continued. Therefore, one of the essential tasks before us now is to acknowledge this fact, consider its possibilities and problems, and draw out its implications for the life and witness of the Church in a pluralistic world. What is the extent of our involvement in such encounters? What is the theological demand of the Christian faith that makes it part of our Christian obedience as we live with men of other faiths? What are the inner resources that sustain us, the criteria which judge our efforts, and the limitations beyond which dialogue ceases to be faithful dialogue? These are a few questions to which some attention should be given here.

I

The Christian interest in other religions is, of course, not new. The early Church seriously grappled with issues raised by its encounters with the religions, philosophies and cultures of the Graeco-Roman world. In recent history the well-known Missionary Conferences—Edinburgh 1910, Jerusalem 1928 and Tambaram 1938—took serious note of other religions.[1] The New Delhi Assembly in 1961 referred to "dialogue as a form of evangelism which is often effective today." [2] Uppsala 1968 pointed out that "the meeting with men of other faiths or of no faith must lead to dialogue. A Christian's dialogue with another implies neither a denial of the uniqueness of Christ, nor any loss of his own commitment to Christ, but rather that a genuinely Christian approach to others must be human, personal, relevant and humble." [3] We must also recognize Vatican II's *Declaration on the Relationship of the Church to Non-Christian Religions.*[4]

With regard to more recent meetings, at least three points may be made. First, there is an increasing participation by our Roman Catholic brethren. Whether at Kandy 1967, or Ajaltoun 1970, or Zurich 1970, Roman Catholics were present not just as observers, but as active participants, bringing in their scholarship, experience and insights from different parts of the world. There are, of course, underlying differences of theological approach, but the fact that Roman Catholics, the Orthodox and Protestants could, together as Christians, meet men of other faiths is itself important. Second, in contrast to some of the earlier debates which moved almost exclusively in Western structures of thought and procedure, not always sensitive to or illumined by insights of Christians from other situations, in recent years people from other parts of the world, particularly from Asia and Africa, with different cultural heritages and with actual experience of dialogues, have made stronger and more persistent contributions. In the period of world missionary conferences, their contributions were more or less interesting footnotes to what was largely a Western debate about other religions. Today they are chapters in the growing ecumenical book. The point that is made here is not that dialogues are more important in Asia or Africa than in the West, but that the issues raised by dialogue are not limited to particular cultural contexts, but have larger ecumenical dimensions. Third, a fact of perhaps even greater significance is the actual participation by men of other faiths in dialogues initiated by Christians. It is no more just talk *about* dialogue by Christians among themselves, but the Christian involvement in dialogue *with* them, discussion of issues in their presence and with their active participation. This does not, of course, preclude theological reflection by Christians themselves, but it is against this background that I now give a few examples of dialogues that have taken place in recent years. They are part of the historic context in which theological reflection on dialogue should take place.[5]

On June 14-16, 1962 a group of Hindu and Christian friends met in a Christian ashram near Kottayam, South India. Twenty-two people, fifteen Christians and seven Hindus, took part in the meeting. The theme was one of the most fundamental issues between Hindus and Christians touching their life and thought at the deepest level: "The Nature of Truth." It was considered under three sub-headings: the nature of truth, the knowledge of ultimate truth, and the relation of ultimate truth to life in the world. It was one of the earliest occasions in India when our Roman Catholic friends joined the Orthodox and Protestants in such a venture. Each day two half-hour periods, one in the morning and one in the evening, were set aside in which participants observed together a period of silent prayer and meditation.

It is noted that "the Hindu and Christian groups came to grips with the fundamental issues in the conversations and sought together to clarify the points of vital difference between *advaitic* (a particular school of Indian philosophy) and Christian understandings of ultimate truth, and explored the meaning of a community of concern and discourse in which dialogues on religious truths and on religious dimensions of cultural and social life could be fruitfully continued." M. M. Thomas, who took part in this dialogue, wrote: "Building a community of discourse with our Hindu brethren is essential if any communication is to take place between Christians and Hindus."[6]

In 1968, on January 27 and 28, at the end of the week of prayer for Christian unity, a group of Roman Catholic, Orthodox and Protestant Christians met together with a group of Muslims at Selly Oak College, Birmingham, U.K. It is significant that such a meeting was possible in Birmingham where people of different religious communities are living together and where, as a result, several problems have come up very sharply in recent years. A few quotations from the report are given here.[7] With the long and violent history of Christian-Muslim relations in Europe and with the memories of the crusades not forgotten, the group felt it necessary to say: "We must never deal with each other simply as stereotyped or pigeon-holed representatives of another tradition. We must seek to know each other and respect each other as individuals. . . . We should be less conscious of our different labels as 'Christians' and 'Muslims' than of our faithfulness to the one God. . . . There might be paradox and even tension in our mutual understanding, but it could be constructive tension." In the context of their day-to-day living in a multi-religious society with all its problems and tensions, two points emerged from the dialogue—the emphasis on certain beliefs common to the Christian and the Muslim, and the need, expressed with a sense of urgency, to continue friendly relations. The report goes on to say: "There was great need for continuing discussion and increasing society's awareness of the relevance of our common assumptions as Muslims and Christians. The supremacy of God, the availability of his revealed guidance, the expectation of an after-life, the definition of right and wrong, of truth and falsehood, the sanctity of family life and all life—such are the issues we must maintain in an increasingly agnostic world. We look forward to further contacts and to working for and praying for a deeper reconciliation of Muslims and Christians in our service to men and to God, in our dialogue with each other and with God."

Several dialogues between Christians and Jews have taken place in recent years. These conversations have not been easy. This is mainly because of historical reasons derived from the history of the Church in the West, partly because of theological differences, and now mostly because of political factors. On October 27-30, 1970, a meeting convened by the International Jewish Committee on Inter-Religious Consultations and the World Council of Churches was held in Lugano, Switzerland. The thirty participants came from England, France, Germany, Holland, India, Israel, Switzerland and the United States of America. The theme of the meeting, mutually agreed to, was "The Quest for World Community—Jewish and Christian Perspectives." Questions touching particularity and pluralism and the relationship between religion, peoplehood, nation-state and land were discussed from different points of view in an atmosphere of friendliness and openness, though not free from tensions generated by strongly divergent views. The fact that Christians and Jews could read together some of the psalms at the beginning of each day emphasized the common roots of our spiritual heritage which, however, needs to be cultivated afresh with new tools and a larger vision of mankind in the Bible, which includes not only Abraham, Isaac and Jacob, but also Adam and Noah.

These examples have been of bilateral conversations between Christians and people of one other faith. But there have also been meetings in which people of several different faiths came together. On October 8-9, 1965, some 30 representatives from six major religions in Korea—Buddhism, Won-Buddhism, Confucianism, Chondoism, Catholicism and Protestantism—gathered together for a two-day session to consider the common tasks before them. The emphasis was not on the "spirituality" of particular religions, but on what men of different religious persuasions could contribute to the solution of the pressing problems of the country. The religions were strongly criticized for their reluctance to be open, and were asked to cooperate with each other in practical tasks. The different religions, it was pointed out, claim to have a message, "and believe that they are called to a mission to save the rest of the world, though they are not yet ready to join the new world which calls us to have open dialogue with our neighbors. . . . This world is our common denominator upon which we are able to communicate with each other. And for us, in Korea, it is this troublesome nation with all its problems that is our field, where we can find the common task for all Korean religions."

Invitations come with increasing frequency to the World Council of Churches to take part in world conferences on religion, some of which deal with specific issues. Such a World Conference on Religion and Peace met in Kyoto, Japan, this year from October 16-22. It was attended by 285 persons belonging to ten major religions and coming from 36 countries. "Blue turbaned Sikh, Orthodox priest with flowing robe and hood, fez-wearing Muslim, shaven-headed Buddhist monk, business-suited rabbi, clergy-collared Protestant, crucifix-adorned Catholic archbishop, orange-robed Hindu swami—they were all there" (*Japan Christian News*, No. 376, Oct. 30, 1970). A Roman Catholic archbishop from India was the chairman of the conference, and among the considerable number of Christians present there were four members of the World Council staff and several who belong to its constituent churches and highest committees. Lest it be misunderstood that this conference was just another "parliament of religions" where the patience of the participants is tested by the number and length of the speeches, it must immediately be pointed out that the main focus was on the practical possibilities of peace, a theme that was discussed in relation to three specific areas—human rights, disarmament and development. The conference message said that they had all come together "in peace out of a common concern for peace" (Report: *World Conference on Religion and Peace*, WCRP/Doc. -030, Kyoto, Japan, October 22, 1970).

The Ajaltoun Consultation on the theme "Dialogue between

Men of Living Faiths," held on March 16-25, 1970, was authorized by the Central Committee at its meeting in Canterbury in August 1969. It took the form of a conversation between Hindus, Buddhists, Christians and Muslims regarding recent experiences and future possibilities of dialogue. The forty participants came from seventeen different countries. The following are some excerpts from the Ajaltoun Memorandum: "The particular object of the Consultation was to gather the experiences of bilateral conversations between Christians and men of the major faiths of Asia, with the full participation of members of these faiths, to experiment with a multi-lateral meeting and to see what could be learned for future relations between people of living faiths. . . . It was the experience of the Consultation that something very new had been embarked upon. It was noted that this was the first time that men of these four faiths had been brought together under the auspices of the World Council of Churches. . . . What was experienced together was felt to be very positive, a matter of general thankfulness and something to be carried forward urgently. . . . The keynote of the Consultation was the understanding that a full and loyal commitment to one's own faith did not stand in the way of dialogue. On the contrary, it was our faith which was the very basis of, and driving force to, intensification of dialogue and a search for common action between members of various faiths."[8]

II

These are a few selected examples of dialogues which have recently taken place in different parts of the world that provide us with the historic context in which we find ourselves today. Two brief observations must be made, however, to put them in a wider perspective. First, there is the question of ideologies, particularly of Marxism. There has also been a series of dialogues between Christians and Marxists. It is important to note, however, that ideologies like Marxism cut across the boundaries of traditional religions, challenging their assumptions, questioning their structures and demanding that they be more concerned with this world and human life. It would be unwise to form "a religious alliance" against ideologies in order to save and to perpetuate traditional religious institutions. But the questions raised by Marxism must be faced within the context of communities where people of different faiths and ideologies seek to live together and look for resources to build their common life.

Second, the impression should not be given that all dialogues are intellectual discourses on "talking" about religious matters. There have also been meetings where no papers were read, where tired vocal cords were exercised to the minimum and where serious efforts were made to break through the structures of language, concepts and debate. Even within "structured" dialogues, people tried to open themselves up to the symbols of religious life and practice, particularly to music and art, to devotion, meditation and the controlled use of silence. But one should recognize that verbal communication is also an essential part of dialogue for sharing in theological ideas, religious experience and practical concerns, without which it is difficult to build up a community of discourse and common involvement.

In all this, the fact that Christians—Roman Catholic, Orthodox and Protestant—are already in dialogue with men of other faiths and are therefore committed to accept its perils and promises is obvious. This must be said even while noting that we are at the beginning of this venture and that, therefore, expectations should not be raised which cannot soon be fulfilled, but which require patient nurturing of new relationships. Conditions that call for dialogue are to be found, however, not just in the countries of Asia and Africa, but also in the West. The presence of settled communities of other faiths in countries that have been traditionally Christian, large groups of migrant workers, thousands of foreign students and many teachers, people connected with international organizations, the "yoga" schools and "centers" of some of the religions of the East in the major cities of the world—all these cannot be ignored, particularly the impression they make on young people and those who reject the institutions of traditional Christianity.[9] Therefore, situations that demand dialogue are not just distant phenomena in some far-off corners of the East, but are actually present next-door as challenges and opportunities.

Further, with great varieties in cultural background and historic situation, and with highly complex attitudes toward the basic questions of life, there is not one single approach to dialogue, although some mutually acceptable frame of reference is essential. Christians themselves—Roman Catholic, Orthodox and Protestant—bring to dialogue different cultural heritages and theological traditions, and therefore it would be most unwise to expect or demand from them unanimity on particular points. People of other faiths have their own approaches to dialogue. Some tend to enter into it on the basis of common human concerns which they feel need urgent cooperative attention. Others participate in it on the assumption of an acknowledged "religious" dimension in life which, according to them, needs to be given priority. Still others, who feel uneasy about some of the consequences of secularization and who are deeply worried about the effects of technology on man's inner life, enter into dialogue in search of "spiritual" resources to guide and shape the quality of human life. Whatever the differences of basis and approach to dialogue on the part of Christians and men of other faiths, answers to some of the vexed questions must be sought in the experience of dialogue itself and not by remaining outside it. Therefore, dialogue should take place in freedom. Without the freedom to be committed to one's own faith and to be open to that of another to witness, to change and to be changed, genuine dialogue would be impossible.

There is a further point that emerges out of the experience of dialogue which must not be forgotten. This is the element of the sinful and the demonic which is present in all human encounters. Therefore, no dialogue can ever be automatically "successful." A concrete example can be given here from India where, generally speaking, it is easy to have dialogue with Hindus. But twice in one year, plans made for a meeting between Hindus and Christians in a university town in North India, which is also a famous pilgrim center, had to be cancelled. The following quotations from the letter of a Hindu friend indicate some of the reasons. Politely declining the Christian invitation, the Hindu friend wrote to his Christian *bhai* (brother): "Do not think that I am against dialogue. . . . On the contrary, I am fully convinced that dialogue is an essential part of human life, and therefore of religious life itself. . . . Yet, to be frank with you, there is something which makes me uneasy in the way in which you Christians are now trying so eagerly to enter into official and formal dialogue with us. Have you already forgotten that what you call 'inter-faith dialogue' is quite a new feature in your understanding and practice of Christianity? Until a few years ago, and often still today, your relations with us were confined either to merely the social plane or to preaching in order to convert us to your *dharma*. . . . For all matters concerning *dharma* you were deadly against us, violently or stealthily according to cases. It was plain to see from your preaching to old Christians or prospective converts, or from your, at best, condescending attitude toward us in your pamphlets and magazines. And the pity was that your attacks and derogatory remarks were founded in sheer ignorance of what we really are, or what we believe and worship. . . . The main obstacles to real dialogue are, on the one hand, a feeling of superiority and, on the other, the fear of losing one's identity."

These are strong words indeed, but they do indicate how fear and distrust can ruin the conditions for genuine dialogue and why openness and love are absolutely essential in our relationships. Some people of other faiths suspect that dialogue is simply a new subtle Christian tool for mission that is being forged in the post-colonial era. On the other hand, there are some Christians who fear that dialogue with men of other faiths is a betrayal of mission and disobedience to the command to proclaim the Gospel. How do we express our obedience to Christ in truth and love, taking into account both these fears? The fear of losing one's identity is experienced not only by Christians, but also by men of other faiths. How do we bring together identity and community in these situations? None of these questions can be discussed in a purely academic way. It is in the living context of continuing dialogue that the meaning of identity should be sought. As Bishop Matthews remarks: "An unseemly anxiety to preserve our heritage is to lose it and, at the same time, to attempt to limit God; but a willingness finally to risk even the loss of our heritage in the service of God and man is to find it. When there is a readiness to risk all, God may be trusted to be faithful in giving all back again in a renewed and enlarged perspective."[10]

These matters lead us to the basic question to which reference was made in the very beginning of this address: the imperative in the Christian faith itself that constrains us to enter into dialogue. Visser't Hooft rightly remarks: "The pluralistic world throws us all back on the primary source of our faith and forces us to take a new look at the world around us. Thus pluralism can provide a real opportunity for a new united witness of the whole Church of Christ in and to the whole world."[11]

III

The fundamental question then is this: "Why are we, as Christians, in dialogue with men of other faiths at all?" It is not enough to merely describe our recent engagements or to give pragmatic reasons for our involvement in the common human concerns of contemporary history. These are, of course, important and provide the context for our obedience, but our concern in dialogue itself should not be determined by intermittent responses to the changing pressures of the world, but in obedience to the Lord and in accordance with the guidance of the Holy Spirit. "A pilgrim people must maintain their differentia as pilgrims," wrote D. T. Niles, "but they must belong to the society among whom their journey is set."[12] Dialogue is one of the crucial areas of relationships between Christians and men of other faiths today where sustained theological reflection must continue not in the isolation of academic discussions, but in the midst of our life together in the community where all are pilgrims on the high roads of modern life.

There are at least three theological reasons why dialogue is and ought to be a continuing Christian concern. First, God in Jesus Christ has himself entered into relationship with men of all faiths and all ages, offering the good news of salvation. The incarnation is God's dialogue with men. To be in dialogue is, therefore, to be part of God's continuing work among us and our fellow men. Second, the offer of a true community inherent in the Gospel, through forgiveness, reconciliation and a new creation, and of which the Church is a sign and a symbol, inevitably leads to dialogue. The freedom and love which Christ offers constrain us to be in fellowship with strangers so that all may become fellow citizens in the household of God. Third, there is the promise of Jesus Christ that the Holy Spirit will lead us into all truth. Since truth, in the biblical understanding, is not propositional but relational, and is to be sought not in the isolation of lonely meditation, but in the living, personal confrontation between God and man, and men and men, dialogue becomes one of the means of the quest for truth. And because Christians cannot claim to have a monopoly of truth, we need to meet men of other faiths and ideologies as part of our trust in and obedience to the promise of Christ.

It is sometimes said that the word "dialogue" is not found in the Bible and that, therefore, it lacks biblical authority. However, there are quite a few other words in the contemporary ecumenical vocabulary which also are not found in the Bible. It has already been said that by dialogue we do not mean just detached, intellectual discourse. While the noun "dialogue" itself is not found in the Bible, the warm relationships and the intense personal encounters suggested by the active verb are very much in evidence throughout the Bible. God's dealings with his people and the nations, the very relationship and obligations implied in the covenant both with Noah and with Abraham, the work of kings and judges, of prophets and priests, the Book of Job, the writings of the prophets and some of the psalms where people talk back and forth to God—surely these do not suggest a one-way traffic of monologues from on high. In the New Testament too, where we see different ways in which our Lord deals with people, the way of dialogue is not contrary to the spirit in which he dealt with Nicodemus, the Samaritan woman, the centurion and his own disciples throughout his ministry. There are occasions, of course, when he refuses to be drawn into discussions and when his presence divides people; therefore, one should not overdo this and claim that everything in the Bible is dialogue. But the Bible gives considerable support to those who do not wish to be theological bulldozers trying to push through the jungle of religions and seeking to flatten mountains of ideologies.

Therefore, there are sound theological reasons why dialogue should be a continuing Christian concern. The basis on which Christians enter into and continue their dialogue with others is their faith in Jesus Christ, the Son of God, who has become man on behalf of all men, of all ages and of all cultures. He is "the true light that enlightens every man" (Jn. 1:9); he is the Word become flesh, "full of grace and truth" (Jn. 1:14); he is the one through whom God "was reconciling the world to himself" (2 Cor. 5:19); he is the one who became obedient unto death, "even the death on a cross" and therefore was "highly exalted" (Phil. 2:8-9); and through him has God made known the mystery of his will "to unite all things in him, things in heaven and things on earth" (Eph. 1:10). It is Christology, not "comparative religion," that is the basis of our concern. Our primary interest is not in "inter-religious conferences"; it is to be with Christ in his continuing work among men of all faiths and ideologies. Christ draws us out of our isolation into closer relationship with all men. In his name people have gone to the ends of the earth as humble participants in his continuing redeeming activity in history. He releases us from all kinds of bondage, including bondage to the safety of the group which shares the same faith, in order to enter into full and free relationship with others. Faith in Jesus Christ involves a way of life that demands obedience as well as a view of life that influences our understanding of God, our neighbors and the world of nature and history of which we are an inextricable part. Christian participation in dialogue is, therefore, part of the concrete living out of the view of life and the way of life that stem from faith in Jesus Christ. "It is *because* of faith in God through Jesus Christ and *because* of our belief in the reality of creation, the offer of redemption, and the love of God shown in the incarnation that we seek a positive relationship with men of other faiths."[13]

Further, there is another aspect to the imperative of the Christian faith which undergirds and directs the quest for community through dialogue. One of the historic consequences of the ministry of Jesus Christ—his life, death and resurrection—is the coming into being of the Christian Church, a community of people bound in fellowship to each other through faith in him. Working for and building up human communities is never easy because of the persistence of sin in all structures of human life. When, in multi-religious societies, religious boundaries are sanctified and perpetuated by tradition, religions themselves become walls of separation rather than bridges of understanding between people. Therefore, the quest for community today cuts across these boundaries, and persons of different faiths reach out to form new communities of greater freedom and love. One of the ways in which Christians can be deeply involved in this struggle is through dialogue. Therefore, dialogue should not be regarded as just a hurried, post-colonial attempt to rub off the smell of colonialism that is still sticking to most of us. Neither is it a tool to show that we identify ourselves with our neighbors through talking about their faiths and quoting their scriptures. Still less should it be considered as merely an emotional reaction to a triumphalistic understanding of mission in the past. It is more than that; it is the expression of our faith in Jesus Christ in and through life in the community. "Christ is our peace, who has made us both one, and has broken down the dividing wall of hostility . . . for through him we both have access in one Spirit to the Father. So then you are no longer strangers and sojourners, but you are fellow citizens with the saints and members of the household of God," says the apostle (Eph. 2:14, 18-19). For Christians, the fight against all that destroys true community, the quest for spiritual resources to undergird all efforts to build community, and the search for the ultimate meaning of truly human existence in community cannot be separated from faith in Jesus Christ. Therefore, Christians must at all times be actively involved in building up a truly universal community of freedom and love.

A further point that needs to be recognized here is our faith in the promise of Jesus Christ about the Holy Spirit: "When the Spirit of truth comes, he will guide you into all truth; for he will not speak of his own authority, but whatever he hears he will speak, and he will declare to you the things that are to come" (Jn. 16:13). This promise not only makes it necessary for us to enter into dialogue, but also to continue in it without fear, but with full expectation and openness. It is not claimed that dialogue is the only way in this quest for truth, nor is it forgotten that discovery of truth is not inevitable. Possibilities of error, distortion and confusion are as present in situations of dialogue as in any human situation. Therefore, one must recognize that there is no guarantee that all dialogues shall automatically lead the participants into fuller truth. But the way in which truth is revealed, understood and communicated in the Bible makes it clear that one should look for "things that are to come" in the areas of personal relationships with God and our fellow men. Dialogue with men of other faiths and ideologies can, therefore, be regarded as at least one of the possibilities open to those who are willing to undertake the journey. Those who fear that the train of truth might be in danger of derailment should note that obedience to truth already revealed in Jesus Christ and trust in his promises outweigh the risks that are present in all human adventures. Our hope in dialogue lies in the continuing work of the Holy Spirit in judgment, in mercy and in new creation.

At this hour of history when the destinies of all people everywhere—and not only of Christians—are being drawn together as never before, and when, because of the massive power of impersonal forces, the need to recognize the ultimate source of man's personal being and community life is so urgent, dialogue offers a helpful opportunity for the renewal of that truly religious quest which Christians believe to be fulfilled by God in Jesus Christ. Therefore, Christians cannot and should not at this juncture withdraw from dialogue; on the contrary, there is every reason to continue in it, to extend it and to deepen it. However, it is only through the guidance of the Holy Spirit, who may lead us into areas as yet strange and unfamiliar to us, and through obedience to Jesus Christ, the crucified and risen Lord, which may mean joining the traffic across the borders beyond which we have not ventured so far, that the continuing Christian dialogue can remain truly faithful dialogue.

NOTES

1. See *Edinburgh 1910: An Account and Interpretation of the World Missionary Conference* by W. H. T. Gairdner (London, 1910)—two sections: Chapter VII, "Carrying the Gospel to All the Non-Christian World," pp. 68ff and Chapter X, "The Missionary Message in Relation to the Non-Christian Religions," pp. 134 ff. *The Christian Message: Jerusalem Report*, Vol. I (London: Oxford University Press, 1928) deals with "The Value of Religious Values in Non-Christian Religions" on pp. 417ff and "Secular Civilization and the Christian Faith" on pp. 284ff. *The Authority of Faith*, Vol. I (International Missionary Council, 1939),

Papers and Findings of the Madras Meeting; see particularly "Findings," pp. 169ff.

2. *New Delhi Report* (London: S.C.M. Press, 1961), Section III, "Witness," p. 84.

3. *The Uppsala Report 1968* (Geneva: World Council of Churches, 1968), p. 29.

4. *The Documents of Vatican II* (New York: Guild Press, 1966), pp. 660ff.

5. The following meetings are referred to in the text: Christian-Hindu, Kottayam, India, Oct. 14-16, 1962; Christian-Muslim, Birmingham, UK, Jan. 27-28, 1968; Christian-Jewish, Lugano, Switzerland, Oct. 27-30, 1970; Christian-Buddhist-Confucian, Seoul, Korea, Oct. 8-19, 1967; World Conference on Religion and Peace, Kyoto, Japan, Oct. 16-22, 1970; and Hindu, Buddhist, Christian and Muslim, Ajaltoun, Lebanon, March 16-25, 1970.

6. M. M. Thomas, *Religion and Life*, Bangalore, Vol. IX, No. 3, Sept. 1962, pp 2ff.

7. All quotations, unless otherwise indicated, are from written reports by actual participants. It is hoped that some of the reports will be published in full before long.

8. *Study Encounter*, Vol. VI, No. 2, 1970, pp. 97-106.

9. There are about 600,000 Muslims in Canada and the United States, 120,000 of them clustered around New York City. The Federation of Islamic Associations in the USA and Canada has planned a sixteen million dollar culture center in New York City (*Religious News Service*, New York, July 15, 1969, p. 10). There are about 500,000 Buddhists in the USA, 8,000 in Germany and 5,000 in England (article by Harty Thomsen, "Non-Buddhist Buddhism and Non-Christian Christianity in Japan," in *Syncretism*, Sven S. Hartman, ed. (Stockholm: Almqvist & Wiksell, 1969, p. 128). In certain parts of Britain, with communities of Hindus, Buddhists, Muslims and Sikhs living with Christian neighbors, the question of religious education in schools has now become more complicated (see *Learning for Living: A Journal of Christian Education*, London, January 1969, Vol. 8, No. 3, article by Mrs. Teresina Havens, p. 31, and *World Faith*, London, No. 81, Autumn 1970, "Statement on Religious Education," pp. 20f).

10. James K. Matthews, *A Church Truly Catholic* (New York, 1969), p. 160.

11. *Ecumenical Review*, Vol. XVIII, April 1966, No. 2, article "Pluralism, Temptation or Opportunity?", p. 149.

12. D. T. Niles, *Upon the Earth* (London: Lutterworth, 1962), p. 79.

13. *International Review of Mission*, Vol. LIX, No. 236, Oct. 1970, theme: Faithful Dialogue, p. 384.

Theological and Missiological Implications of China's Revolution

Donald E. MacInnis

The prospect of rapprochement with China—qualified now by a new cultural revolution—has generated enormous interest in the West about what has taken place in that land of 800 million persons from which much of the West has been cut off for twenty-two years. Many American Christians, in particular, have never been able to understand what happened to their largest overseas mission field, where by the end of 1952 the number of missionaries had dropped from a peak of 10,000 to zero. Among "China watchers" in the West, few are better able to interpret China events than Donald E. MacInnis, who had three periods of missionary service in China (the last in Foochow in 1948-49), then was in Taiwan from 1953-66, and is now director of the China Program for the National Council of Churches in the United States. MacInnis (whose book *Religious Policy and Practice in Communist China: A Documentary History* is a basic text in this field) sees religious analogies in what is happening in China today and asks, in view of what has been achieved, whether "China has created its own secular religion with a dynamic for moral transformation that outstrips the institutional church." He reminds Christians that "if God works within the secular history of the world . . . then we must believe that his saving action for his people in China has never ceased." Certainly there are important lessons to be learned from the China experience that will benefit the Christian mission in other developing nations. Dr. MacInnis read this paper to the 1973 annual meeting of the American Society of Missiology, and it first appeared in the October 1973 issue of the ASM's quarterly journal, *Missiology: An International Review* (Pasadena, California).

For many years following the replacement of the Nationalist government of Chiang Kai-shek by the Communist government of Mao Tse-tung, most Americans, deeply influenced by the cold war mentality, took a bleak and somber view of the People's Republic of China. Americans acquiesced to Senator Joe McCarthy's purge of our top China specialists in the State Department, several of them sons of missionaries. They were driven from their jobs because, as we now know, they recognized the true nature of the Communist revolution as a broad popular uprising under Communist leadership against intolerable injustices, corruption and human misery. In the 1950's Americans were not ready or willing to see beyond the presumed threat of an international Communist conspiracy directed from Moscow. Today China and Soviet Russia are bitter enemies, while Americans and Chinese visit each other's countries in a climate of open cordiality.

American Christians had an added problem in understanding the events of those years, for our largest mission field had been China. By the end of 1952 the number of missionaries serving in China had dropped from a peak of nearly 10,000 to zero. Many Americans, conditioned by reports about Stalin's Russia, expected nothing but disaster for the Chinese people. However, outside observers now report a different story.

Recent visitors to China are impressed with many material changes in the face of the land and the vastly improved standard of living for the people. But their most vivid impressions, especially for those who have lived in the old China, are the changes in attitudes, values and the spirit of the people. James Reston, senior editor of the *New York Times*, was overwhelmed by "the staggering thing that modern China is trying to do. They're not trying merely to revolutionize people and establish a sense of social conscience, but they're really trying to change the character of these people. The place is one vast school of moral philosophy."

Most of the values of the new China do not clash with our own. Dr. Han Suyin, writing for Americans, speaks of an immediacy of understanding of new China by visiting Americans, "astonishing in its vivid depth of feeling." She discovers a warm people-to-people affinity rooted in common attitudes and values, the first being a respect and yearning for morality.

The Puritan tradition in the West matches in many respects a Chinese moral tradition which pre-dates the Communists, but which since 1949 has been raised to the level of top national priority. Visitors to China marvel at the code of honesty, the social discipline, the lack of public corruption, crime and violence, the absence of pornography and sex exploitation. Miss Han alludes to the "old American dream," the hunger for moral regeneration, for goodness and virtue to become again exciting, and the search by youth for a new, moral revolution and sense of purpose. The slogans of the recent cultural revolution still dominate the public scene. "Fight selfishness" and "Serve the people" appeal to Westerners appalled at the squalor of our human relations, the loss of community concern and the alienation of youth.

If this is true, we ask, can such profound and basically "spiritual" changes take place without the witness and leadership of an authentic religious community? Or is it true, as some observers believe, that China has created its own secular religion with a dynamic for moral transformation that outperforms the institutional Church?

Americans, totally cut off from China for twenty-two years, are hungry for authentic information and insights about the revolutionary changes that have transformed a once-bankrupt nation. Although an estimated several hundred thousand visa applications have been filed with the Chinese authorities, only about 3,000 Americans have visited China since the ping pong team's tour in 1971. There are obvious limitations on what they can see and learn in a visit of four weeks. Yet it is essential for us to begin to understand what happened in China between 1950 and 1973.

What is the real China today? Americans have been bombarded with a range of views and opinions, from uncritical partisans of new China to the bitter critics. The one voice we have scarcely heard is that of the Chinese themselves. This is an historical problem. We have looked at China through lenses manufactured in the USA, while the Chinese have viewed us from their own ideological assumptions. However, since Mr. Nixon's visit and the new climate of rapprochement, the Chinese press has been totally devoid of pejorative news stories or references about the United States. At the same time distinguished and respected Americans, like James Reston, Ambassador John K. Galbraith, Professor Ross Terrill and Barbara Tuchman have written vivid and compelling first-hand reports on their impressions of China today.

Yet these reports by Americans are still not the full story. Nor do they necessarily reflect the Chinese view of what happened to them and their nation. American Christians, deeply concerned for China's millions and for friendly people-to-people relations with them, need to understand why a tiny revolutionary party, organized by a handful of men in 1921 and with only minimal help through the years from the Soviet Union, could sweep to power with almost no opposition. We need to know, from their viewpoint, why religion was seen to be superfluous and diversionary to the main tasks of unifying a prostrate, disintegrated nation. If we can see that, then it will be possible to move beyond the mental blockage posed by the loss of our largest single mission field, the image of violence and suffering in the revolutionary turnover period, and the cold war assumptions that ruled our thinking for many years following the Korean War.

My assumption is that we do want to move beyond that sterile and static position to a new and open search for understanding of God's on-going action in today's world, including China. We find ourselves in an agonizing struggle for objectivity as we consider, on the one hand, the diminution of the Church in China, while we read authentic reports of remarkable achievements in solving problems of famine, disease, poverty, illiteracy and mass misery. We are gripped by inner tension as we consider the broad gains in social justice, public health, education and social services for the masses of the Chinese people, achievements made by a secular state which at the same time denigrates institutional religion and allows no foreign missionaries or evangelism. But even on our own Christian "turf," in the area of values, morality and compassionate human relations, James Reston and others tell us that China challenges conventional religion.

How do you and I view China? Can we accept the fact that the People's Republic of China is not just another dynasty whose cycle will run out like all the others, opening doors once more for free access to China by foreigners? Stanley Mooneyham, editor of *World Vision* magazine, in response to a form letter asking him: "Will you be one of the preachers and captain one of the 1,000 three-man teams for an evangelistic crusade in one of the 1,000 cities of China?" wrote in June, 1971:

This reminds me of a question asked by a sensitive Asian Christian recently: "Does God always have to come through New York?"

The evangelical opportunists—well-meaning and fired by zeal, but with little knowledge—will rush their crash programs into the marketplace to take advantage of the awakened Christian interest in China. I applaud their burden and zeal. I am appalled by their huckster approach. For those who would now rush to kick down the Bamboo Curtain . . . some words of caution are in order.

First almost nothing has changed in China, except that China wants some limited contact with the rest of the world on her terms. . . . Second (and paradoxically), almost everything has changed in China. There is little or no indication that we [Americans] understand this. Time did not stop in China when the Communists came to power. The social and cultural landscape has been radically altered. Unless we find out how and to what extent China has changed, we will waste valuable time preparing to evangelize the China of 1948 which no longer exists. We must do our homework, a discipline for which evangelicals are not largely known.

The People's Republic of China is not just another in an endless cycle of China's imperial dynasties. Profound changes have transformed the psycho-cultural identity of the Chinese people. No mere change in top leadership (which will come, of course) can ever reverse that. The recent cultural revolution was far more than a political campaign or power struggle. The goal was a massive shift in psycho-historical perceptions, a virtual spiritual conversion of China's millions. The first of the sixteen points in the 1966 Communiqué that launched the cultural revolution began: "The current great proletarian cultural revolution is a great revolution that touches people to their very souls."

It appears that China's youth, mobilized in 1966 into militant groups of Red Guards across the nation, over-responded to the summons to attack the "four olds"—the remnant traces of bourgeois feudalism: old ideas, old culture, old customs and old habits. In a widespread and indiscriminate assault on every remaining sector of pre-revolutionary culture, Buddhist temples, Moslem mosques and Christian churches were closed by roving Red Guard groups. Religious scriptures and objects of all kinds were seized and destroyed, and clergy and believers were harassed. The phenomenon of the Red Guards peaked in 1967; since then they have scarcely been mentioned. In the past two or three years China's leaders and press have condemned what is now called ultra-leftism or over-zealousness. One by-product of this new policy is the gradual reopening of some Buddhist temples and monasteries, Moslem mosques and a few Christian churches.

But there is no assurance that institutional religion will be allowed to function openly and freely. Although the Constitution guarantees "freedom of religious belief," it also guarantees "freedom not to believe." Evangelism outside one's church or temple or home has not been permitted since 1951. Yet public religious worship under severe limitations did continue up to the Red Guard period in 1966. There is no evidence that China's leaders made organized religion a particular target during the three-year period of the Cultural Revolution. Religion is not mentioned in the sixteen-point Communiqué, nor has Chairman Mao or any other leader spoken of religion in subsequent communiqués or directives. One concludes that China's religious believers, by 1966, were seen to be either thoroughly absorbed in the collective tasks of socialist nation-building, or too insignificant in numbers or influence to pose any challenge.

Although Maoism is not a religion, and Mao himself scorns the cult of Mao that flourished a few years back, there are religious analogies in China today. Leaving aside the more obvious and superficial analogies (a scripture, a canon, a dogma, rituals, etc.), revolutionary China has its own self-contained belief system which embraces a creation theology, a soteriology and an eschatology. Mao's concept of continuing revolution, based on Marx's dialectic view of history and Mao's own elaboration of that theory in his essay "On Contradictions," is both an analysis of historical origins and growth, and a dynamic ideology for transforming human history—a secular "creation theology" reminiscent of Teilhard de Chardin's.

The official doctrine in China today affirms a theory of universal salvation that took its first great step with China's "liberation" in 1949. The Chinese believe that class struggle is central to the present stage of transition to Communism, and that the individual, regardless of class background, can be transformed; "dou-pi-gai"—struggle-criticism-transformation—is a process of self-analysis and encounter-group struggle that is designed to correct bourgeois, individualistic and selfish attitudes. Since, theoretically, every person can be transformed (saved), then society, the nation and the world can be saved. The goal is to change one's central concern from "self" to concern for others; from the self and family as one's focus of loyalty and commitment, to the collective, the people. "Serve the People" is the title of Chairman Mao's best-known essay.

Finally there is a secular eschatological hope, although the millennium is still seen to be a long way off. China's leaders reiterate: "We are still only a developing nation." Mao himself has said that there will have to be other cultural revolutions in the years ahead, perhaps for another three hundred years. But the dramatic gains in personal security and livelihood for China's rural and working people and their families are, to them, a tangible foretaste of the ultimate utopia.

But the Chinese do not see these as religious analogies. Religion, for the leaders, party cadres and youth generation, is a relic of the past. An Australian visitor to a Buddhist monastery, now only a museum filled with gilded images, asked his guide what she thought of it all. "Buddha belongs to the past. He has nothing to do with our society today," she said.

He disagreed with her, suggesting that the word Buddha simply meant "enlightened one" and was a name for a person who understood all things with perfect clarity. "Why, Chairman Mao, if you like, is a kind of Buddha," he said. She swung around with a look of utter horror on her face and snapped: "Chairman Mao and Buddha have nothing whatever in common!"

China's official view of religion today is thoroughly Marxist, documented from the writings of Engels, Marx and Lenin. In his 1927 "Report on an Investigation of the Peasants' Movement in Human," Mao described the spontaneous peasant uprising in that province against the domination of four systems of authority—the "four thick ropes" of the feudal-patriarchal system binding the Chinese people: (1) the political power-holders from township level on up; (2) the authority of the clan, focused in the ancestral temple and male heads of households; (3) the religious authority "ranging from the king of hell down to the town and village gods"; (4) the domination of women by men.

Mao's report describes the smashing of idols by the aroused peasants in the 1927 peasant movement, the appropriation of temples for use as village schools and offices for the peasants' associations, and the prohibition of local superstitious customs. For Mao, the pragmatist, religious and superstitious practices were sheer economic waste, squeezing money from the impoverished masses, tying up land and buildings for religious uses, and diverting resources, personnel and energies from productive labor. For Mao, the Marxist, religion was pre-scientific nonsense. Yet he cautioned against excessive zeal and the use of force: "It is the peasants who made the idols, and when the time comes they will cast the idols aside with their own hands; there is no need for anyone else to do it for them prematurely."

Secure in the conviction of the final triumph of communism, Mao has tolerated religion, certain that it would wither and die in the process of socialist construction and socialist education. The short-term survival of religion during the transition period was of no real concern to him. "Whether you believe in this religion or that religion, all of you will be respected," he told a Tibetan delegation in 1952.

In earlier years his mode of dealing with religion was ridicule. Liberation comes from only one source, he said—the united power of the peasants. In 1927 he witnessed the Hunan peasants demonstrating "people's liberation" theory in actual practice, and his report is electric with excitement. He saw a corrupt system disintegrating before the collective assault of the peasants. One element in that system, as he saw it, was a web of ancient superstitious religious practices utilized by the landed gentry and political power-holders to oppress and exploit the people. Have the gods helped you to throw off your burdens, he asked, or is your new freedom due solely to your own efforts?

> The gods? Worship them by all means. But if you had only Lord Kuan and the Goddess of Mercy and no peasant association, could you have overthrown the local tyrants and evil gentry? The gods and goddesses are indeed miserable objects. You have worshiped them for centuries, and they have not overthrown a single one of the local tyrants or evil gentry for you! Now you want to have your rents reduced. Let me ask: How will you go about it? Will you believe in the gods or in the peasant association?

For Mao, the sole source of liberation for the people is the people themselves. In his well-known essay, "The Foolish Old Man Who Removed the Mountains," he rewrote an ancient fable about an old man who tried to dig up two great peaks that obstructed the way to his house. In the fable God was so moved by the old man's conviction that his sons, or their sons or grandsons, could finish the task that he sent down two angels who did the job. Mao's version saw two great mountains lying like a dead weight on the Chinese people: one was imperialism, the other was feudalism. "We must persevere and work unceasingly," he wrote, "and we, too, will touch God's heart. Our God is none other than the masses of the Chinese people. If they stand up and dig together, why can't these two mountains be cleared away?"

If there is any mystical element in Mao's personal belief system, it is his faith in the people. In his 1965 interview with André Malraux, he said:

When I said "Chinese Marxism is the religion of the people," I meant that the Communists express the Chinese people in a real way if they remain faithful to the work upon which the whole of China has embarked as if on another Long March. When we say "We are the Sons of the People," China understands it as she understood the phrase "Son of Heaven." The People has taken the place of the ancestors.

Malraux concluded his account of the interview with this local maxim: "Gods are all right for the rich; the poor have the Eighth Route Army."

The most dynamic religious force in twentieth-century China came from abroad. For this reason, Christianity was doubly condemned, particularly Roman Catholicism with its political and diplomatic apparatus centered in the Vatican. The missionaries, Catholic and Protestant, were charged with "cultural imperialism." There is reference to the "cultural imperialism" of the foreign missionaries in a textbook written jointly by Mao and a group of comrades in 1939:

The imperialist powers have never slackened their efforts to poison the minds of the Chinese people. This is their policy of cultural aggression. And it is carried out through missionary work, through establishing hospitals and schools, publishing newspapers and inducing Chinese students to study abroad. Their aim is to train the intellectuals who will serve their interest and to dupe the people.

In a proud, ancient and self-sufficient culture like China's, any foreign religion had hard going. Christianity, protected by the "unequal treaties" and Western gunboats patrolling the inland waters of sovereign China, battled sullen resentment and open opposition, particularly from the Confucian scholar-gentry, from the beginning.

The campaign to eradicate imperialist influence in Chinese Christian circles began in a drive for full financial and leadership autonomy to free the churches from all ties with foreign churches. The Protestant Three-Self Reform Movement and the

National Catholic Patriotic Association, constituted in 1954 and 1957 respectively, centralized the administrative supervision of all Christians under the Religious Affairs Bureau of the State Council and formalized the complete independence of Chinese churches from foreign control and support. By the end of 1952 all missionaries had left China and all educational, medical and other institutions had been nationalized.

China's Christians were caught in an agony of conflicting loyalties. As Chinese, they naturally supported the unification and rebuilding of their country under the new government. As Christians, concerned for the welfare of their people, they welcomed the elimination of famine, epidemic disease, edemic poverty and the exploitation of millions by the rich and powerful.

At the same time, the advent of power of a Marxist regime threatened the existence of all religions. Yet sensitive Chinese Christians had been uneasy in a social and political situation primed for explosion long before the Communist victory in 1949. Y. T. Wu, a YMCA leader who became general secretary of the Protestant Three-Self Patriotic Movement after 1950, wrote this in 1948: "Why do I say that the situation of the Chinese Christian church is tragic? Because China is today face to face with the greatest change in its history, and in this period of great change the Christian Church, besides the negative reactions of feeling sorry for itself and trying to escape reality, has nothing to say or do."

The *Christian Manifesto*, issued by a group of Protestant leaders meeting in Peking in July 1950, celebrated the new independence of the Chinese church. The *Manifesto* exemplifies the doctrine of collective self-reliance that has marked every aspect of China's nation-building since 1949. The *Manifesto* proclaimed that the Chinese church would henceforth support the "common political platform" of the new government by (1) recognizing the history of imperialism in China, especially American imperialism through the Church, (2) by practicing three-self autonomy (self-support, self-government, self-propagation), and (3) by practicing self-respect, self-reliance, and self-criticism.

Christian churches and organizations in China should take

effective measures to cultivate a patriotic and democratic spirit among their adherents in general, as well as a psychology of self-respect and self-reliance. . . . At the same time, self-criticism should be advocated, all forms of Christian activity re-examined and readjusted, and thoroughgoing austerity measures adopted, so as to achieve the goals of a reformation in the Church.

Twenty-three years later the institutional Church in China is barely visible, although we know that Christians continue to practice their faith quietly in their homes. Does this mean that God's ongoing action of creation and salvation (which are inseparable) is not at work among China's millions today? Few Christians in the West would affirm that. If God works within the secular history of the world—and the biblical record surely supports this—then we must believe that his saving action for his people in China has never ceased. If God is concerned for social justice, liberation and human fulfillment—the salvation of all his people —then evidence of his grace and work is manifest in China. Salvation is a process of continuing transformation—of the people, of our world, of our institutions, and even of the Church.

Catholic theologians, in a recent Vatican statement, believe that some of Chairman Mao's directives "affirm human values" and that their common understanding of fundamental human rights, as defined by the United Nations Charter, provides a platform for positive dialogue between the Church and China's leaders.

God's action in history may not be sharply visible through an institutional Church in China today, yet he is not confined to any single instrument, even the Church. His power in love on behalf of the people cannot be doubted. In his own time and wisdom the Church in China will once again boldly witness to Jesus Christ. For now, his power in love on behalf of the people of China cannot be doubted. Perhaps they had China in mind when the Secretariat for Interfaith Dialogue of the East Asia Christian Conference wrote this paragraph in 1970:

Jesus Christ, Lord and man of history and of the cosmos, can never be brought in or added to man's cultural and spiritual life. It need, therefore, cause no surprise that we may discern his presence everywhere, prior to that moment toward which we look forward eagerly when men will recognize his presence. This discernment of Christ's work since history began in all our societies and spiritual "worlds" awaits a sensitiveness to the Spirit to which we need to give more serious attention in our Christian churches and communities.

How can we relate to the people of China today and tomorrow? What are the implications for Christian world mission?

First, we know that the traditional forms of Christian mission to China cannot be restored for three reasons: (1) because of China's Marxist view of religion and the memory of superstitions and abuses in the name of religion in traditional China; (2) because of China's view that missionaries were linked with Western imperialism and the "century of humiliation" that followed the Opium War; (3) because of China's stress on self-reliance; they neither seek nor accept foreign aid of any kind.

Second, the main burden for Christian witness in China will be carried by Chinese Christians themselves. As Stanley Mooneyham put it: "If God widens the crack in the curtain enough to allow any of us to go through, we will likely find an incredibly pure church. . . . It might be more appropriate to respectfully ask to sit at their feet than to stand in their pulpits."

Third, we must learn from the China experience as we carry forward the Christian world mission in other developing nations. We need to re-examine our assumptions, our methods and relationships. There are strong moves toward autonomy among churches in Africa, Asia and Latin America. The mood of self-reliance and national pride, the resentment of foreign power and influence, and the resurgence of indigenous cultures are all reflected in the national churches.

Finally, even as we praise God for all signs of his continuing work of creation and salvation in the secular world, we reaffirm our conviction that beyond the needs of the body and mind— food, shelter, employment, schooling, health care, justice—is the human dilemma, man's cry for liberation from the existential dichotomy between personal ideals and dreams, and man's finitude and sinfulness, mirrored in the social dichotomies between ideals of social justice and the realities of human selfishness. Sociological, economic, and political solutions for the predicament of man overlook the problem that man confronts in himself. The disintegration of traditional culture and morality in the West demonstrates a crisis of values that is more existential than social. The elimination of social and economic inequities will still leave man searching for self-understanding and ultimate meaning. Man's search for liberation is shadowed by his poignant awareness of ultimate mystery and his own weakness, finitude and mortality. Salvation for each person, and for all mankind, has been given and will be *fully* known only in God's work of grace and love in Jesus Christ.